THE MEASUREMENT AND VALUATION OF HEALTH STATUS USING EQ-5D: A EUROPEAN PERSPECTIVE

The Measurement and Valuation of Health Status using EQ-5D: A European Perspective

Evidence from the EuroQol BIOMED Research Programme

Edited by

Richard Brooks

Strathclyde University,
Glasgow, Schotland, U.K.

Rosalind Rabin

EuroQol Group Business Management,
Rotterdam, The Netherlands

and

Frank de Charro

Erasmus University Rotterdam,
Rotterdam, The Netherlands

KLUWER ACADEMIC PUBLISHERS
DORDRECHT / BOSTON / LONDON

A C.I.P. Catalogue record for this book is available from the Library of Congress.

ISBN 1-4020-1214-4

Published by Kluwer Academic Publishers,
P.O. Box 17, 3300 AA Dordrecht, The Netherlands.

Sold and distributed in North, Central and South America
by Kluwer Academic Publishers,
101 Philip Drive, Norwell, MA 02061, U.S.A.

In all other countries, sold and distributed
by Kluwer Academic Publishers,
P.O. Box 322, 3300 AH Dordrecht, The Netherlands.

Printed on acid-free paper

Printed in the Netherlands.

Table of contents

List of contributors vii

Foreword ix

Acknowledgements xi

List of tables and annexes xiii

List of figures xvii

Glossary of terms xix

1. **Introduction** 1
   Richard Brooks

2. **Guidelines for analysing and reporting EQ-5D outcomes** 7
   Paul Krabbe and Tom Weijnen

3. **EQ-5D: Modes of administration** 21
   Caroline Selai, et al.

4. **Guidelines for value sets in economic and non-economic studies using EQ-5D** 29
   Paul Kind

5. **Test-retest performance of EQ-5D** 43
   Susan Macran

6. **Construction of the EQ-net VAS and TTO databases** 55
   Tom Weijnen, et al.

7. **Comparison of EQ-5D VAS valuations: analysis of background variables** 81
   Harri Sintonen, et al.

8. **A European EQ-5D VAS valuation set** 103
   Wolfgang Greiner, et al.

9. A comparison of EQ-5D time trade-off values obtained in Germany, The United Kingdom and Spain 143

Jan Busschbach, et al.

10. What concepts does the EQ-5D measure? Intentions and interpretations 167

Julia Fox-Rushby and Caroline Selai

11. Producing other language versions of the EQ-5D 183

Michael Herdman, et al.

12. Exploring the results of translating the EQ-5D into 11 European languages 191

Rosalind Rabin, et al.

13. EQ-5D in selected countries around the world 207

Richard Brooks, et al.

14. Summary and future EQ-5D work 229

Richard Brooks and Frank de Charro

References for all chapters 245

Appendices 259

Index 301

List of contributors

Xavier Badia Health Outcomes Research Europe, Barcelona, Spain

Richard Brooks Department of Economics - Strathclyde University, Glasgow, Scotland, United Kingdom

Jan Busschbach Institute for Medical Psychology & Psychotherapy - Erasmus Medical Center - Erasmus University Rotterdam, Rotterdam, The Netherlands

Frank de Charro Centre for Health Policy and Law - Erasmus University Rotterdam, Rotterdam, The Netherlands

Stephen Joel Coons Department of Pharmacy Practice and Science - College of Pharmacy - The University of Arizona, Tucson, Arizona, U.S.A.

Paul De Cock Center for Preventative Health - Academic Hospital - University of Leuven, Leuven, Belgium

Nancy Devlin Department of Economics - City University, London, United Kingdom

Willy De Weerdt Department of Rehabilitation Sciences - University of Leuven, Leuven, Belgium

Paul Dolan ScHARR - University of Sheffield, Sheffield, United Kingdom

Julia Fox-Rushby Health Policy Unit - London School of Hygiene & Tropical Medicine, London, United Kingdom

Idoia Gaminde Gobierno de Navarra - Sección de Planificación y Evaluación - Recinto "Hospital de Navarra", Pamplona, Spain

Wolfgang Greiner Institut für Versicherungsbetriebslehre - Universität Hannover, Hannover, Germany

Paul Hansen Department of Economics - University of Otago, Dunedin, New Zealand

Michael Herdman 3D Health Research, Barcelona, Spain

Naoki Ikegami Department of Health Policy & Management - Keio University School of Medicine, Tokyo, Japan

Jennifer Jelsma Division of Physiotherapy - Department of Allied Sciences - University of Cape Town, Cape Town, South Africa

Jeffrey Johnson Institute of Health Economics, Edmonton, Alberta, Canada

Paul Kind Outcomes Research Group - Centre for Health Economics - University of York, York, United Kingdom

Paul Krabbe Department of Medical Technology Assessment - University Medical Centre Nijmegen, Nijmegen, The Netherlands

Susan Macran Outcomes Research Group - Centre for Health Economics - University of York, York, United Kingdom

Carlo Marra Centre for Health Care and Epidemiology - Faculty of Medicine - University of British Columbia, Vancouver, British Columbia, Canada

Martin Nieuwenhuizen Centre for Health Policy and Law - Erasmus University Rotterdam, Rotterdam, The Netherlands

Arto Ohinmaa Department of Public Health - University of Alberta, Edmonton, Alberta, Canada

Siem Oppe Centre for Health Policy and Law - Erasmus University Rotterdam, Rotterdam, The Netherlands

Rosalind Rabin EuroQol Group Business Management, Rotterdam, The Netherlands

Montserrat Roset Health Outcomes Research Europe, Barcelona, Spain

Caroline Selai Institute of Neurology - University College London, London, United Kingdom

Harri Sintonen Department of Public Health - University of Helsinki, Helsinki, Finland

Aki Tsuchiya SHEG - ScHARR - University of Sheffield, Sheffield, United Kingdom

Tom Weijnen Centre for Health Policy and Law - Erasmus University Rotterdam, Rotterdam, The Netherlands

Alan Williams Centre for Health Economics - University of York, York, United Kingdom

John Yfantopoulos Department of Health Economics - University of Athens, Athens, Greece

Foreword

Multidisciplinary collaboration is a very fraught activity, and no-one in their right minds should embark upon it without some compelling reason. Great personal as well as intellectual tensions can easily be generated by having to deal with people who don't even agree with you about how a problem is to be formulated, let alone how best to tackle it, and what counts as evidence. The matters that are taken for granted within one discipline, are often the very things that constitute the controversial core of another discipline. Terms such as "value", "validity", "explanation", and "significance" turn out to have quite different connotations in the different sub-cultures, and may even be rejected as irrelevant in contexts in which others regard them as central.

In a strictly academic environment this sort of argumentation is the stuff of life, and is typically how people sharpen their wits and hone up their rhetorical skills, as well as helping to widen the realm of knowledge. But if you want something to emerge that might be of practical use for those in the world of action, then at some point the talking has to stop and a decision has to be made. It is extremely rare for the EuroQol Group to be unanimous about anything, and this is both a weakness and a strength. The weakness is that if any sizeable minority dig their heels in and refuse to budge on some point, the Group as a whole cannot move forward on it. The strength comes from the fact that in a hard-hitting multi-disciplinary forum you will never be unaware of the risks you are taking by going down one path rather than another (and such risks are inescapable). A dissenting minority is always free to go off and collect evidence that might help resove such issues, and bring it back to a subsequent meeting so as to generate reconsideration of such matters. Indeed, they will be encouraged to do so, because the Group is more influenced by empirical evidence than by fine rhetoric.

What I find as almost miraculous is that only a handful of people have left the Group because they could not stomach the way it worked and/or the direction in which it was going. I think there are two principal reasons for this. One is a strongly shared commitment to the main task, which is to improve the lot of struggling humanity by providing an easy to use, easy to understand, and easy to obtain instrument for measuring what people value most in health-related quality of life. The other is mutual respect and tolerance for others who persist in not accepting your views, and a willingness to explain in plain language (and repeatedly if nesessary) something which to you is patently obvious. This has proved to be a great bonding experience for the Group, and is a testimony to adopting the rule of reason as a survival strategy.

It has been these qualities that enabled a group of very diverse scholars (by age, sex, nationality, discipline, interest, and temperament) to set up and collaborate on the Biomed project, the fruits of which are contained in this book. I doubt whether there will be many individual readers who will find it all very interesting and illuminating, but I would be very disappointed if there were not something here that would be of interest to everyone concerned with outcome measurement in health care, or with the measurement of population health. I commend it with that possibility foremost in my mind.

Alan Williams
University of York
September 2002

Acknowledgements

The editors wish to acknowledge the European Union for funding the work described in this book under the Biomed 2 programme - PL 963118 - concerted action.
Dennis Kennedy assisted with the layout and graphical work.

List of tables and annexes

Table 2.1. The suggested application of the 3 components of the EQ-5D classified by type of research study and design 11

Table 2.2. Frequency distribution (profile) of the EQ-5D descriptive system for single observation studies 15

Table 2.3. Frequency distribution (profile) of the EQ-5D descriptive system for comparison of more than one population or repeated measurements 16

Table 2.4. EQ VAS score 17

Table 3.1. The conventional interpretation of the kappa statistic 26

Table 4.1. Summary of choice factors in selecting EQ-5D weights for economic studies 38

Table 4.2. National population value sets 40

Table 5.1. EQ-5D test-retest frequencies (MVH survey) 45

Table 5.2. Number of (positive/negative) changes by EQ-5D dimension (MVH survey) 46

Table 5.3. Percentage change in EQ-5D dimensions between time 1 and time 2 by change in EQ VAS time 1-time 2 (MVH survey) 47

Table 5.4. Percentage change on EQ-5D between time 1 and time 2 by serious illness at time 1 (MVH survey) 48

Table 5.5. EQ-5D test-retest frequencies (rheumatoid arthritis study) 49

Table 5.6. Number of (positive/negative) changes by EQ-5D dimension (rheumatoid arthritis study) 50

Table 5.7. Percentage change on EQ-5D dimension between time 1 and time 2 by change in the EQ VAS time 1-time 2 (rheumatoid arthritis study) 51

Table 5.8. Reliability coefficients for sample members who reported no change in their arthritis over 3 months (rheumatoid arthritis study) 51

Table 5.9. Percentage change on EQ-5D between time 1 and time 2 by self-reported change in arthritis (rheumatoid arthritis study) 52

Table 5.10. Mean EQ VAS scores at time 1 and time 2 by self-reported change in arthritis (rheumatoid arthritis study) 52

Table 6.1. EQ-5D health states 56

Table 6.2. Sample features in the VAS and TTO databases 65

Table 6.3. Respondent characteristics in the EQ-net VAS database 68

Table 6.4. Respondent characteristics in the TTO database 70

Table 6.5. Exclusions and inconsistencies in the EQ-net VAS database: exclusions and inconsistencies calculated on standard states 72

Table 6.6. Exclusions and inconsistencies in the EQ-net TTO database 74

Table 6.7. Respondent characteristics by exclusions in the EQ-net VAS database 75

Table 6.8. Respondent characteristics by exclusions in the EQ-net TTO database 77

Table 7.1. Exclusions by respondent characteristics 86

Table 7.2. The distribution of respondent characteristics by studies after exclusions 87

Table 7.3. Weighted linear regression of VAS values on background variables for all studies (coefficients with $p < 0.01$ depicted) 92

Table 7.4. Weighted linear regression of VAS values on background variables and dummies for the non-ranked studies (coefficients with $p \leq 0.01$ depicted) 94

Table 7.5. Outcomes of the SVD-analysis of 18 health state evaluations for 11 studies 95

Table 7.6. Absolute differences between the original scores and the representation by the first component 96

Table 8.1. Effects of the transformation procedures on the mean, median and measure for skewness (0 : a normal distribution; > 1 and < -1 : a skewed distribution). Standard states only 105

Table 8.2. The dummy variables and their scores in the model 108

Table 8.3. Number of health states by number of inconsistencies 110

Table 8.4. Influence of the number of inconsistencies on the regression results (coefficient from the regression and 95% confidence interval) 111

Table 8.5. Exclusions and inconsistencies 112

Table 8.6. Share of respondents with a background characteristic in the different studies. Before and after exclusions 115

Table 8.7. Results from OLS regression on the VAS values. Model with background variables (linear regression) 116

Table 8.8. Results from OLS regression on the VAS values. Model without background variables (linear regression) 117

Table 8.9. Results of CANALS solutions compared with results from OLS regression 119

Table 8.10. Reconstructed dummy-weights from the CANALS transformation and regression 120

Table 8.11. Analysis with dummies for EQ-5D dimensions only. Multilevel analysis on 82910 health states valued in more than 1 study 124

Table 8.12. Observed mean and median values (linear regression); estimated and rescaled estimated values and differences between the observed mean and estimated values. The standard states 128

Annex 8.1. Number of valuations per sample in the analysis 132

Annex 8.2. Mean, median, estimates and difference between mean or median and estimates 134

Annex 8.3. Estimated and rescaled estimated values for all 243 EQ-5D health states 136

Table 9.1. Mean TTO values, SD and number of observations after exclusions 150

Table 9.2. Background variables 153

Table 9.3. Multi-level parameter estimates of the 4 model specifications 154

Table 9.4. Differences between countries on the individual dimensions and levels of the EQ-5D 158

Table 9.5. Model 3 with continuous variables for EQ VAS and age 159

Table 10.1. UK-based studies, by EuroQol Group members, collecting qualitative data alongside the EQ-5D 173

Table 11.1. EQ-5D language versions: June 2002 186

Table 12.1. Differences between Finnish, Dutch and UK (Frome) postal valuations for a set of EQ-5D health states using the EQ-5D VAS 199

Table 12.2. Differences between Spanish (Cat_Hos and Navarra) interview-based valuations and UK (Frome) postal valuations for a set of EQ-5D health states using the EQ-5D VAS 200

Table 12.3. Differences between Spanish (Cat_Cor) and UK (MVH) interview-based valuations for a set of EQ-5D health states using TTO 201

List of figures

Figure 2.1. Graphical presentation of the mean outcomes (and standard errors of the mean) for the 5 dimensions of the EQ-5D for a clinical or cost-effectiveness pre-post design 15

Figure 2.2. EQ-5D descriptive system 17

Figure 2.3. Example of clinical data presentation combined with mean outcomes for the EQ VAS 18

Figure 2.4. Example of presentation of longitudinal EQ-5D index measures 19

Figure 4.1. Values, valuations and applications 36

Figure 5.1. Change in VAS scores (MVH survey) 46

Figure 5.2. Change in VAS scores (rheumatoid arthritis study) 50

Figure 7.1. Mean values of standard states by study and overall 88

Figure 7.2. Mean VAS valuations from standard studies and those based on RIT 89

Figure 7.3. Mean EQ VAS valuations by age groups 89

Figure 7.4. Mean EQ-5D VAS valuations by age and EQ VAS combined 90

Figure 7.5. Mean VAS valuations by education 91

Figure 7.6. Average study scores for health states. Derived from the first component of a SVD-analysis 97

Figure 7.7. Proportionality constants for studies. Derived from the first component of a SVD-analysis 98

Figure 8.1. Transformations of the categories on the EQ-5D dimensions from CANALS analysis with linear restriction on the VAS values 121

Figure 8.2. Monotonic VAS-transformation resulting from a CANALS analysis with a full set of parameters 122

Figure 8.3. Monotonic VAS-transformation resulting from a CANALS analysis with a reduced set of parameters, including the EQ-5D dimensions and the RIT dummy 123

Figure 8.4. EQ-5D health states ranked according to mean, median and estimated VAS values 126

Figure 8.5. EQ-5D health states ranked according to difference between mean and median observed values and estimated VAS values 126

Figure 8.6. Estimated and estimated rescaled values. Rescaled with mean and median value for dead. All 243 EQ-5D health states 128

Figure 9.1. EQ-5D health states ranked according to mean TTO values after exclusions 152

Figure 9.2. EQ-5D health states ranked according to mean VAS values 152

Figure 9.3. Aggregated background coefficients model 3 (Own VAS ≥ 85) 156

Figure 9.4. The values of the German, Spanish and UK dummies for different background variables form model 4 157

Figure 9.5. EQ-5D health states ranked according to mean positive TTO values 160

Figure 9.6. EQ-5D health states ranked according to mean negative TTO values 161

Figure 13.1. Plot of predicted and observed TTO scores (divided by 10). The UK predicted scores from the MVH are included for comparison 225

Glossary of terms

ANOVA	Analysis of variance
ANCOVA	Analysis of covariance
CANALS	Model from SAS programme TRANSREG
CASM	Cognitive assessment of survey methods
CEA	Cost-effectiveness analysis
CI	Confidence interval
CUA	Cost-utility analysis
DALE	Disability adjusted life expectancy
DALY	Disability adjusted life year
df	Degree of freedom
diff.	Difference
EQ-5D descriptive system	Standard layout for the five dimensional classification system, each of which records 3 levels of severity (page 2 of EQ-5D)
EQ-5D index	Index value attached to an EQ-5D state according to a particular set of weights
EQ-5D self-report questionnaire	EQ-5D (consists of EQ-5D descriptive system and EQ VAS and EQ SDQ if desired)
EQ-5D valuation questionnaire	Standard layout consisting of EQ-5D, EQ-5D VAS, EQ SDQ and instructions
EQ-5D VAS	VAS of standard layout for recording an individual's rating of hypothetical EQ-5D health states
EQ-net	EuroQol Biomed network programme
EQ SDQ	Standard set of socio-demographic questions for use with EQ-5D valuation questionnaire. A modified version may be used with EQ-5D
EQ VAS	Standard vertical 20 cm visual analogue scale (similar to a thermometer) (page 3 of EQ-5D)
Exp.	Experienced
HFA	Health Funding Authority (New Zealand)
HRQoL	Health-related quality of life
ICC	Interaclass correlation coefficient
IQR	Inter-quartile range
IQOLA	International Quality of Life Assessment
MANOVA	Multivariate analysis of variance
MCS-12	Mental composite summary scores of the SF-12
Neg.	Negative
NHP	Nottingham Health Profile
Not excl.	Not excluded
ns	Not significant
NZ	New Zealand

OLS	Ordinary least squares
PCS-12	Physical composite summary scores of the SF-12
PE	Parameter estimates
Pos.	Positive
PTO	Person trade-off
QALY	Quality-adjusted life-year
QLHQ	Quality of Life and Health Questionnaire
QoL	Quality of life
Q-TWIST	Quality-adjusted time without symptoms of disease
RCT	Randomised controlled trial
RIT	Ranked, interview-based, ten years duration
ROC	Receiver operating characteristic
SAS	Statistical analysis system
SD	Standard deviation
SE	Standard error
SF-12	Short Form 12
SF-36	Short Form 36
Sig.	Significant
SIP	Sickness Impact Profile
SOPs	Standard operating procedures
SG	Standard gamble
SVD	Singular value decomposition
TTO	Time trade-off
TWIST	Time without symptoms of disease
VAS	Visual analogue scale
UK	United Kingdom
UK MVH	United Kingdom measurement and valuation of health study
UK A1, A3	UK MVH A1 and A3 value sets
US	United States
WHO	World Health Organisation
WHOQOL	WHO Quality of Life instrument

1
Introduction

Richard Brooks

The EuroQol Group first met in 1987 to test the feasibility of jointly developing a standardised non-disease-specific instrument for describing and valuing health-related quality of life. From the outset the Group has been multi-country, multi-centre and multi-disciplinary. Although the majority of the current members of the Group are from European countries, the increasing worldwide use of the instrument developed by the Group - EQ-5D - has resulted in new members from across the world joining in the enterprise.

Two papers from the Group (EuroQol Group, 1990; Brooks *et al*, 1996) have set out how the Group developed its instrument and the key issues involved in this development. The second paper made clear the generic nature of EQ-5D, paid particular attention to issues in valuation (the valuation task, the number of health states, alternative scaling/valuation approaches), and reviewed the evidence then available on how the instrument measured up to the key methodological requirements of practicality, reliability, and validity. The paper also took up some key issues that the Group was addressing, namely modelling the valuation data, the effect of duration, and the valuation of 'dead'. The paper thus showed how the EuroQol 'enterprise' comprised an ongoing research programme pursued in the context of our original aims. This book reports on our continuing efforts to fulfil these aims.

The 1996 paper also included a brief review of the limited number of papers that had been published by the mid-1990s in the (clinical) application of EQ-5D. The number of applications has now burgeoned, with the instrument evidently being widely regarded as a simple, practical way of measuring health-related quality of life (HRQoL).

It is worth stressing a number of points concerning the development of EQ-5D. First, its generic nature - from the outset we sought a multi-dimensional instrument covering, if possible, physical, mental, and social attributes of HRQoL. Second, we were also convinced that it would be necessary to develop a (cardinal) index which would ultimately allow us to provide HRQoL valuations, such as quality-adjusted life-years (QALYs). This was a key decision, given that many of the developments in HRQoL measurement prior to the inception of the Group had focused on the profile approach. Third, given the heavy focus on the meaning of 'health' and its relationship with HRQoL in present-day discourse, we should stress that the format of EQ-5D was not developed in isolation from key trends in health status and HRQoL measurement up until the late 1980s, with the Group members from differing disciplinary backgrounds bringing to bear and drawing upon their collective experience in these areas.

R. Brooks et al. (eds.),
The Measurement and Valuation of Health Status Using EQ-5D: A European Perspective, 1–5.

Fourth, the Group was anxious that HRQoL be measured and valued by people themselves, that is, not relying upon 'expert' valuations. This is evidenced not only in the descriptive part of the instrument where respondents fill in boxes concerning their own health, but also in the valuation task, where a variety of sample designs, especially population-based, have been employed.

In summary, the Group has been innovative in the area of health status measurement. We have always been strongly focused upon valuation as well as measurement, recognising that if decision-making in the health (and related) sectors is to be appropriately informed, then health status needs to be valued at individual, group and societal levels. EQ-5D includes the capability to generate values at all these levels, and is currently one of a small number of generic indices which can be used in evaluation approaches requiring social values (e.g. economic evaluations).

Originally a 6-dimensional instrument was formulated, but by 1991 the 5-dimensional format now known as EQ-5D had been developed and has remained in place, apart from some minor format changes.

THE EQ-5D INSTRUMENT

A brief outline of the nature of the instrument and its uses follows. The full UK English version is provided as Appendix 1. A glossary of terms precedes this introduction. Readers are also referred to the Group's website - www.euroqol.org - where more detailed information is presented.

EQ-5D is a standardised instrument for use as a measure of health outcome. Applicable to a wide range of health conditions and treatments, it provides a simple descriptive profile and a single index value for heath status that can be used in the clinical and economic evaluation of health care as well as population health surveys. EQ-5D has been specially designed to complement other HRQoL measures such as the SF-36, NHP, SIP or disease-specific measures. It is designed for self-completion by respondents and is ideally suited for use in postal surveys, in clinics, and in face-to-face interviews. It is cognitively simple, taking only a few minutes to complete. Instructions to respondents are included in the questionnaire. Although EQ-5D was intended for self-completion, the EuroQol Group recognises that this is not always the appropriate mode of administration: some studies have been conducted by telephone, and some have used observers and proxies instead of the respondents themselves.

A clear distinction should be made between the EQ-5D self-report questionnaire (commonly known as 'EQ-5D') designed as a measure of health outcome and the EQ-5D valuation questionnaire (designed to collect valuations for health states defined by EQ-5D). Nowadays these are distributed as separate versions to avoid confusion.

THE EQ-5D SELF-REPORT QUESTIONNAIRE (EQ-5D)

EQ-5D essentially consists of 2 pages, i.e. the EQ-5D descriptive system (often referred to as 'page 2') and the EQ VAS (often referred to as 'page 3'). These pages are combined with a cover page ('page 1') and optional demographic questions.

The descriptive system records the level of self-reported problems on each of the 5 dimensions of the classification (mobility, self-care, usual activities, pain/discomfort, anxiety/depression). Each dimension is divided into 3 levels (no problems, some or moderate problems, extreme problems or unable). This information can be used in the following ways:

(i) As an EQ-5D health profile for individuals or groups, either at a single point in time, or over a period of time; differences in such profiles can be used to describe health outcomes.

(ii) Health states defined by the 5-dimensional descriptive system can be converted into a weighted health state index by applying scores from 'value sets' elicited from general population samples.

A convenient way of identifying health states is employed: by assigning the numbers 1,2,3 to each level in each of the 5 dimensions we can label health states using 5-number descriptors ranging from 11111 to 33333 (a total of 3^5 or 243 states). Thus 12121 is the state ' no problems in walking about, some problems washing or dressing, no problems performing usual activities, moderate pain or discomfort, not anxious or depressed'. 'Unconscious' and 'death' are also included in the valuation exercise to give a total of 245 states addressed by EQ-5D.

The EQ VAS records the respondent's self-rated health status on a graduated (0 -100) visual analogue scale (VAS), where the endpoints are labelled 'best imaginable health state' and 'worst imaginable health state'. This information can be used as a quantitative measure, and differences in this scale can be used as a measure of outcome, as judged by the individual respondents.

THE EQ-5D VALUATION QUESTIONNAIRE

A fuller version of the instrument contains the valuation task (pages 4-7). These pages provide a technique for valuing health states and have been used to value heath states in population studies. Valuations elicited in this way can be applied to health states generated by the EQ-5D descriptive system to produce a weighted health state index. Sets of values are available for a number of countries (see the website for current availability).

Finally, pages 8-9 (EQ SDQ) include sections for other information including age, sex, and level of education which enable a fuller picture of respondent samples to be obtained.

USES OF EQ-5D

EQ-5D is being widely used for:

(i) *Monitoring* the health status of patient groups at different moments in time, e.g. referral, admission, discharge, follow-up of outpatients.
(ii) *Evaluation and audit* of health care, by measuring changes in health status in individual patients and in groups of patients.
(iii) *Assessing* the seriousness of conditions at different moments in time.
(iv) Providing relevant information for *resource allocation* at a variety of levels.
(v) Assisting in providing evidence about *medical effectiveness* in processes where drugs or procedures have to be approved.
(vi) Establishing levels of *population health status* both locally and nationally.

Details of published material by a wide range of users are available on the website.

EQ-NET PROJECT

This book is specifically devoted to the EQ-net project undertaken by the EuroQol Group over the period 1998-2001, and funded by the European Union under the Biomed II scheme. The aim of the project was to further the development of EQ-5D in the key areas of valuation, application, translation and communication. The design of the project reflected the continuing study concerns of Group members to review in detail all aspects of the EuroQol enterprise.

The EQ-net project also reflected the Group's keenness to react to the demands from users and potential users of EQ-5D for clear guidelines on how to use and apply the instrument in a variety of settings and policy contexts (population, clinical, economic appraisal). Chapters 2-4 address these concerns. Thus in the field of applications, the project has facilitated the production of guidelines for the design, analysis and reporting of EQ-5D in clinical and economic studies as well as population health surveys. Although EQ-5D was originally designed for pencil and paper self-report, the Group recognises the demand for guidelines in regard to alternative modes of administration. A small task force of EQ-net participants has been considering this issue and has prepared guidelines for EQ-5D proxy, observer and telephone versions. Computer-assisted methods to collect EQ-5D data have also been investigated. Chapter 5 reports on the reliability of EQ-5D in the context of its test-retest performance.

Focus on valuation issues has been a paramount feature of our work. A major effort has concentrated on harmonising and integrating the results of the various European valuation projects carried out by Group members during the last 10 years. During this time, Group members have been engaged in deriving values from different groups (e.g. patients and general population samples) for EQ-5D health states in several European countries. It was shown that values for a specific set of health states, then known as 'the common core' (referred to in subsequent chapters as 'standard states'), were similar in a number of Northern European countries. The research, mostly funded nationally, was fragmented, however, and the Group recognised the desirability of integrating the results in some way that might produce a standardised set of European valuation data. The EQ-net project provided support for this in the form of a network resource that managed and integrated the data as well as providing assistance to the participants performing the tasks. The results of these endeavours are shown in Chapters 6-9.

The Group has been mindful of the worldwide debate on conceptual issues in health and HRQoL measurement and valuation. Such issues are closely related to linguistic and terminological matters in the case of an instrument such as EQ-5D, which has a large number of language versions. The translation aspect of the EQ-net project, concerned with linguistic and conceptual issues, is reported upon in Chapters 10-12. This work focused on producing further translations and adaptations of EQ-5D that aim to achieve semantic equivalence. The EQ-net translation sub-project also facilitated the updating and refining of the guidelines for the translation procedure as well as defining the concepts contained in EQ-5D.

The key area not specifically included in the book is that of communication. Briefly: the project has facilitated the strengthening of communication between the Group and users generally. This has been achieved by the production of an external newsletter, distributed to more than 1000 people on the Group's mailing list, the development of the website, the organising of breakfast meetings and/or training sessions during international conferences and the convening of a user meeting in Amsterdam. Evidently a lot of this communication has concerned topics and issues treated in detail within the other three key areas.

Finally, in order to indicate the worldwide spread of EQ-5D, and the issues raised due to this development, we asked a number of analysts across the world to write about the use of EQ-5D in each of their countries. Their material appears in Chapter 13.

The concluding Chapter 14 summarises the work accomplished during the EQ-net project as presented in this book. We also take the chance to suggest how the Group is proceeding with its ongoing work, an enterprise that has undoubtedly been strongly influenced by our experiences in pursuing the EQ-net project.

2
Guidelines for analysing and reporting EQ-5D outcomes

Paul Krabbe and Tom Weijnen

2.1 INTRODUCTION

Application of the EQ-5D

The EQ-5D is used in different fields of research, each field with its own scientific traditions. These traditions are reflected in different methods of analysis, application, and presentation. The particular interest of a researcher may determine whether 1 or more of the 3 parts (descriptive system, VAS, index) of the EQ-5D will be applied. This chapter presents an overview of the major types of application of the EQ-5D. First, 3 fields of research are discussed, each orientated to a particular research question. Second, the 3 main types of study design are outlined. Third, guidelines for the collection of EQ-5D data are presented. Fourth, guidelines for analysing and reporting EQ-5D outcomes are presented for each of these different research strategies.

Guidelines for analysing and reporting of EQ-5D outcomes are important in order to facilitate comparisons between studies. There is a tendency to standardise the reporting of study results and for this purpose Standard Operating Procedures (SOPs) are sometimes presented. The EuroQol Group, however, has decided not to develop SOPs, but instead to offer guidelines. One part of the guidelines comprises the main body of results that the Group considers should be presented in each study, the other part is more indicative.

Study areas

Broadly, 3 different fields of research can be recognised where the EQ-5D can be applied: clinical studies, economic studies, and population health studies. Each focuses on answering a specific research question.

Clinical studies

Clinical studies are predominately focused on the effectiveness of medical interventions. Increasingly, HRQoL measures are integrated into this type of study to record the 'global' or 'generic' health status of patients. Information is no longer solely presented about clinical effects and indicators, HRQoL outcomes are also measured. The descriptive system of the EQ-5D can be used for this purpose. Under experimental conditions, such as RCTs, EQ-5D measures are increasingly being incorporated as secondary outcome measures. Longitudinal designs are frequently used in clinical

R. Brooks et al. (eds.),
The Measurement and Valuation of Health Status Using EQ-5D: A European Perspective, 7–19.

studies in order to monitor follow-up after a medical intervention. Measurement on the 5 distinct dimensions of the EQ-5D can also be informative in describing the dynamics of HRQoL during treatment and follow-up.

Economic studies

Economic studies have been used alongside clinical studies. Such studies are explicitly concerned with comparisons between alternative medical interventions. Full economic evaluation requires the assessment, measurement and valuation of both inputs to a medical intervention, and the outcomes of these interventions. Outcomes can be valued in monetary terms (in cost-benefit analysis), in 'natural' units such as lives saved (in cost-effectiveness analysis) and in utility terms (in cost-utility analysis). Some analysts are reluctant to use the term 'cost-utility analysis', preferring to include such work under cost-effectiveness analysis. Whichever terminology is used, the effect of an intervention is judged by valuing health status before and after the intervention. This valuation of health status is undertaken by assigning a single numeric value (formally called 'utility') between zero (say, dead) and 1 (say, perfect health) for different health states. The EQ-5D instrument has been expressly developed for application in these types of economic analysis.

Population health studies

Population health studies differ from the other 2 fields of research, as they are not focused on the effectiveness or cost-effectiveness of a particular medical intervention. These studies are predominantly concerned with quantifying the burden of diseases, monitoring disease-specific trends or changes and comparisons between regions and countries. Generic instruments such as the EQ-5D enable such comparisons to be made in HRQoL terms.

Study designs

Different study designs can be identified that are associated with the 3 fields of research mentioned above. The application of the EQ-5D is suitable both for observational studies and RCTs. The choice for a particular study design simply affects the soundness of the comparisons that can be made between different study groups or between measurement at different points of time. Thus the type of study design determines the kind of research questions that can be properly addressed and the associated statistical testing that is appropriate for these purposes.

Observational designs

In clinical studies that include HRQoL measures, observational designs are frequently carried out to determine the differences in HRQoL between different patient groups. Because comparison is focused on patient groups, this precludes randomisation of patients to the different groups. Hence no repeated or multiple measurements are planned and no experimental design is conducted (true experiment with randomisation of patients). In addition, measurements are often collected solely at a single point in time. The omission of a pre-measurement may be reasonable in cases where there is no actual treatment. Studies in the field of population health are predominantly of this type. However, even clinical studies may be based on an observational design because the goal of the study is to focus on the description of a stable (chronic) patient population (e.g. rheumatoid arthritis, dementia).

Experimental designs

In the case of an experimental design such as the RCT, a control group is required to determine possible biases, e.g. the placebo effect. In addition, the attribution of the subjects (patients) to the experimental group and the control group should be performed by randomisation of the patients to control for possible differences in patient characteristics between the groups. The benefits of the RCT are that possible biases can be properly controlled, and adequate statistical testing can be performed. All RCTs are characterised by a measurement before and a measurement after an intervention. The main reason for using both measures is to hold the starting points constant in subsequent analysis of experimental effects. Where the RCT is properly conducted the difference between the 2 measurements expresses the effects due to the intervention. Possible biases detected in the control group can be used to adjust the effect detected for the treatment group. Statistical analysis for this type of data should be performed on the data for both measurements and not on the change scores. This topic will be discussed in more detail in section 2.3.

Quasi-experimental designs

A relatively large number of studies are not based on the RCT but rely on various other types of design in which control or comparison groups are identified or constructed without applying randomisation. RCTs may not be applicable due to practical circumstances, time pressures, cost constraints or ethical considerations. A quasi-experimental design may also result when a study that starts out as an RCT does not end up that way, e.g. when there is a failure in randomisation. In order to overcome, at least partially, the potential biases that may arise from not obtaining a randomised attribution of subjects to the research groups, quasi-experimental designs deal with adaptations and extensions of the classical pre/post-measurement design (Cook and Campbell, 1979; Neal and Liebert, 1986).

One way to control for the comparability of treatment groups is to match the research groups. Another way is to collect measurements several times before and after a specific intervention. This type of quasi-experimental method has been termed 'simple interrupted time series design'. To date this type of design has rarely been applied in HRQoL measurement.

2.2 DATA COLLECTION

The EQ-5D

In clinical, economic, and population health studies the EQ-5D can be applied to measure health status. For economic studies of the cost-utility variety a key feature of the EQ-5D is fully used, which is that peoples' health states can be transformed to single numbers representing utilities. However, there are many situations where simply reporting respondent information on the 5 dimensions might offer significant information. In this case the role of the EQ-5D is mainly to function as a generic HRQoL instrument. Furthermore, it is important to recognise that the EQ-5D has been specially designed to complement other HRQol instruments.

EQ-5D descriptive system

On this part of the EQ-5D (page 2), the respondent is asked to indicate his/her health state by ticking in the box against the most appropriate statement in each dimension. The 5 EQ-5D dimensions comprise 3 levels, generating a total of 243 theoretically possible health states.

EQ VAS

The EQ VAS offers a simple method for obtaining and scoring self-rating of current health status. the VAS scale used is a vertical 20 cm. 'thermometer' (page 3). This page can be used in conjunction with the 5-digit classification of the descriptive system to build an accurate profile of the respondent's health status. The EQ VAS has endpoints of 100 ('best imaginable health state') at the top and 0 ('worst imaginable health state') at the bottom. The respondent rates his/her current health state on the EQ VAS by drawing a line from the box marked 'your own health state today' to the appropriate point on the EQ VAS.

EQ-5D index

Another variable that can be derived from the variables of the EQ-5D descriptive system is the EQ-5D index. The EQ-5D index is a health status index that can be used to calculate QALYs. In the economic evaluation of health care, QALYs can be used to compare the results of different health programmes. QALY calculations are based on information generated from quality of life indices combined with information about the number of life years gained from an intervention. EQ-5D self-classified health states from the descriptive system may be converted to a single summary index by applying scores from a standard set of preference weights derived from general population samples. In principle this index could be treated as a way of determining QALYs. There are different sets of weights available (see Chapters 4, 8 and 9).

If the health status index is based on a set of weights derived from values from general population samples, this implies that the index can be regarded as a *societal* valuation of the respondent's health state, in contrast to the respondent's or patient's own assessment of his/her health state (EQ VAS scores). If economic studies are being conducted from a societal perspective, the relevant EQ-5D index could be applied. Table 2.1 tabulates the suggested application of component parts of the EQ-5D with respect to the 3 different types of study.

Table 2.1. The suggested application of the 3 components of the EQ-5D classified by type of research study and design

		Design		
		Observational	Experimental	Quasi-experimental
Study	Clinical	Descriptive system VAS	Descriptive system VAS	Descriptive system VAS
	Economic	NA[a]	Index	Index
	Population	Descriptive system Index VAS	NA[a]	Descriptive system Index VAS

a. NA: Not Applicable

Missing data

Assessment of health status is rapidly becoming an integral part of many studies, especially in RCTs and economic studies. However, difficulties with data collection and compliance appear to be important obstacles to the successful implementation of health status assessment.

For the EQ-5D we can distinguish 2 main types of missing data: 1) item non-response for missing data in a questionnaire where a response has not been provided for at least 1 question; 2) unit non-response when the whole questionnaire is missing for a person.

With repeated data collection 3 different situations can arise:

(i) Late entry into the study.
(ii) Missing information.
(iii) Drop-out from the study.

Efforts to minimise the proportion of missing data and also the systematic biases that may cause this phenomenon are very important and should be a major concern for any study and for any outcome measure (Curran *et al*, 1998).

Because the EQ-5D descriptive system is based on only 5 independent dimensions, methods of handling missing data for 1 or more of the 5 dimensions are not adequate. In most cases a missing answer on 1 of the dimensions will lead to the complete rejection of the questionnaire. Only in repeated or longitudinal studies can some of the proposed solutions to overcome missing questionnaires be applied (at least partially). To analyse longitudinal HRQoL data, multi-level analysis may be used to overcome this problem (Goldstein, 1995).

2.3 ANALYSIS

Statistical models

Several statistical models are available to analyse and test various assumptions. In general, the analysis of variance (ANOVA) model is suited to test for mean differences between groups. If we are dealing with only 2 groups, ANOVA and the t-test are identical. An extension of this basic statistical model, the analysis of covariance (ANCOVA), may be appropriate when dealing with pre-assessments (see next section), which is the case in many clinical studies. For those situations where responses for the same person are collected on several occasions, the multivariate analysis of variance (MANOVA) model is required. MANOVA is also suitable for testing for mean differences between groups of persons and their repeated measures in a single analysis (Tabachnick and Fidell, 1989).

The same type of statistical analysis can also be performed by applying regression analysis with dummy coding. Because the method of coding, especially in the MANOVA type of analysis, is rather technical and requires substantial knowledge of the underlying statistical theory, this approach is only recommended for suitably trained researchers. However, the advantage of applying regression analysis may be the imputation of various variables to control for covariates. In addition, regression analysis provides a prediction model, which on some occasions may be the purpose of the study. Conventionally, regression analysis was carried out by using the linear optimal least squares (OLS) regression model. A more advanced regression model, that is being used more frequently in quality of life studies and outcomes research, is the multilevel or hierarchical model (Goldstein, 1995). By using this type of regression model the structure of the data can be specified (e.g. which health states are valued by which persons) and the model can handle missing data to some extent.

In clinical studies the primary outcome of research is often the occurrence of a particular event. For this purpose a statistical analysis is available called survival analysis. Conventionally, this analytical technique was developed for situations where the main outcome of the study was whether a patient died or was still alive. But other mutually independent events can also be considered (e.g. threshold clinical measures, disease-free, toxicity). Efforts have focused on the integration of both quality and quantity of life into a single analysis to be used for treatment comparisons. This has led initially to the development of the TWIST method and its extension into the quality-adjusted time without symptoms of disease and toxicity of treatment (Q-TWIST) method (Gelber *et al*, 1998). Q-TWIST was originally designed to incorporate aspects of HRQoL into adjuvant chemotherapy for the treatment of operable breast cancer (Goldhirsch *et al*, 1989), but the methodology has also been useful in other disease settings. As in an ordinary survival analysis, the focus of the method is on time, but rather than evaluating a single endpoint such as overall survival or disease-free survival, multiple outcomes corresponding to changes in HRQoL are considered. The multiple outcomes partition the overall survival time into clinical health states that may differ in HRQoL. Each clinical health state is assigned a weight that corresponds to its value in terms of HRQoL. The EQ-5D may be regarded as an appropriate instrument for this purpose.

Measuring change

The measurement of change has been a topic of considerable confusion in the medical literature. A number of articles (e.g. Guyatt *et al*, 1998) have argued that measurement of change in health status is, in most situations, the appropriate goal of research. The concept of responsiveness to change has provoked considerable controversy. Opinion about change scores and responsiveness is by no means unanimous (Hays and Hadorn, 1992; Wright and Young, 1997). For several years there has been an extensive debate in the fields of psychology, education, and more recently in epidemiology and clinimetrics, about the usefulness and appropriateness of difference scores as opposed to the raw data yielded from pre-post (experimental) designs (Norman *et al*, 1997). Though clinicians are considerably more familiar with the use of change (difference) scores and their interpretation from a methodological point of view, it should be recognised that statistical testing based on pre-measures and post-measures is more appropriate and in addition more capable of detecting statistically significant effects (Streiner and Norman, 1995), reflecting the greater power of such statistical tests. The underlying mechanism is that the simple subtraction of post-measurements from pre-measurements to create a difference score as a measure of the overall effect of treatment assumes that the effect of treatment will be the same, except for random error, for all subjects. This assumption can be shown to be false in many, if not most, circumstances (Streiner and Norman, 1995).

A variety of statistical tests are applicable to test treatment effects, including chi-square, paired t-tests, and repeated measures of ANOVA or ANCOVA. A more complex and informative method of analysis is based on using multiple regression. The research question posed can be exactly the same as in the former tests, but in addition, the multiple regression model is able to control for a selection of confounding factors (covariates), which should at least include the pre-measures. For the EQ-5D the change between successive measurements should preferably be performed with statistical tests that take into account the variance of the measurements and the association between the measurements.

Treatment groups

If data stems from an observational design, in most cases we are not confronted with a comparison between groups. Here the main objective is to evaluate or monitor the health status of the entire group under study. However, in clinical studies the main objective is often to detect an effect for a particular treatment. For methodological reasons this is investigated for 1 experimental group and 1 control (placebo) group, or is conducted for 2 or more groups of patients, each treated with a different modality. Similar study designs are also found in economic studies and sometimes even for population health studies, for example studies focused on the comparison of strata comprising people with low versus high education levels. In those situations where comparison between groups forms a central interest of the study more advanced statistical techniques are required.

To test for statistical significant differences between groups for outcomes collected at 1 point in time the standard t-test will be sufficient. For the EQ-5D this test can be applied for all 3 components of the instrument, i.e. the EQ-5D descriptive system, EQ VAS, and EQ-5D index. Non-parametric statistical tests can be considered if the distributions of the scores are highly skewed (Siegel and Castellan, 1988). More advanced statistical models are required if the research question is to focus on the effect of a particular intervention (pre-post measurement) in comparisons of 2 or more groups. Here MANOVA modelling is the appropriate technique. Unfortunately, for these more complex statistical analyses, no non-parametric counterparts are available.

2.4. REPORTING

Descriptive system

The data from the descriptive system may be presented as a profile (Figure 2.1). The distribution of the scores on the 5 dimensions can thus be analysed. It is strongly recommended that the scores on the descriptive system are always reported for the 3 levels in each dimension (e.g. as in Table 2.2).

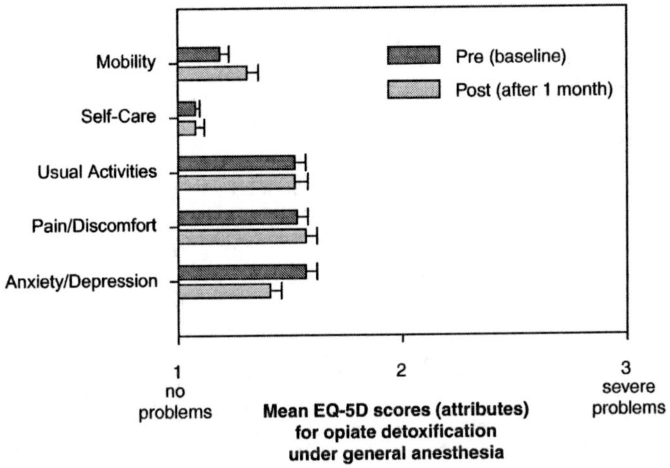

Figure 2.1. Graphical presentation of the mean outcomes (and standard errors of the mean) for the 5 dimensions of the EQ-5D for a clinical or cost-effectiveness pre-post design[1]

Table 2.2. Frequency distribution (profile) of the EQ-5D descriptive system for single observation studies[a]

EQ-5D profile	Mobility	Self-Care	Usual Activities	Pain/ Discomfort	Anxiety/ Depression
No problems	42 (20%)	83 (40%)	27 (13%)	76 (36%)	137 (66%)
Some problems	150 (73%)	118 (56%)	83 (40%)	115 (55%)	60 (29%)
Extreme problems	13 (6%)	8 (4%)	97 (47%)	18 (9%)	10 (5%)

a. Coast *et al*, 1998

1. Laheij *et al*, 2000

Scores obtained with the descriptive system can be compared with the scores of a reference group (e.g. Table 2.3).

Table 2.3. Frequency distribution (profile) of the EQ-5D descriptive system for comparison of more than 1 population or repeated measurements

EQ-5D profile	Dutch[a] (general population)	Migraine patients[b] (Dutch population)	Migraine[c]
Mobility			
no problems (%)	95.1	83.0	83.0
some problems (%)	4.7	16.3	16.3
confined to bed (%)	0.2	0.7	0.7
Self-Care			
no problems (%)	96.7	97.2	97.2
some problems (%)	2.9	2.8	2.8
unable to (%)	0.3	0.0	0.0
Usual Activities			
no problems (%)	85.8	72.4	72.4
some problems (%)	11.7	26.4	26.4
unable to (%)	2.4	1.2	1.2
Pain/Discomfort			
none (%)	68.0	49.5	49.5
moderate (%)	30.5	46.6	46.6
extreme (%)	1.5	3.9	3.9
Anxiety/Depression			
none (%)	83.6	73.0	73.0
moderate (%)	15.7	24.6	24.6
extreme (%)	0.7	2.5	2.5

a. Essink-Bot *et al*, 1993
b. Essink-Bot *et al*, 1995
c. Criteria International Headache Society. Based on: Essink-Bot *et al*, 1995

For many repeated measures results may be more easily represented in figure form rather than unwieldy tables, e.g. Figure 2.2.

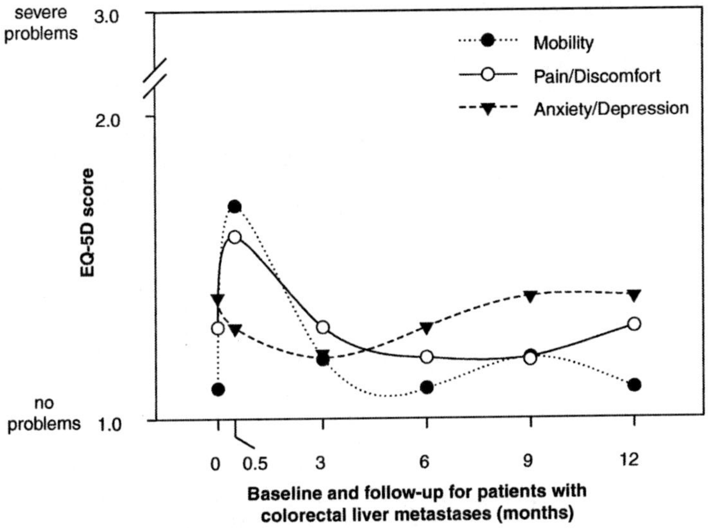

Figure 2.2. EQ-5D descriptive system[2]

EQ VAS

The scores on the own EQ VAS indicating the patient's assessment of his or her health state can be presented as mean scores with standard deviations. If researchers think it is more appropriate to report medians (e.g. to deal with the high skewness of the distribution of the VAS scores), both measures should be presented. Where more than 1 measurement has to be undertaken for the same group of persons, EQ VAS scores can be presented as in Table 2.4, or can be depicted graphically (Figure 2.3).

Table 2.4. EQ VAS score[a]

	Baseline		Period		Endpoint	
	Experi-mental group	Control group	Experi-mental group	Control group	Experi-mental group	Control group
Mean EQ VAS score (SD)	66.7 (17.6)	70.1 (17.9)	50.1 (24.2)	50.9 (24.8)	73.1 (18.9)	74.3 (18.2)
Median EQ VAS score (IQR)	70 (55-80)	70 (60-85)	50 (30-70)	50 (30-70)	80 (60-88)	75 (65-90)

a. Laheij *et al*, 2000

2. Langenhoff *et al*, 2001

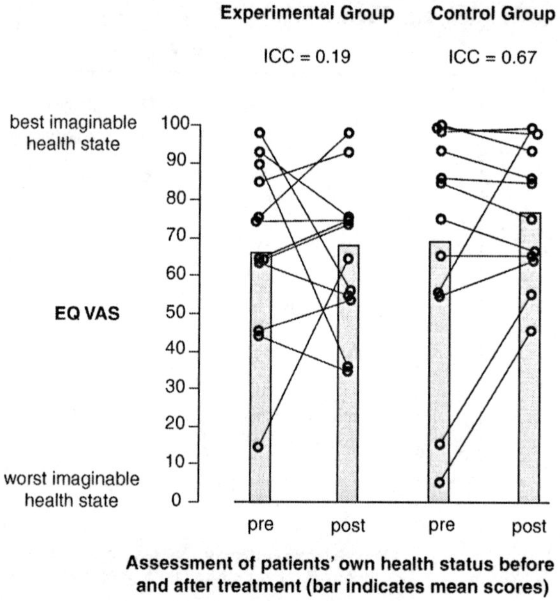

Figure 2.3. Example of clinical data presentation combined with mean outcomes for the EQ VAS[3]

EQ-5D index

Results for the EQ-5D index can be presented in similar ways to the EQ VAS scores. If EQ-5D index values are measured by a longitudinal design, a figure could be informative (e.g. Figure 2.4).

---

3. Krabbe, 1998

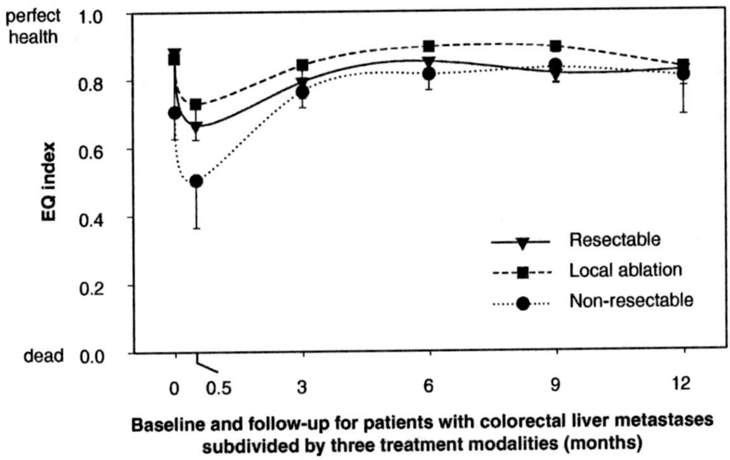

Figure 2.4. Example of presentation of longitudinal EQ-5D index measures[4]

2.5 SUMMARY

This chapter has indicated that EQ-5D can be used in 3 major areas of study - clinical, economic, and population health. A number of research designs were briefly discussed and the components of the EQ-5D were slotted into these designs. Data collection with the EQ-5D was described, followed by a discussion of a number of statistical techniques required for the analysis of these data. Finally, some suggestions concerning how to report EQ-5D data were presented. In the next chapter we consider how to administer the EQ-5D.

4. Langenhoff *et al*, 2001

3
EQ-5D: Modes of administration

Caroline Selai, Idoia Gaminde, Michael Herdman, Jeffrey Johnson and Rosalind Rabin

3.1 INTRODUCTION

Chapter 1 briefly described the conceptual underpinning and the development of EQ-5D so that the reader will be aware that in developing EQ-5D, the EuroQol Group had a number of specific goals. EQ-5D was originally designed to be a self-administered questionnaire, to be used in postal surveys. There are many instances, however, when self-reported completion of a paper-and-pencil questionnaire is either impractical or not possible. Self-report may not be possible because the respondent is physically incapacitated or cognitively impaired. Administration of paper-and-pencil versions of a questionnaire is sometimes not the most efficient method of data collection and may not be practical in large multi-centre trials. If we alter the mode of administration of a questionnaire, why is this change important?

Small differences in the wording, layout and/or administration of a questionnaire can influence the results. In between-group comparisons, for example, it is essential to ensure that the conditions under which the questionnaire is administered are as similar as possible in the different groups. In longitudinal studies, where the same questionnaire is administered on several occasions to the same group, every effort must be made to ensure that the conditions of administration are as similar as possible on each administration. Where this is not the case, the onus is on the researcher to prove, empirically, that the use of alternative formats or different modes of administration make no substantial difference to the results obtained.

This chapter provides recommendations for researchers wishing to collect clinical data using the EQ-5D descriptive system and the EQ VAS. Recommendations for researchers wishing to collect EQ-5D valuation data are not included here: they are provided in Chapter 4. This chapter has two aims:

(i) To give a brief overview of the literature on alternative modes of administration (i.e. anything different from pencil-and-paper self-report) relevant to EQ-5D.

(ii) To make recommendations for researchers intending to collect EQ-5D data using any of the alternative modes of administration. Scripts to be used for telephone administration, for interviews and proxy-report are included as appendices.

R. Brooks et al. (eds.),
The Measurement and Valuation of Health Status Using EQ-5D: A European Perspective, 21–27.

3.2 ALTERNATIVE MODES OF ADMINISTRATION

Self report, other than pencil-and-paper questionnaire received as part of postal survey.

Alternative modes of self-report include:

(i) Face-to-face interview.
(ii) Telephone interview.
(iii) Self-completion in the presence of an interviewer.

EQ-5D data have been collected using a variety of modes of administration. Face-to-face interview might be chosen if, for example, a respondent has motor difficulties which would make completion of a questionnaire difficult (e.g. a patient with Parkinson's disease). Telephone interviews can increase the response rate (compared to impersonal postal surveys) and they minimise data loss that may occur anywhere along the journey from the respondent's home, to the post-office, back to the researcher's desk. Sometimes, EQ-5D might be part of a battery of questionnaires that is administered at the respondent's home (or patient's bedside). This mode of administration might be chosen by a doctor or a nurse who is also performing a clinical examination. In this case, EQ-5D is completed in the presence of an interviewer.

Very few papers have reported on the advantages or limitations of the different forms of administration, and there has been little research into possible differences in scores due to modes of administration with regard to EQ-5D. It has generally been taken for granted that there are no differences. In a recent study, Wu *et al* (1997a), compared the mode of administration (self versus interview), the type of interview (face-to-face versus telephone) and self-administration versus proxy-rated interviews of the EQ VAS. They found no differences in the VAS scores by mode of administration (self versus interview), or by the type of interview (face-to-face versus telephone) but they found a 6 point difference in VAS scores between self-ratings and proxy-ratings of the patients' health state, with proxies rating patients lower. This did not quite reach statistical significance ($p = 0.06$). Data on the EQ-5D descriptive system were not reported in this paper.

Recommendations

Given the paucity of studies that have systematically compared the different modes of administration of EQ-5D use, we recommend that when different modes of administration are used, a variable indicating mode of administration should be recorded in the data set. Data should always be analysed separately before aggregating, and researchers should report consent rates, data completeness and other potential sources of bias for the different modes of administration. Where possible, an experimental design that tests for differences between modes of administration is recommended.

For telephone interviews, adherence to the script reproduced in Appendix 2 is recommended. For self-completion of EQ-5D in the presence of an interviewer, it is recommended that the respondent is handed EQ-5D, but that the interviewer should not give any additional verbal instructions. Only in this way is it possible to ensure uniformity of presentation and thus minimise bias introduced by help from the interviewer. Adherence to the scripts reproduced in Appendices 2-4 is recommended in regard to telephone interviews, interviewer present and face-to- face interviews

3.3 COMPUTER-ASSISTED DATA COLLECTION

Computer-assisted modes of administration are likely to play an increasing role in survey data collection. The resources spent in time (labour), and checking for error in the manual coding of paper-and-pencil questionnaires, data-entry and data-analysis are greatly reduced.

Computer-assisted modes may include both respondent self-report (with the respondent either alone in front of the computer or an interviewer present in the room) and proxy report. For a good review of the technological innovations relating to this mode of administration, see de Leeuw and Nicholls (1996).

In theory, the use of computer-assisted methods should introduce little bias in terms of framing effects. Depending on the design, computer-assisted tools are just screens which should display the same stimuli (i.e. sections of EQ-5D) as those seen on paper. To be consistent, the computer screen should display the 20cm vertical EQ VAS. Any researchers who have questions about presenting EQ-5D computer stimuli on a computer screen, should report to the EuroQol Business Management. Since there are likely to be rapid developments in the field of information technology, it is recommended that all researchers planning to develop a computer-assisted version of EQ-5D should contact the EuroQol Business Management for an update. Researchers are also advised to check the EuroQol Group website.

It is also recommended that the format of computer-assisted data collection versions (i.e. the wording and layout) should be exactly the same as the corresponding recommended pencil-and-paper version. For example, if EQ-5D is to be self-administered (not interviewer-assisted), then the computer programme should be self-running with the computer screens appearing as if the respondent was completing a paper and pencil task.

Standardised instructions should be written and a standardised screen used. For example:

(i) Introductory screen with explanation/instructions.
(ii) Overview.
(iii) Display of 2 components presented simultaneously on 1 screen, i.e. the EQ-5D descriptive system and the EQ VAS.
(iv) Screen requesting background variables.
(v) If proxy respondents are to be used, there should be a separate proxy version that is designed using the same format as one of the pencil-and-paper proxy protocols (see Appendices 5 and 6).

3.4 PROXY REPORT

In some cases, where the respondent is physically incapacitated or severely cognitively impaired, it is necessary to collect data via proxy report, i.e. someone who knows the respondent well, usually a relative, carer, nurse or clinician. There is a literature on the benefits and limitations of proxy reports of health status and quality of life (Magaziner *et al*, 1998). The overall picture is that there is generally fairly good proxy-patient agreement for concrete, observable items such as 'ability to walk' but poor agreement for non-observable items such as pain and affect (e.g. anxiety and depression). Given this general finding, we would anticipate patient-proxy agreement to be better for some dimensions on EQ-5D than for others. Over and above these expectations there might prove to be reasons why the structure or the wording of EQ-5D leads to particularly poor or better-than-expected patient-proxy agreement. All such findings should be documented and reported.

To date there have been few studies reporting proxy ratings of EQ-5D. Proxy data have been reported in a study of children with imperforate anus (Stolk *et al*, 2000), and in studies of patients with stoke and dementia.

Stroke

In a recent study that compared patient self-report to proxy scores in stroke patients (Dorman *et al*, 1997), data was available for 130 patient-proxy dyads. Agreement between responses from the patients and those from their proxies was better for patients who were able to self-complete EQ-5D than for those patients for whom EQ-5D had to be administered by interview. For both groups, agreement was best for the self-care dimension and worst for the dimension that assessed psychological outcome. For the more severely affected patients, agreement was only fair for the pain and social functioning dimensions and no better than chance alone for the psychological functioning dimension ($k = 0.05$). Patients tended to rate their own health status as better than their proxies did ($p < 0.05$). Dorman *et al* found moderate agreement between responses from patients and those from their proxies for the more directly observable dimensions of EQ-5D, and that proxy agreement was less good for the more subjective dimensions. They concluded that, in general, information about some dimensions obtained from a proxy may be sufficiently valid and unbiased to be useable in most types of trials and surveys.

Dementia

The assessment of quality of life of patients with dementia is complex. Despite the many methodological issues, there are several HRQoL assessment techniques in development. Studies have shown that patients with mild-to-moderate dementia can rate their own HRQoL but that proxies are needed for patients with severe dementia. EQ-5D was administered in 2 studies to both patients with dementia and their carers (Coucill *et al*, 2000; Coucill *et al*, 2001; Selai, 2000a; Selai *et al*, 2001). Overall, the findings generally supported the results reported in the literature i.e. better agreement for observable items and poorer agreement for pain/discomfort and anxiety/depression. Two particular findings emerged from these studies. First, in both studies there was very poor agreement for the usual activities dimension. Qualitative data revealed that both patients and carers were asking, "what is usual?" Since dementia leads to a gradual loss of abilities, it was not clear what 'usual' activities meant. Second, it was found that differences emerged not only because the patients and proxies had different perceptions of the degree of problem (e.g. patient ticked 'moderate' but proxy ticked 'extreme'). In addition, there were differences in interpretation of the scope of the question. For example, some patients thought the question about mobility referred to 'ability to walk'. Some of the proxies also thought it referred to this but some proxies said they were thinking about orientation (e.g. patient's ability to find their way home from the shops, an ability involving a number of cognitive skills). So some of the discrepancies arose from differences in interpretation of the question. The methodological issues are currently the subject of debate in the HRQoL literature. We recommend that reporting of experimental design, methods and results be explicit and detailed.

Additional methodological considerations:

Differences may occur according to who the proxy is (spouse, health professional, etc.) and whether he or she lives with the patient or just visits. There is also a big difference according to the instructions given to the proxy (not often explicitly reported). For instance, is the proxy reporting either (a) how he or she (i.e. the proxy), judges the HRQoL of the patient or (b) how he or she (i.e. the proxy) thinks the patient would judge his or her own HRQoL? In the case of dementia, there are problems due to denial and loss of insight. At a certain point of (severe) dementia the proxy might say that he/she thinks that the patient has an extreme problem in the area of social life but that he/she recognises that the patient has lost insight and seems quite happy, (oblivious, unaware). The proxy might therefore decide that the patient would rate himself or herself as having 'no problem' with his/her social life.

Recommendations

It is recommended that the relationship of the proxy to the patient (spouse, professional carer) is clearly documented. Also, it is recommended that the precise instructions to the proxy be reported. We have drawn up two proxy scripts:

(i) Asking the proxy to rate how he or she (i.e. the proxy) would rate the patient's HRQoL (Appendix 5).

(ii) Asking the proxy to rate how he or she (i.e. the proxy) thinks the patient would rate his or her own HRQoL if he/she (i.e. the patient) was able to communicate it (Appendix 6).

In general, it is recommended that proxy ratings are obtained for both of these. In projects where proxy ratings are collected in addition to patient self-report, it is recommended that strength of agreement be calculated and reported. Agreement should be assessed using the Cohen's kappa statistic for each of the EQ-5D dimensions. Confidence intervals should be produced as well. The conventional interpretation of the kappa statistic is shown in Table 3.1 (Altman, 1991).

Table 3.1. The conventional interpretation of the kappa statistic (Altman, 1991)

Value of k	Strength of agreement
< 0.20	Poor
0.21 – 0.40	Fair
0.41 – 0.60	Moderate
0.61 – 0.80	Good
0.81 – 1.00	Very good

3.5 RECALL PERIODS

EQ-5D was designed to record the HRQoL of the respondent on the day of administration. It has been suggested that in cases where health status fluctuates, the researcher might want to know how the respondent is today and his or her health status when he or she is more 'ill'. An example of this is the 'on' and 'off' periods of fluctuating health status in Parkinson's disease. Respondents have therefore been asked to recall a former health state (or think of a 'typical' health state) and give a rating for that period. Asking a respondent to recall and rate a previous health state introduces potential bias since a respondent may have a poor memory of his or her previous health condition. There is a large literature on memory and mis-memory for health states and the cognitive processes involved in surveys (Tanur, 1994).

Two studies using EQ-5D among critically ill patients had a complex design introducing both patient-proxy reports and a recall period. In one study, patients and proxies were asked to rate retrospectively the patient's health state prior to the "illness, intervention or accident which led to his or her admission to the ICU" (Badia *et al*, 1996). Agreement between patients and proxies regarding their prior health state was moderate to good in physical and pain areas and fair for anxiety/depression.

In a second, similar study, the instructions to the proxies were standardised (Diaz-Prieto *et al*, 1998). They were told to "think of your relative or friend and check the statements that best describe his or her health state 3 months prior to the current hospital admission". In this study, in all cases, EQ-5D was administered by the doctor attending the patient. Patient-proxy agreement was moderate for mobility, self-care and usual activities and fair for pain/discomfort and anxiety/depression.

3.6 SUMMARY

The interpretation and comparison of data (using any instrument) across studies is only possible if the *same* instrument has been used in each study. Any deviation from the standard instrument or from the standard mode of administration could introduce 'noise' into the data. We recognise that there are occasions when other versions of EQ-5D or other modes of administration are necessary or desirable. We have made suggestions for alternative formats and adherence to these scripts is strongly recommended.

4
Guidelines for value sets in economic and non-economic studies using EQ-5D

Paul Kind

4.1 INTRODUCTION

Values play a critical role in influencing all aspects of the planning and delivery of health care. The term 'values' is taken here to embrace a variety of forms of preference, sometimes but not always formally codified, sometimes held privately by individuals and otherwise pooled with others, sometimes represented in a quantitative numeric form and elsewhere represented descriptively or in an ordinal form. Our own private preferences shape the way that we respond to our own health experiences as patients. Health care workers are not insulated from the contaminating effects of their private values on the judgements that they make in the course of their professional activities. Politicians and policy makers too, will be aware of these same tensions. It is the usual state of affairs that such preferences remain largely obscured and the rules by which they are manipulated and traded are undocumented. The emergence of standardised measures of health status such as EQ-5D promises to introduce a degree of order to this otherwise confused information void. The strength of such measures lies partly in their capacity to generate numeric data in terms of a single index. In this, its most sophisticated form, EQ-5D explicitly incorporates information on preferences derived from one or other of its many potential sources. However, there are simpler methods of treating the data generated by EQ-5D but even these less complex formats rely in part upon the exercise of preferences. As with all generic measures of HRQoL 'values' form a consistent theme in the collection, processing, analysis and presentation of EQ-5D. This chapter is intended as a guide to the use of EQ-5D in its several formats and in the different types of application for which it was designed or has proven to be of value.

4.2 EQ-5D PRESENTATIONAL FORMATS

The EQ-5D descriptive system defines a total of 243 health states formed from the unique combinations of its 5 component dimensions. This fundamental classification is extended by a further 2 states (unconscious and dead). The basic information captured by the EQ-5D in its self-completion form comprises (a) the recorded level of problem on each of the 5 dimensions and (b) a rating of self-assessed health status on a 0-100 visual analogue scale. If EQ-5D is completed by an observer then these data may be absent in those instances where the subject of the assessment is unconscious or dead. Where present, the information for each dimension consists of a single digit number in the range 1 to 3 corresponding to the level of problem on that dimension.

R. Brooks et al. (eds.),
The Measurement and Valuation of Health Status Using EQ-5D: A European Perspective, 29–41.

These data may be treated as 5 separate items that constitute a profile of HRQoL and are usually represented graphically. When taken together these same data uniquely define 1 of the 243 possible EQ-5D health states. For reference purposes, this health state is labelled by combining the 5 separate digits that indicate the level of problem recorded for each dimension. Hence the health state 11232 is defined by responses indicating no problem with dimensions 1 and 2 (mobility and self-care), a moderate problem with dimensions 3 and 5 (usual activities and anxiety/depression) and an extreme problem with dimension 4 (pain/discomfort). In its most sophisticated form, this EQ-5D health state can be transformed into a single index score, once the rules for determining the relative value for each dimension/level have been determined.

Taken together, the 5 dimensions of the EQ-5D descriptive system can be manipulated in 4 formats:

(i) Single digit representation of level of problem on each dimension.
(ii) Collective representation of level of problem as a profile.
(iii) Encoded representation of profile as a unique health state.
(iv) Conversion of health state to corresponding weighted index.

The second source of information on HRQoL within EQ-5D is generated through the directly-assessed rating made on the standardised visual analogue scale that complements the descriptive record of problems dealt with above. This global rating yields a score in the range 0 to 100 (respectively the worst and best imaginable health states).

A number of assumptions regarding value can be introduced for each of these formats. The EuroQol Group has adopted an explicit position about the legitimacy of these assumptions but this does not preclude the possibility that others may wish to take a counter view. The key feature of these value assumptions is that they are reasonably transparent. Others who may wish to interpret EQ-5D differently will need to make clear any alternate value assumptions of their own. The basic data element of EQ-5D is the coded level of problem on each dimension. The numerals 1 to 3 are in fact no more than numeric labels with no intrinsic arithmetic properties. The numerals might just as well be substituted by the characters x, y and z. The numeric labels correspond to the hierarchical structure of the level of problem within each dimension (level 3 < level 2 < level 1). The use of the label as a cardinal score was never intended. To do so in this way would be to force a value system on to the data in ways that run counter to the express intentions of the Group. Interpreting the level codes as numbers implies for example, that within each dimension a level 2 problem lies midway between no problem and extreme problem. Furthermore, since the same assumption would be applied to each dimension in turn, the application of this value transformation implies that the value associated with a given level of problem is identical across all dimensions. These assumptions are dangerously appealing to the uninformed user but are to be generally avoided. Where they are encountered it should be recognised that such assumptions reflect the values of the researcher and consequently have limited status.

The danger of over interpretation is not limited to the imposition of numeric values on the basic descriptive components of EQ-5D. Once the encoded digits have been combined to identify a single health state the newly defined numeric label appears to have even more strongly pronounced arithmetic features. Again, the interpretation of these labels as numbers is misleading. The placement of numerals within the state label implies no specific value. For example, mobility is the first dimension that is assessed within EQ-5D. The state 31111 can safely be treated as worse than the state 21111. The magnitude of the difference between these 2 states cannot be inferred by subtracting 1 health state label from the other to yield the apparent 'score' of 10000. This type of manoeuvre imposes the assumption that the value of each dimension decreases concurrently with the order in which the dimensions are rated so that mobility would carry a higher value than, say, usual activities or self-care. Not only would such an interpretation run counter to the rationale of the Group, but it would leave researchers open to a more fundamental criticism. The ordinal relationship between EQ-5D health states is not defined in all cases. The state 22333 is logically superior to state 11222 since on all dimensions the first state indicates more extreme problems than the second. Such a clearly defined ordinal relationship does not hold for the states 11333 and 33111 where dominant patterns are partial in each state. To treat such ambiguous states as though they were numbers would clearly be an illegitimate operation.

Finally, the descriptive information generated by the first part of the EQ-5D may be converted into a single aggregate index (EQ-5D index) once the relative value of dimensions (and levels within dimensions) has been established. Such values may arise from specific investigation, for example from surveys conducted with the general population. Equally, where no appropriate external set of values exists, researchers may be tempted to utilise their own reasonable assessment of the scores to be associated with level changes within dimensions. Given the range of value sets that are now available from studies in which such values were explicitly investigated, there is no longer scope for considering the use of researcher-based value assumptions as having any particular legitimacy.

4.3 TYPES OF USE

EQ-5D is by definition a generic measure and hence there are few natural constraints to the potential range of applications in which it could be usefully deployed. It was designed for self-completion and this has remained its primary mode of administration although it is now recognised that there are circumstances where this is impractical for one reason or another. This is not a particular limitation of EQ-5D but rather a general problem for the measurement of HRQoL. Such situations are encountered when respondents are not able themselves to complete the EQ-5D as with say, trauma patients or individuals with cognitive problems, or in the frail elderly or very young. Since EQ-5D was originally designed for delivery via a printed questionnaire, the advent of alternative modes of administration through telephone or computer-assisted interview introduces other considerations that were considered in Chapter 3.

In general, the observation of HRQoL falls into 2 categories:

(i) When conducted on individual subjects who may or may not be located within the health care system as patients, or on 1 or more groups of subjects.
(ii) When conducted at a single point in time, or as a repeated linked measurement over time.

EQ-5D could be used as a point estimate of HRQoL in a single individual. Where reference data are available, such as population age/sex averages, then such information is useful in establishing the proximity of that individual to those average levels. This practice is analogous to the use of clinical parameters when used in testing 'normal' values seen in a patient, for example in their blood-pressure or body mass. Similarly, EQ-5D might be used as a marker of global health status when assessing patients in disease areas such as in oncology or rheumatology, where standard classifications are used to indicate clinical disease severity. EQ-5D might be measured periodically to monitor HRQoL over time, for example at key stages of referral, hospital admission, discharge and follow-up. When repeated in this way, then such monitoring information could be utilised to infer changes in HRQoL. These outcome data will vary according to the format in which the EQ-5D information is processed. The subject of discussion in this chapter is predominantly related to the use of EQ-5D in its weighted index form.

Individual EQ-5D data can be aggregated to provide information about the health status of population subgroups of interest. Establishing reference material for the general population is an important part of the development of EQ-5D in any country setting. Such information is now available for several countries, in some instances having been collected in multiple surveys thus providing insights into changes in public health over time. These reference data can be useful in informing the assessment of health inequalities and in the determination of resource allocation. In clinical studies, when mean change in HRQoL is a designated primary or secondary end-point, then EQ-5D can provide the requisite information. Once again it would be possible to consider other EQ-5D formats, but it is the weighted index form that is reviewed here. Studies in which outcomes data are generated may be used to provide information for economic analysis, for example in establishing cost-effectiveness. Where this type of analysis is required by regulatory bodies it is likely that there will be particular requirements that affect the choice of the reported EQ-5D format and the selection of the reference source for values used to compute the weighted index.

There remains a third broad class of application in which EQ-5D has a role. The EuroQol Group came into being largely to explore the cross-national similarities and differences in the values attached to health states. There are important issues to be addressed here when the values themselves form the basis of study. Attention to the proper replication of valuation methods may be more important than concern with the selection of any particular method. Comparability of sampled populations may be a more substantial problem than the achievement of national representation.

4.4 SOURCES AND TYPES OF VALUES

As has been already noted, it is possible to conceive of several *ad hoc* arrangements that might be used to impose a value structure on EQ-5D data. The Group has from the outset been concerned with the investigation of values for EQ-5D health states and research groups within its network have at one time or another adopted several valuation methods, these methods include:

(i) VAS using a vertical 20cm graphical rating scale.
(ii) Ranking.
(iii) Paired comparisons.
(iv) Time Trade-Off (TTO).
(v) Standard Gamble (SG).
(vi) Person Trade-Off (PTO).

The EuroQol Group adopted the first of these (VAS) as its standard valuation method. Since the process of directly eliciting values for all EQ-5D health states would be procedurally onerous, a number of factorial designs have been adopted in research supported by the Group. Data derived using these different sets have formed the basis of separate modelling studies designed to estimate values for health states that were not directly observed. An analysis of the data from these various studies is the subject of Chapter 8. VAS ratings, generally obtained from postal survey responses to a mailed questionnaire, form the greater part of the valuation data held within the EuroQol Group. These data are available in 2 forms. In its standard form, the postal questionnaire records individual ratings for each of 16 health states. In addition, respondents are asked to record their value for the state 'dead' using the same VAS rating scale. These ratings yield scores that lie between 0 and 100. Mean and median scores for EQ-5D health states based on all respondents in a valuation survey can be readily computed. For certain purposes, however, it is necessary to present values for EQ-5D health states on a reworked scale in which the logically best health state (11111) has the value 1 and dead has the value 0. This transformation is usually performed on individual respondent data prior to aggregation. However, individual respondents sometimes fail to record ratings for all health states presented in the questionnaire. This is generally not critical but where values for either 11111 or dead are missing, then any remaining scores cannot be transformed. There is a particular tendency for respondents who are older and/or less well educated, to omit a rating for 'dead' so that these vulnerable population subgroups are at additional risk of being censored as a consequence of the transformation process. In selecting the most appropriate source of transformed EQ-5D values it might be prudent for the user to take account of any possible biases introduced by this route.

4.5 QUESTIONS OF AGGREGATION

The source of reference values and the methods used to obtain them are two central issues in assessing the robustness of any measure of health status that claims to be a preference-based instrument. However, one further issue is relevant. Supposing that values have been obtained from an appropriate reference source then these will have to be represented by some sort of average. The aggregate form of these data might be one of several different measures of central tendency. The choice of such measures is often seen as being driven exclusively by statistical considerations, for example, where distributions are non-normal then the median would be preferred to the mean. There are related secondary aspects of such a choice in that appropriate statistical tests would be non-parametric with consequent limitations for the generalisation of results. In the area of preference measurement the choice of average measure is not entirely a statistical one - other perspectives can be legitimately applied. If the measurement of values for health states were treated as akin to a ballot of the sort encountered as part of the electoral process then the median value would be the natural corresponding choice. In some circumstances a case might even be made for the mode. The form of measure of central tendency may well be influenced by other factors, notably where incomplete sets of values have been used to interpolate values for health states. Since this type of modelling is common practice within the EuroQol Group it is recommended that end-users take note of any constraints that might arise as a result of the methodology adopted in estimating values for the complete set of EQ-5D health states.

4.6 APPLICATION

It is assumed here that EQ-5D has been collected with a view to measuring health status (HRQoL), sometimes for individuals or groups of individuals, and sometimes at several points of time. When used to measure health outcomes it is useful to note that this can be conducted in several frameworks, by different professionals with different objectives. Whilst it may reasonably be argued that a distinction between clinical and economic evaluation is artificial, it remains the case that health care professionals use health outcomes data in forms that are different to those adopted by health economists. Nothing is lost by retaining the option to adopt different values with which to make the conversion from ordinal ratings to a weighted index. This then is the entry point for the flow chart shown in Figure 4.1.

4.7 EQ-5D IN ECONOMIC STUDIES

In an economics application the choice of value set is in part determined as a consequence of the form of analysis that is selected. Cost-utility analysis requires an index to act as the quality-adjustment factor in computing QALYs. This in turn means that the value set must have been generated using a recognised utility measurement procedure[1]. Most often CUA will adopt a societal perspective and in these circumstances the index adjustment should be made using utility weights that are those of the general population. In those studies that adopt the patients' perspective utility weights from relevant population subgroups will be necessary. For example, a clinical trial that incorporated patient self-assessed health status might use a utility measurement procedure to elicit that assessment. In these circumstances the utility weight is based primarily on the actual health state in which the patient is located. This position contrasts with estimates obtained through procedures that describe hypothetical health states of which the respondent may or may not have first-hand experience.

In reaching a decision regarding which utility weights should be adopted it is worth taking a number of considerations into account. Firstly, it should be noted that the EuroQol Group makes no recommendation in respect of any utility procedure. Unless there is clear evidence to the contrary, for these purposes it should be assumed that all such methods have equal status. Furthermore, since different researchers within the Group have adopted different utility measurement procedures at one time or another, there are a number of alternate value sets from which a choice could be made. The primary consideration here is the analytic perspective that is being taken in the planned CUA. Where utility weights for the relevant population or population subgroup exist then these clearly should be weights that are used in the analysis.

---

1. For these purposes TTO, SG or PTO

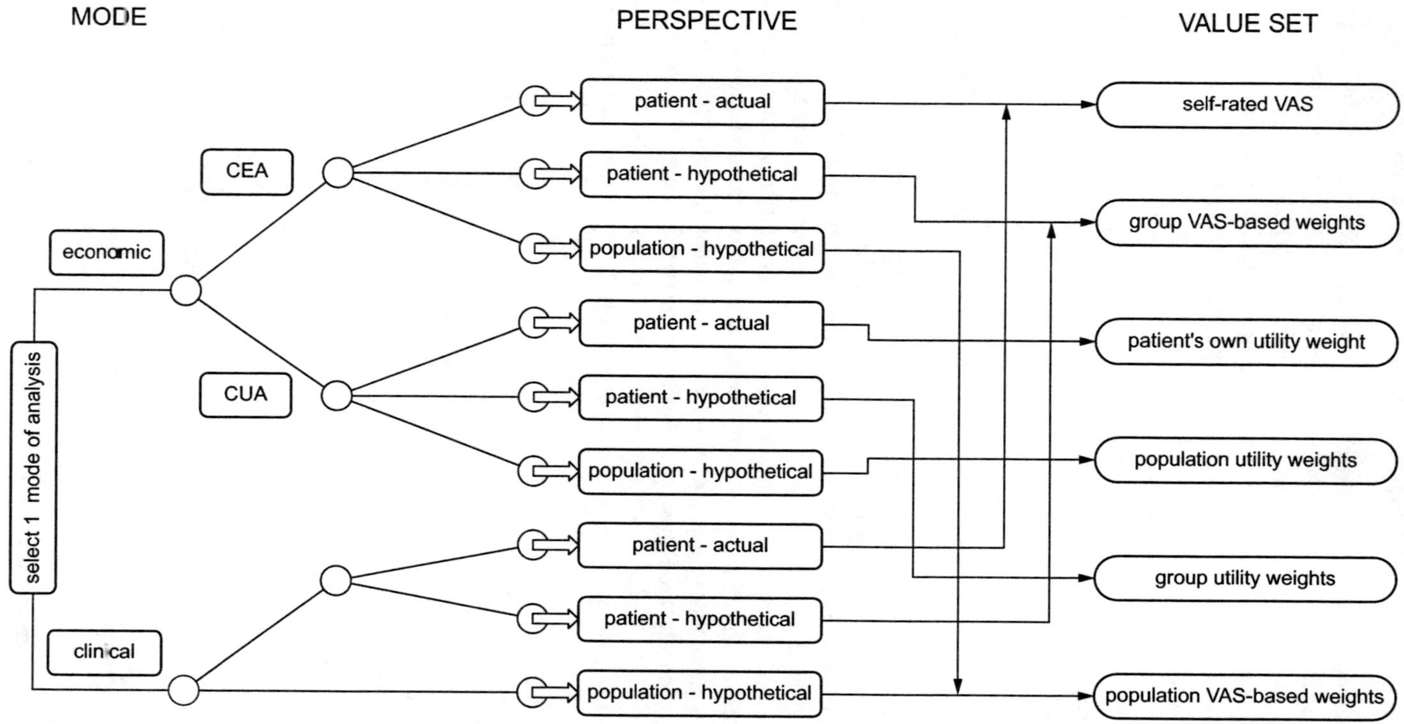

Figure 4.1. Values, valuations and applications

Where no utility weights are already to hand, there are further choices that can be exercised. Firstly, utility weights from an alternative source might be adopted *pro tempore* as surrogates for the correct local values. Given the sound technical basis of the UK MVH study it would be natural to look no further than the UK TTO A1 valuation set in these circumstances (MVH Group, 1995). However, it should be admitted that the utility weights in the MVH study were collected from a representative sample of the UK population some 10 years ago, so that the use of these utility weights in a contemporary, non-European setting may be problematic. Secondly, utility weights might be estimated from the results of work undertaken in the EQ-net project that sought to derive a unified set of values based on a pooling of data generated in different valuation studies conducted in different countries (see Chapters 8 and 9). Both these courses of action involve an element of risk that needs to be carefully considered before any final decisions are taken.

Where cost-effectiveness is the form of analysis that is adopted, then the requirement of utility weights no longer applies, and other forms of valuation can be regarded as legitimate means of computing the index form of EQ-5D. Valuing changes in EQ-5D health states using VAS methods is entirely consistent with the use of any naturally occurring, convenient outcome parameter as the measure of benefit in a cost-effectiveness study[2]. Once again it is possible to contemplate 3 possible valuation scenarios – the patient's own individual perspective, that representing the collective view of patients[3] as a group, and a societal perspective that represents the community as a whole. Again, where valuation sets are available the source of weights can be readily identified. The situation becomes more complex when no values are directly available for the relevant population or subgroup. Short of commissioning an independent valuation survey – which would probably be the most appropriate strategic response – the use of a pre-existing valuation set is indicated. The problem here, however, is that of choosing between a number of second-best solutions. General population surveys have been conducted in several countries, but not always using a common standard methodology, so that close examination of the reported methods and analysis is recommended before a selection is made from amongst these competing sources. The EQ-net methodology reported in this book offers a route away from these difficulties, but introduces further complexities of its own. However, in the absence of any locally determined VAS scores, values based on the analysis of cross-European EQ-5D data may prove the best alternative.

Finally, since EQ-5D enables respondents to record their own self-rated health status using a 0-100 VAS scale, it could be envisaged that a change in this rating might be used as a measure of patient benefit. In that case a CEA analysis might present results

---

2. If cost per unit change in blood pressure (BP) then why not cost per unit change in EQ-5D?
3. This could equally well be generalized to stand for any designated subgroup of interest, say caregivers or family instead of patients as direct beneficiaries

in terms of a cost per unit change in self-assessed health status. Table 4.1 summarises the options in selecting EQ-5D weights for economic studies.

Table 4.1. Summary of choice factors in selecting EQ-5D weights for economic studies

	Cost-utility analysis	Cost-effectiveness analysis	Cost consequences
Format	Index	Index	Profile or Index
Utility weights	Yes	Optional	Optional
Source	General population	General population Population subgroups Self-assessment	General population Population subgroups Self-assessment
Normalised scores	Yes	Optional	Optional
0 –100 scale	No	Optional	Optional
Suggested default source	UK TTO A1	EQ-net VAS	Optional
own VAS	No	Optional	Optional

4.8 EQ-5D IN NON-ECONOMIC STUDIES

Health status measurement is a key activity in the planning and delivery of care. In addition to the role that EQ-5D has in evaluation, as indicated in the previous section, it is well suited to generating information for use in many other settings including clinical decision-making, informing public health policy and in clinical studies. For example, the issue may simply be to compare the health status of an individual with normative data based on population averages for someone of similar background. Such reference values are available for laboratory tests and it is wholly unexceptional to report say, a patient's blood serum levels and at the same time indicate the 'normal' range. Management or treatment decisions may stem from such information. In using EQ-5D to compare the health of patient groups or local populations with such normative reference values, we can establish variations that can impact on the formation of policy. Where such activity is put into place more systematically, then health authorities can utilise the information to monitor progress in achieving national targets for health improvements. Comparisons *between* provider units in different locations or between consultant specialties *within* a single institution can result in significant information that might be applied for benchmarking or performance management. There is a self-evident need for outcomes data in clinical studies and, as indicated in the previous section, EQ-5D has a specific role where economic analysis is concerned. However, its usefulness is not confined to application in cost-effectiveness studies. EQ-5D is capable of contributing important outcomes data in clinical studies in its own right.

For the majority of non-economic studies the issue of valuation can be more readily resolved. Where EQ-5D responses are to be converted to a single index the valuation method *per se* is less of an issue. First and foremost, the valuation method should conform to the standard EuroQol methodology based on VAS ratings obtained through postal surveys. Valuations for EQ-5D health states are available for several countries where large representative samples of the general population have been invited to take part. Where national value sets exist then these should provide the principal reference source. Once again, there are many alternate sets of values that might be considered where no local set is to be found and these include primarily the EQ-net VAS values and the UK VAS A3 (MVH Group, 1995). Such value sets are clearly proposed as pragmatic choices in the absence of local values but inevitably carry some risk that they will fail to properly represent the view and preferences of the population in which they are being applied. It is to be hoped that the absence of local value sets will signal the need to fill this information gap.

In non-economic studies of a national population it is essential to maintain consistency in selecting a set of values. In longitudinal studies, the same set of values should be applied throughout. Similarly, where cross-sectional studies are separated by time or geography, it will be important to use a common value set when deriving estimates of health status. The practicalities of standardisation have been addressed within the EQ-net project but there remain fundamental questions, as yet unresolved, about the conceptual basis for a single universal set of health state values. The impact of selecting a single value set must be addressed no matter which of the many options is adopted. Failing to do so leaves us little further advanced than the researchers who impose their personal private preferences in valuing health.

4.9 TAILPIECE

A key question, not specifically addressed in Figure 4.1, is that of the availability of value sets for use in different countries. A number of value sets based on surveys of the general population have already been established as listed in Table 4.2. However, given that work to develop similar value sets for other countries and population subgroups is always likely to be in process then prospective users should consult the EuroQol Group website (www.euroqol.org).

Table 4.2. National population value sets

Country	Population	N	Valuation method	Reference
Denmark	General	1179	VAS	Wittrup-Jensen *et al,* 2002
	General	1332	TTO	Wittrup-Jensen *et al,* 2002
Canada	General	1700	VAS	Pickard *et al*, 2001
Finland	General	1630	VAS	Ohinmaa *et al*, 1996
Germany	General	370	VAS	Schulenburg *et al*, 1996
	General	124	VAS	Claes *et al*, 1999
	General	339	TTO	Claes *et al*, 1999
Japan	General	621	TTO	Tsuchiya *et al*, 2002
Netherlands	General	993	VAS	Essink-Bot *et al*, 1993; Busschbach *et al*, 1999
	Students	126	VAS	Busschbach *et al*, 1997
New Zealand	General	919	VAS	Devlin *et al*, 2000a
Spain-Catalunya	General (includes patients)	600	VAS	Badia *et al*, 1995a
	General (includes patients)	294	VAS	Badia *et al*, 1998
	General	979	TTO	Badia *et al*, 2001
Spain-Navarra	General	300	VAS	Gaminde *et al*, 1996
Sweden	General	542	VAS	Björk & Norinder, 1999
UK	General (GP practice)	122	VAS	Gudex, 1992
	General	3395	TTO	MVH Group, 1995; Dolan, 1997
	General	3395	VAS	MVH Group, 1995
	General	238	TTO	Macran & Kind, 2000
	General	238	VAS	Macran & Kind, 2000
	General	1764	VAS	Macran & Kind, 2001
US	General	905	VAS	Johnson *et al,*2000a
Zimbabwe	General	2384	VAS	Jelsma, 2002a
	General	2384	TTO	Jelsma, 2002a

Users of EQ-5D have a rich array of value sets from which to select one or more that are relevant to their needs[4]. The starting point in this selection process has to be the anticipated uses to which the EQ-5D data are to be put. The basic information comprises 5 data items indicating the level of self-reported problems on each of the EQ-5D dimensions. For the purposes of this guidance, the required format is taken to be the single index no matter the intended form of application. The question at issue then, is to determine which of several alternative valuation sets is best suited for the task of converting the 5 ordinal ratings into a weighted composite score.

Whilst ideally a set of weights that represent the general population's preferences might be the system of choice, what is to be done if such a system is not accessible? These second best choices can be resolved as follows.

For economic studies, in the absence of a set of national population-based utility weights, then select a set of utility weights for a population that most closely approximates it. In the absence of a suitable candidate, adopt the most robust valuation set (*pro tempore* the UK TTO A1 set).

For economic studies where cost-utility analysis is not anticipated, then a VAS set of weights can be used. In the absence of a locally appropriate set of values then adopt the most robust valuation set (either UK VAS A3 set or the EQ-net VAS set).

In non-economic studies where VAS values are required, then act as in the last paragraph. If relevant to the form of non-economic study, the use of self-rated VAS data should be considered.

For economic or non-economic studies in which the values for health states are required from particular population subgroups then it may be possible to synthesise by analysing pre-existing value sets collectively owned by members of the EuroQol Group. Contact the EuroQol Business Management for assistance.

---

4. Although Table 4.2 indicates a potentially diverse source of data, values for *all* EQ-5D health states may for technical reasons not be available for all countries. Contact the EuroQol Business Management for the current state of play.

5
Test-retest performance of EQ-5D

Susan Macran

5.1 INTRODUCTION

In order to assess the usefulness of a measure there is a need to determine its measurement (or psychometric) properties. This usually involves examining its reliability (the extent to which the results it provides are reproducible) and its validity (the extent to which it measures what it is intended to measure). The reliability and validity of a measure can be assessed in a number of different ways and the book by Streiner and Norman (1995) provides a readable guide. This chapter reports on the exploration of 1 aspect of reliability, the test-retest reliability or the reproducibility of scores, for the EQ-5D descriptive system and the EQ VAS. Although 2 previous studies have examined the test-retest reliability of health state values elicited using the EQ-5D VAS (Van Agt *et al,* 1994; Dolan *et al,* 1994), until now there have been no published findings on the reliability of the EQ-5D descriptive system and the EQ VAS.

An important requirement of the EQ-5D and indeed all health outcome measures, is that the measurements they produce are sensitive to change. When assessing the performance of a measure users need to know the extent to which any change reflected by a measure is due to 'real' change or due to some sort of measurement error. Such a characteristic is usually assessed by calculating the test-retest reliability of a measure. Test-retest reliability calculates the consistency of a measure over time, and is most commonly assessed by administering a measure to the same group of individuals on 2 occasions separated by a time period which is short enough to assume that the individuals' health will not have changed. This time interval is probably the most important consideration when assessing the test-retest reliability of a measure. If the interval is too short, respondents may remember what they answered on the first occasion, while if it is too long, the characteristic that is being measured may have changed. As the most appropriate time interval is dependent both on the task and the nature of the characteristic being measured there are no standard rules for determining this period.

Test-retest reliability is summarised by calculating a reliability coefficient, which defines the ratio of the variability in the 2 scores for a respondent to the total variance and thus the proportion of the total variance in the scores which is due to 'true' difference. Reliability coefficients range from 0 to 1.0, where 0 indicates no reliability and 1.0 indicates perfect reliability (no measurement error). While there are a number of methods for calculating such coefficients, the intra-class correlation coefficient (ICC)

R. Brooks et al. (eds.),
The Measurement and Valuation of Health Status Using EQ-5D: A European Perspective, 43–54.

is usually considered the most appropriate for continuous data, while Cohen's kappa or weighted kappa coefficient (Cohen, 1960; Cohen, 1968) is best for nominal data.

As well as merely reporting a reliability coefficient it can also be informative to examine the performance of a measure over time in other ways, for example, by simply examining changes in scores across the 2 occasions relative to some external change criterion. Indeed in some cases, reliance on just a standard reliability coefficient may give a misleading impression of a measure's performance depending on the task in hand. It has been suggested (Guyatt *et al*, 1989; Deyo *et al*, 1991) that properties such as reliability and validity are not sufficient to indicate a measure's suitability for measuring longitudinal change. Instead, the responsiveness of a health outcome measure, or ability to detect important clinical changes (which may be identified by patients, clinicians, or physiological measurements) over time is also an important characteristic.

This chapter presents analysis of the test-retest performance (reliability and responsiveness) of the EQ-5D descriptive system and the EQ VAS. The data presented in this paper are taken from 2 data sets where EQ-5D was administered on 2 separate occasions. One is a sample of the general population and the other is a clinical sample of individuals with rheumatoid arthritis. For both samples the time interval over which the data was collected was 3 months. Data in the former was originally collected to test the test-retest performance of the EQ-5D VAS valuations, while in the case of the latter sample, data were collected with the express purpose of assessing the test-retest performance of EQ-5D.

Sample 1 is taken from the 1993 MVH survey (Dolan *et al*, 1994) which interviewed a representative population sample of 3395 adults living in Great Britain. A sub-sample of 221 individuals, selected to be representative of the main sample, was re-interviewed 3 months after the initial interview in 1991.

Sample 2 is taken from a sample of individuals with rheumatoid arthritis (Hurst *et al*, 1997) who were attending as out-patients in Edinburgh, Lothian and Fife in Scotland. 224 patients completed EQ-5D at home prior to a routine clinic appointment 3 months apart in 1995.

5.2 THE DATA

Sample 1 – MVH survey

221 individuals completed EQ-5D on 2 occasions, 3 months apart. The sample was: 55% female; median age 43 years (range 19 years to 87 years); 11% were educated to at least degree level and 28% had no qualifications.

Table 5.1 compares the frequency of reported problems on each of the EQ-5D dimensions for the sample at time 1 and time 2. Overall there was very little change in scores, although the sample as a whole appears to have become slightly healthier. Table 5.1 also presents test-retest reliability scores in the form of kappa coefficients, for each of the dimensions. In terms of reliability some dimensions performed much better than others. In this general population sample the mobility dimension was the most reliable and the pain dimension the least reliable. 84 individuals (38% of the sample) changed their response on at least 1 dimension between time 1 and time 2, and there were 132 changes in total. 61% of the changes were positive, i.e. the majority of cases who changed reported improved health at time 2. Of those individuals who changed, the majority (63%) only changed on 1 dimension. No individuals changed on all 5 dimensions.

Table 5.1. EQ-5D test-retest frequencies (MVH survey)

	No problems	Moderate problems	Extreme problems	N	Kappa (SE)
Mobility - Time1		Mobility - Time 2			0.75 (0.06)
No problems (%)	97	2	1	178	
Some problems (%)	24	76	--	42	
Extreme problems (%)	--	100	--	1	
Self-Care - Time 1		Self Care - Time 2			0.65 (0.12)
No problems (%)	98	2	< 1	208	
Some problems (%)	31	61	8	13	
Extreme problems (%)	--	--	--	--	
Usual Activities - Time 1		Usual Activities - Time 2			0.59 (0.07)
No problems (%)	94	5	< 1	186	
Some problems (%)	31	65	3	29	
Extreme problems (%)	17	50	33	6	
Pain/Discomfort - Time 1		Pain/Discomfort - Time 2			0.49 (0.06)
No problems (%)	90	10	< 1	146	
Moderate problems (%)	41	56	3	68	
Extreme problems (%)	--	71	29	7	
Anxiety/Depression -Time 1		Anxiety/Depression - Time 2			0.57 (0.07)
No problems (%)	94	6	--	174	
Moderate problems (%)	41	59	--	44	
Extreme problems (%)	--	67	33	3	

Table 5.2 presents the number of positive/negative changes experienced by the sample broken down by EQ-5D dimension. The pain/discomfort dimension experienced the most number of changes (accounting for 38% of the changes observed) followed by the anxiety/depression and the usual activities dimensions. Changes on the pain/discomfort, anxiety/depression and mobility dimensions tended to be largely positive, while changes on the usual activities and self-care dimensions were equally distributed between positive and negative.

Table 5.2. Number of (positive/negative) changes by EQ-5D dimension (MVH survey)

Number of dimensions changed	Mobility		Self-Care		Usual Activities		Pain/ Discomfort		Anxiety/ Depression	
	Pos.	Neg.	Pos.	Neg.	Pos.	Neg.	Pos.	Neg.	Pos.	Neg.
1	2	1	1	2	2	2	21	7	10	5
2	5	--	--	1	4	4	7	4	7	2
3	3	3	2	2	5	5	5	4	1	3
4	1	2	1	1	2	1	--	2	2	--
Total	11	6	4	6	13	12	33	17	20	10

The mean EQ VAS scores of the sample improved from 81.2 (SD=17) at time 1 to 83.8 (SD=17) at time 2. In terms of conventional criteria, the EQ VAS showed good reliability with an ICC of 0.84 (95% CI 0.65-0.78). Just over three-quarters of the sample (76%) showed a change in their EQ VAS scores across the 2 time points: for 50% of cases EQ VAS scores improved and for 26% of cases it worsened. Most changes were in the order of 10 points on the VAS scale or less, although some cases showed large changes (see Figure 5.1). Although individuals who experienced positive changes exhibited the widest distribution of change scores, those who experienced negative changes were more likely to show large changes of 20 points or more.

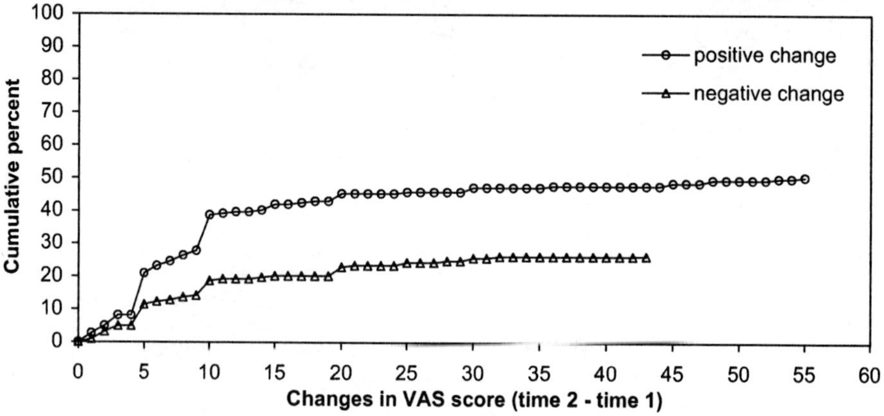

Figure 5.1. Change in VAS scores (MVH survey)

Table 5.3 examines the relationship between a change in EQ VAS scores between time 1 and time 2 and change in the number of problems reported on the EQ-5D dimensions. Respondents who experienced a change of more than 3 points in their EQ VAS scores between time 1 and time 2 were more likely to experience a change in the number of problems reported on the EQ-5D dimensions than those who experienced no change or a change of 3 points or less on the EQ VAS. Those who experienced a negative change on the EQ VAS were more likely to change on 2 or more dimensions than those who experienced a positive change.

Table 5.3. Percentage change in EQ-5D dimensions between time 1 and time 2 by change in EQ VAS time 1-time 2 (MVH survey)

	No change[a]	Better[b]	Worse[b]
No change EQ-5D dimensions	73	59	49
Change on 1 dimension	17	30	23
Change on > 1 dimension	10	11	28
N	81	92	47

a. Change of 3 points or less
b. Change of more than 3 points

31 cases (14%) reported that they had a serious illness at time 1. Table 5.4 shows that these individuals were far more likely than the rest of the sample to experience a change in their level of reported problems on the EQ-5D dimensions between time 1 and time 2: 70% compared to 33% experienced a change on at least 1 dimension. Table 5.4 also shows that these sample members were also more likely to experience a change (both positive and negative) in their EQ VAS scores between time 1 and time 2. 97% of those with a serious illness experienced a change of more than 3 points on the EQ VAS compared with only 72% of those with no serious illness.

9 cases reported that they had experienced a new serious illness since they first completed EQ-5D at time 1. However, this number was too small for any meaningful analysis.

Table 5.4. Percentage change on EQ-5D between time 1 and time 2 by serious illness at time 1 (MVH survey)

	Serious illness at time 1	
	Yes	No
No change on EQ-5D dimensions	29	67
Change on 1 dimension	42	21
Change on > 1 dimension	28	12
No change on EQ VAS	3	27
Negative change on EQ VAS	39	24
Positive change on EQ VAS	58	48
N	31	190

Sample 2 – Rheumatoid arthritis study

224 individuals completed EQ-5D on 2 occasions, 3 months apart. The sample was 81% female with a median age of 55 years (range 21 years to 87 years). The mean duration of arthritis amongst sample respondents was 13 years (SD 12).

Table 5.5 compares the frequency of reported problems on each of the EQ-5D dimensions for the sample at time 1 and time 2 plus the kappa reliability coefficients. At the aggregate level there was very little change in the number of reported problems over the 3 months, although the sample as a whole reported slightly better health status. Fewer individuals reported extreme problems and slightly more individuals reported moderate problems. With respect to reliability, EQ-5D performed less well for this clinical sample than it had for the general population sample. The coefficients were lower for each of the dimensions and the pain/discomfort and anxiety/depression dimensions showed particularly poor reliability.

Table 5.5. EQ-5D test-retest frequencies (rheumatoid arthritis study)

	No problems	Moderate problems	Extreme problems	N	Kappa (SE)
Mobility - Time1		Mobility - Time 2			0.63 (0.06)
No problems (%)	74	25	--	51	
Some problems (%)	7	90	2	161	
Extreme problems (%)	--	50	50	12	
Self-Care - Time 1		Self-Care - Time 2			0.65 (0.05)
No problems (%)	79	20	--	83	
Some problems (%)	16	81	3	111	
Extreme problems (%)	--	27	73	30	
Usual Activities - Time 1		Usual Activities - Time 2			0.52 (0.05)
No problems (%)	65	35	--	34	
Some problems (%)	13	79	8	133	
Extreme problems (%)	--	35	65	57	
Pain/Discomfort - Time 1		Pain/Discomfort - Time 2			0.46 (0.05)
No problems (%)	54	45	--	11	
Moderate problems (%)	4	86	10	153	
Extreme problems (%)	5	41	54	59	
Anxiety/Depression - Time 1		Anxiety/Depression - Time 2			0.40 (0.05
No problems (%)	79	18	2	116	
Moderate problems (%)	32	60	7	96	
Extreme problems (%)	8	83	8	12	

160 individuals (69%) of the sample changed their responses on at least 1 EQ-5D dimension between time 1 and time 2 (compared to only 38% in the MVH survey) and there were 268 changes in total (compared to 133 changes in the MVH survey). As with the previous sample, the majority (59%) of changes was positive. Just over half (53%) of those who changed only experienced changes on 1 dimension, although 1 individual experienced changes on all 5 EQ-5D dimensions.

Table 5.6 presents the number of positive and negative changes experienced by the sample by EQ-5D dimension. Most changes occurred on the anxiety/depression dimension, which accounted for just over a quarter (27%) of the total changes, followed by the pain and usual activities dimensions. Changes on the anxiety/depression and pain/discomfort dimensions tended to be largely positive (as in the MVH survey), however, changes on the usual activities dimension were more likely to be negative.

Table 5.6. Number of (positive/negative) changes by EQ-5D dimension (rheumatoid arthritis study)

Number of dimensions changed	Mobility		Self-Care		Usual Activities		Pain/ Discomfort		Anxiety/ Depression	
	Pos.	Neg.	Pos.	Neg.	Pos.	Neg.	Pos.	Neg.	Pos.	Neg.
1	5	3	8	2	8	10	12	7	12	17
2	4	6	9	12	6	12	13	6	17	9
3	5	7	6	4	8	11	7	7	11	3
4	3	1	2	2	1	3	1	--	1	2
5	1	--	1	--	--	1	1	--	1	--
Total	18	17	26	20	23	37	34	20	42	31

The EQ VAS scores from the sample as a whole improved from a mean of 57.1 (SD=23) at time 1 to a mean of 59.5 (SD=21) at time 2. 90% of the sample showed a change in their EQ VAS scores between times 1 and 2 (compared to 75% in the MVH sample). For 41% of cases their self-rated health worsened and for 51% of cases their self-rated health improved. As with the previous sample, most of the changes (46%) were in the order of 10 points on the VAS scale or less (16% had a change of less than 4 points between time 1 and time 2) although 5% of cases showed large changes of 40 points or more (Figure 5.2). The EQ VAS again showed good reliability although not as good as in the MVH sample (ICC 0.78, 95% CI 0.72-0.83).

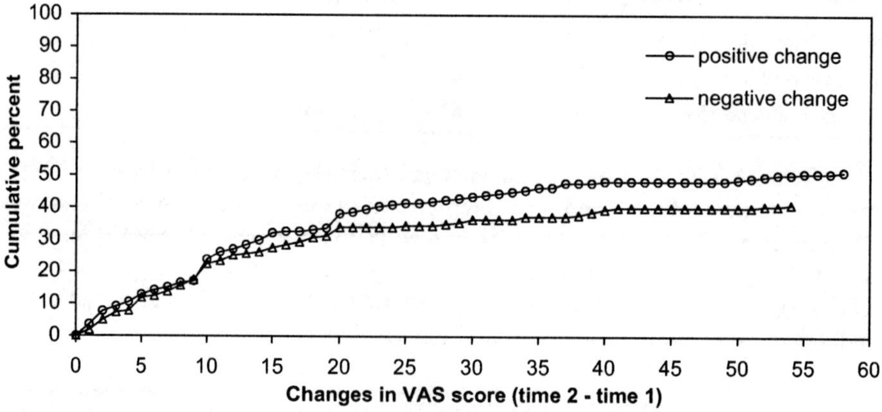

Figure 5.2. Change in VAS scores (rheumatoid arthritis study)

Table 5.7 shows that sample respondents who experienced no change or a change of less than 4 points in their EQ VAS scores were just as likely as those who experienced a negative change in their EQ VAS scores to experience a change in the number of problems they reported on the EQ-5D dimensions; although the latter were more likely to experience changes on more than 1 dimension. In the MVH sample those who experienced no change in their VAS scores were much less likely to experience a change in the number of problems reported on the dimensions. Also, in contrast to the MVH sample, those who experienced a positive change in their VAS scores were more likely to experience a change on 1 or more of the dimensions than those who experienced a negative change in their scores.

Table 5.7. Percentage change on EQ-5D dimension between time 1 and time 2 by change in the EQ VAS time 1-time 2 (rheumatoid arthritis study)

	No change[a]	Better[b]	Worse[b]
No change EQ-5D dimensions	34	21	33
Change on 1dimension	45	37	33
Change on > 1dimension	21	42	34
N	58	90	73

a. Change of 3 points or less
b. Change of more than 3 points

At time 2, sample respondents were asked whether they felt their arthritis had become better, worse or stayed the same over the past 3 months. 93 individuals reported no change in their arthritis, 57 said that their arthritis had improved, and 73 reported that their arthritis had become worse. Table 5.8 presents the reliability coefficients (kappa and ICC) for EQ-5D for respondents who said that their arthritis had not changed. Compared to the coefficients for the whole sample reported in Table 5.9, the coefficients had improved, especially those for the usual activities and the pain/discomfort dimensions. The anxiety/depression dimension still exhibited the worst reliability.

Table 5.8. Reliability coefficients for sample members who reported no change in their arthritis over 3 months (rheumatoid arthritis study)

EQ-5D dimension	Reliability coefficient
Mobility	0.67 (0.09)[a]
Self-Care	0.71 (0.06)[b]
Usual Activities	0.70 (0.07)[b]
Pain/Discomfort	0.67 (0.09)[b]
Anxiety/Depression	0.43 (0.08)[b]
EQ VAS	0.82 (0.74-0.88)[b]

a. Kappa coefficient (standard error)
b. ICC (95% CI)

In this sample we were also able to examine the responsiveness of the EQ-5D to clinical change. Table 5.9 shows that 39% of respondents who reported no change in their arthritis between time 1 and time 2 also experienced no change in the number of problems reported on each of the EQ-5D dimensions and 34% experienced no change in their VAS scores. In contrast, 21% of sample members who reported that their arthritis had changed (either positively or negatively) had no change on the dimensions (χ^2 $p < 0.05$) and 20% had no change on the VAS (χ^2 $p < 0.001$). There was no difference between sample respondents who said that their arthritis had become better or worse in terms of the change in number of problems they reported on the dimensions. However, 68% of individuals who said that their arthritis had become better also experienced a positive change in their VAS scores, while 53% of those who reported that their arthritis had become worse experienced a negative change on the EQ VAS.

Table 5.9. Percentage change on EQ-5D between time 1 and time 2 by self-reported change in arthritis (rheumatoid arthritis study)

	Self-reported change in arthritis over 3 months		
	No change	Better	Worse
No change on EQ-5D dimensions	39	21	22
Change on 1 dimension	40	35	38
Change on > 1 dimension	21	44	40
No change on EQ VAS	34	19	20
Negative change on EQ VAS	28	12	53
Positive change on EQ VAS	35	68	25
N	93	57	73

Table 5.10 compares the mean EQ VAS scores at time 1 and time 2 according to whether respondents reported that their arthritis had become better, worse or remained unchanged in the past 3 months (Deyo *et al*, 1991). T-tests revealed that the difference in scores between time 1 and time 2 was significant for those who reported a change in their arthritis but not for those who said that their arthritis remained the same.

Table 5.10. Mean EQ VAS scores at time 1 and time 2 by self-reported change in arthritis (rheumatoid arthritis study)

Self-reported change in arthritis	EQ VAS time 1 Mean (SD	EQ VAS time 2 Mean (SD)	Difference time 1 - time 2 Mean (SD)	N	t (sig.)
No change	59.87 (21.12)	63.02 (17.18)	-2.59 (14.97)	93	-1.6 (ns)
Better	56.68 (22.84)	71.79 (17.34)	-13.10 (17.39)	57	-5.65 (< 0.001)
Worse	52.11 (24.30)	45.37 (20.89)	6.94 (19.06)	73	3.15 (< 0.01)

5.3 DISCUSSION

Overall the data presented here suggest that the EQ-5D demonstrates acceptable test-retest reliability (or reproducibility) when administered to both a general population and a clinical sample over a 3-month period. Reliability coefficients were slightly higher for the general population sample than for the clinical sample, although coefficients for the latter improved when the sample was restricted to those who reported no change in their condition over the test period. For both samples the mobility and self-care dimensions showed the most reliability over time and the pain/discomfort and anxiety/depression dimensions the least reliability. This finding was not entirely unexpected as the aspects of health measured by these latter 2 dimensions are arguably the most labile and as such would be the first to reflect any change in an individual's health status. The observation that the reliability coefficients improved (particularly for pain/discomfort) when the arthritis sample was restricted to those who said that their arthritis had not changed over the 3-month period would also support this interpretation. It is probable that a shorter test-retest period would improve the reliability of these 2 dimensions. Self-reported health using the EQ VAS showed a high degree of reliability for both samples.

Deciding on the appropriate test-retest period in analyses of this kind is difficult. Opinions in the literature regarding the best interval vary from a few hours to a couple of months. However there would seem to be little use in demonstrating that a measure has good test-retest reliability over the period of a day or a few hours when the states it is intended to measure have durations of weeks or months. A 3-month test interval was selected for the arthritis sample because it was felt that it would give an indicator of the performance of EQ-5D under conditions comparable to those found in routine clinical practice, where a 3- to 4-month period between measurements is commonplace. The principal aim of the MVH survey was to test the stability of health state valuations over time (obtaining test-retest data on the EQ-5D was a secondary outcome) and a retest period of 3 months was chosen as the most appropriate for that task.

Deyo *et al* (1991) suggest a retest interval of 1 to 2 weeks for health status measures which are to be used longitudinally. They argue that this period should be long enough to minimise any recall effects, whilst also providing an indicator of the degree of non-specific score change that naturally occurs in a measure. The data presented here give some idea of the type of changes in response in the EQ-5D that might be expected in a clinical or general population sample over a 3-month period. Although the size of the changes should not be compared directly, the overall pattern of change in responses over the test period is very similar for the 2 samples. For both samples most of the changes between time 1 and time 2 were positive. However, whether this is a characteristic of the samples, the retest period, or of the EQ-5D, is impossible to tell.

It has been suggested that the responsiveness (the ability to detect small levels of clinical change) of a health outcome measure is also an important component of its psychometric performance and should be routinely reported alongside reliability (Deyo *et al*, 1991). However, high levels of responsiveness and reliability are not necessarily synonymous and sometimes it is necessary for researchers to make a trade-off between the 2 depending on their intended use of the measure. The analysis presented in this chapter examined the responsiveness of the EQ VAS amongst patients with arthritis. In this sample, individuals' self-reports as to whether their arthritis improved, worsened or remained unchanged over the 3-month test-retest period were used as the external criterion of change against which to validate the EQ-5D. Although such self-reported change is by no means a 'gold standard' most would find it difficult to question or contradict a patient's judgement. The data demonstrated that the EQ VAS was responsive, at least for individuals with arthritis. Those who said that their arthritis had changed (either positively or negatively) also experienced significant changes on the EQ VAS compared with those who said their arthritis remained unchanged. In addition, the EQ VAS appeared to be more responsive for those who reported that their arthritis had improved than for those who said that it had worsened. Both groups had similar mean EQ VAS scores at time 1, so this finding could not be explained by some sort of floor effect in self-reporting of health at time 2. While we used t-test comparisons as a simple measure of responsiveness, Deyo *et al* (1991) also suggest calculating effect size and the use of receiver operating characteristic (ROC) curves as a means of further exploring this aspect of an instrument's psychometric performance.

In conclusion, this data demonstrates that the EQ-5D exhibits acceptable measurement properties over a 3-month period in both a clinical and a general population sample; its measurements are both reproducible, and in the case of the EQ VAS responsive, to self-reported clinical change. Although generic health outcome measures such as EQ-5D are often criticised because of their perceived lack of responsiveness, these data suggest that with respect to individuals with arthritis this is not the case. However it should be stressed that there are no absolute standards of reliability nor should reliability be thought of as a characteristic that a measure possesses in and of itself. The reported reliability of a measure is always context specific. For instance, large samples or short retest periods tend to produce higher reliability coefficients than small samples or long retest periods. As such, reliability coefficients should always be interpreted with caution outside the context of the specific populations for which they were calculated.

Acknowledgements

The author would like to thank Nigel Hurst for the rheumatoid arthritis sample and John Yfantopoulos for his comments on an earlier draft of the paper.

6
Construction of the EQ-net VAS and TTO databases

Tom Weijnen, Martin Nieuwenhuizen,
Arto Ohinmaa and Frank de Charro

6.1 INTRODUCTION

One of the objectives of the EQ-net project was to create an integrated database containing valuation data gathered previously in different European countries and in different studies. This database would enable secondary cross-national and comparative data analysis to be undertaken.

The EQ-5D offers a standardised framework to compare values for health states elicited with VAS and TTO methods in different European countries. This framework basically consists of the valuation of health states, which are defined by the descriptive system of the EQ-5D, together with a standardised set of questions on respondent characteristics.

The standard valuation method of the EuroQol Group has been to use the EQ-5D valuation questionnaire in a postal survey. With this questionnaire a set of 18 states shown in Table 6.1 can be valued. This set comprises 15 states: 13 unique health states defined by the EQ-5D, plus 'dead' and 'unconscious'. 11111, 33333 and dead are each valued twice.

For various reasons valuation studies have departed from the standard postal VAS method. For example, the set of states to be valued may have differed from the standard set, some studies have been interview-based rather than postal, and in some studies the respondent was asked to rank the health states before the VAS valuation.

This chapter describes the construction of the EQ-net databases. Separate databases were constructed for VAS and TTO valuations. 11 studies from 6 countries were included in the VAS database. The TTO database includes 3 studies. The main features of the 11 studies in the VAS and TTO databases are summarised in sections 6.2 - 6.4. Section 6.5 contains information on the background variables in the databases. Section 6.6 reports on the number of exclusions and inconsistencies. An analysis is undertaken on the shares of exclusions by respondent characteristics and sample features in section 6.7.

R. Brooks et al. (eds.),
The Measurement and Valuation of Health Status Using EQ-5D: A European Perspective, 55–79.

Table 6.1. EQ-5D health states

EQ-5D health state		Page no. of the EQ-5D valuation questionnaire
1	11111A	Page 5
2	11111B	Page 6
3	21111	Page 6
4	12111	Page 6
5	11211	Page 5
6	11121	Page 5
7	11112	Page 6
8	11122	Page 5
9	21232	Page 5
10	22233	Page 5
11	22323	Page 6
12	32211	Page 6
13	33321	Page 5
14	33333A	Page 5
15	33333B	Page 6
16	Unconscious	Page 6
17	DeadA	Page 5
18	DeadB	Page 6

6.2 THE EQ-5D DATABASES

The data in the EQ-5D database consists of valuations of the EQ-5D health states and respondent characteristics of 11 valuation studies conducted in 6 European countries: Finland, Germany, the Netherlands, Spain, United Kingdom and Sweden. Variables, which describe salient features of the conduct of the studies, have also been added to the database. Since different definitions of the background variables with respect to working status and education have been used it was necessary for comparability purposes to re-code the differing definitions: this process is described in section 6.5.

All the available valuations of health states have been included in the database. This means that some studies included more values than the standard 18 states (see Table 6.1), some had values for more than the 18 states, but not all the standard 18 states were valued, and some did not have 2 values for 11111, 33333 and dead.

Exclusions

In January 1999 the EuroQol Group established a standard set of exclusion criteria. The leading principle was to minimise the number of exclusions. These criteria are:

(i) The respondent gave all states the same value.
(ii) The respondent valued less than 3 states.
(iii) The respondent had more than 3 inconsistencies in the states valued.

The criteria take into account responses with incomplete or unreliable data (i) (ii) and responses with too many inconsistencies in the logical order of the states valued (iii). The valuation of a health state is inconsistent if the value is higher than the value of a health state that is dominant to that state, according to logical ordering of the health states. For example if health state 11122 is valued higher than state 11112, the first state is valued inconsistently. The third criterion is based on the observation of Ohinmaa and Sintonen (1999) that in the Finnish data there was a threshold level of 3 inconsistent valuations beyond which the results of modelling in deriving values for all 243 states were affected significantly.

Hence 3 other variables were added to the database. One variable indicates whether a respondent has incomplete or unreliable data. The second is for respondents with inconsistent valuations. Finally, the combination of respondents with incomplete or unreliable data and respondents with inconsistent valuations is indicated by a separate yes/no variable. This variable is used to determine the total number of respondents in the database who were excluded from analysis.

There are 2 main databases. One database contains the VAS valuations from the 11 VAS studies, the other contains the TTO valuations from the 3 TTO studies. The EQ-net VAS database has 2 versions. One version is the database with only the 18 states listed in Table 6.1 and with the number of inconsistencies calculated on these states. The analysis of the VAS data in this chapter and Chapter 7 is restricted to the standard 18 states, so only these states have been taken into account in calculating inconsistencies and applying the exclusion criteria. The other version is the database with all the available VAS values and with the inconsistencies calculated on all the available values per respondent. For the analyses in Chapters 8 and 9 inconsistencies are calculated using all these available values per respondent. The inconsistencies in the EQ-net TTO database have been calculated on all the available TTO valuations per respondent. The relevant calculations are reported in section 6.6.

The background variables in the 2 versions of the EQ-net VAS database are the same. Those background variables in the TTO database concerning respondent characteristics also do not differ from the background variables on these characteristics in the EQ-net VAS databases, although other study features may differ.

6.3 THE EQ-NET VAS DATABASE.

In the EQ-net VAS database, 3 studies were postal samples in which the standard EQ-5D valuation questionnaire with the 18 states was used. In one postal sample only 17 states were valued and in 2 postal surveys more than the 18 states were valued. There were 5 interview-based studies. In 2 interview-based studies 18 health states were valued of which 17 belonged to the Table 6.1 set. Two interview-based studies replicated the UK MVH study in which the VAS valuations were carried out after the respondents ranked the health states they were asked to value.

The following sections describe the most important features of the different studies in the EQ-net VAS database. These features are: place and time of data collection, response rates, and the total number of health states valued. A short description has also been given of the study designs and whether or not all the 18 states were valued.

Catalonia: Cornellà de Llobregat

In the Cornellà de Llobregat study (Cat_Cor) 2 trained interviewers recruited 300 individuals, both patients and non-patients, attending a primary care centre during October-December 1996 (Badia *et al*, 1998). Individuals were recruited according to age and sex quota sampling so as to be representative of the Catalan general population. Inconsistent responses led to the exclusion of 6 respondents, giving a final sample of 294. Respondents first ranked 15 health states and then valued these states. Of these 15 health states, 13 states were randomly chosen from the subset of 43 EQ-5D health states used in the UK MVH study. Every respondent valued the states 11111, 33333, unconscious and dead. A total of 45 VAS values was thus elicited. This was also the case for the 2 other interview ranked TTO studies for which VAS data were included in the EQ-net VAS database.

Catalonia: l'Hospitalet del Llobregat

This Catalonian study (Cat_Hos) took place at a primary health care centre in l'Hospitalet del Llobregat, an industrial city in the metropolitan area of Barcelona (Badia *et al*, 1995a). Doctors proposed patients who might be interested in joining the study and, if the individual agreed to participate, he or she was sent to an adjacent room and asked to fill out the questionnaire under the supervision of a trained nurse. Other persons (12% of the sample) replaced individuals who did not understand the evaluation task. The criteria used to decide upon such substitution were large numbers of inconsistencies in the rating of the health states (10%), and failure to value one or more health states (2%). The sample size was fixed at 600 valid questionnaires. Quota sampling was used with sex, age, occupational class, and patient/non-patient status as control variables. Respondents valued 18 health states, including 11111, 33333, and dead, twice each. One of the 18 health states (22322) does not belong to the Table 6.1 set, so only 17 of the set were valued.

Finland

The data from Finland originates from the Finnish EuroQol valuation study (Finland). The Finnish valuation questionnaire was sent by post in November 1992 to a sample of 4000 persons over 16 years of age chosen randomly from the computerised population registry (Ohinmaa *et al*, 1996). The sample was divided into 17 sub-samples. These sub-samples each received a different questionnaire. The data included in the EQ-net VAS database were from 11 sub-samples totalling 2530 persons. After 2 reminders 1630 questionnaires were returned from the 11 sub-samples, a response rate of 64.4%. Some health states were common to every questionnaire, while some states were unique to various sub-samples. The 18 states, including unconscious, twice 11111, twice 33333, and twice death, were part of a total of 49 health states valued.

United Kingdom: Frome IV

The Frome IV study (UK_FR) was 1 of a series of studies carried out in a general practice population in Frome, UK (Gudex, 1992). The purpose of the study was to see whether an extra dimension of energy/tiredness should be included in the EQ-5D descriptive system. This postal survey was carried out in June-August 1991. Questionnaires were sent out to people chosen randomly from the computerised register of the Frome general practice. Respondents were required to be aged 16 years and over. Five different versions of the questionnaire were posted to 340 people, who received each version of the questionnaire. Questionnaires differed with respect to the wording of the mobility dimension and with respect to the number of dimensions. In the EQ-net VAS database, data from the standard version of the questionnaire, with the 18 states, were included. From the 340 questionnaires, 122 (35.9 %) were returned. No reminders were sent.

United Kingdom: MVH

The second UK data set (UK_MVH) included in the EQ-net VAS database is from the MVH study (Dolan, 1995). This was a representative sample of the non-institutionalised adult population of England, Scotland and Wales (Williams, 1995). Anticipating a response rate of 55% and a sample size of 3235, 6080 addresses were selected from the Postcode Address file (Gudex *et al*, 1997). Of the 6080 addresses, 756 were outside the scope of the survey, being non-residential, empty/derelict, untraceable or even not yet built. This resulted in a total of 5324 addresses. 3395 interviews were completed, a response rate of 63.7%. Trained interviewers conducted the interviews between August and November 1993. Each interview comprised: completion of page 2 (the descriptive system), ranking of states, VAS rating of states, TTO rating of states and provision of personal background data.

All respondents valued the states unconscious, dead, 11111 and 33333. Each respondent also valued 2 of the 5 mildest states and 3 randomly selected states from 3 sets of mild (set 1), moderate (set 2), and severe states (set 3). Hence each respondent valued 15 states.

Germany: 1994

There are 2 standard German studies. The first (Ger_94) was carried out to validate the German version of the EQ-5D (Schulenberg *et al,* 1996). 1000 households across Germany were randomly selected using data from the German telephone company (Telekom). Those members of the households who were 18 or older and who had their birthday first were asked to fill out the questionnaire. The questionnaires were sent out by mail in June 1994. After 1 month a reminder with a new questionnaire was sent out to all non-respondents. A further 2 weeks later the remaining non-respondents were contacted again by phone and asked to return the questionnaire. Out of the 1000 questionnaires, 370 questionnaires were returned and 155 persons refused by mail or by phone to fill out the questionnaire. For the 370 returned questionnaires, 123 respondents answered within the first 4 weeks, 131 were returned after the first reminder and another 116 after the telephone reminder. Respondents were asked to value 18 health states, including unconscious and twice the states 11111, 33333 and dead. One of these 18 health states was not a standard state (12121).

Germany: 1997

This 1997 study (Ger_97) followed the same principles as the 1994 study with the exception that no reminders were sent. Questionnaires were sent out by mail in April 1997 to 1000 households randomly selected from Telekom (Claes *et al*, 1999). To avoid a bias resulting from sample selection by telephone numbers, those members of households who were 18 or older and who had their birthday next were asked to fill out the questionnaire. Because no reminder was sent out a lower response rate was expected: 124 respondents returned the questionnaire. Within the first 4 weeks 109 questionnaires were returned, which is highly comparable with the responses in the first 4 weeks of the 1994 survey (123 out of 1000 questionnaires). Respondents had to value the 18 states, including unconscious and twice the states 11111, 33333, and dead.

Germany TTO

For this study (Ger_TTO) a random sample was selected of 4000 addresses, derived from Telekom (Claes *et al*, 1999). In order to represent urban and rural regions equally, the selection was based on postal zip code areas. It was ascertained that half the selected persons were female. The selected persons were informed in writing about the study and were asked for their willingness to participate using a reply card. The return amounted to 9.5% or 380 addresses. No reminder was sent out. The interviewers agreed upon interview dates with the participants by telephone. If it was not possible to find a mutual date for a meeting, or after 3 fruitless attempts to contact the person, the interview was cancelled. Appointments were made for 339 interviews, a response rate of 8.5%. Moreover, 5 interviews had to be aborted prematurely, because the participants could not master the task.

The face-to-face interviews were conducted in north Germany between October 1997 and March 1998. Respondents were asked to value up to 15 different health states from a sample of 43 states. Participants were first asked to give some information about their socio-economic backgrounds. Then they were given selected cards with the description of the health states. These cards had to be ranked before the valuation task on the VAS scale was undertaken. During the valuation task modification of the rank order was permitted at any time. 36 health states were valued, of which 12 were standard states. The state 'dead' was not valued. TTO rating of states was also undertaken.

Navarra

The data in this study (Navarra) were elicited from the general population in the Navarra region in September 1995, using quota sampling by age and sex (Gaminde and Cabasés, 1996). Respondents were interviewed at home by a qualified interviewer. One of the characteristics of the EQ-5D questionnaire is that it was developed to be self-administered. This starting point was maintained during the interview, with a passive role for the interviewer. The interviewer rang the bell, asked if that person minded undertaking the task, the task was explained, and the respondent filled out the questionnaire. The interviewers only helped when asked by the respondents, and then only for clarification. No ranking or criteria for exclusion were applied during the process of data gathering, apart from excluding those not wishing to fill out the questionnaire. Information is not available on the number of people who so refused. 300 interviews were carried out. Respondents had to value 18 states, including unconsciousness and twice the states 11111, 33333, and dead. The standard state 22323 was not valued.

The Netherlands

The Dutch data (Netherl.) are from the Rotterdam survey, carried out in January 1991 (Bonsel *et al*, 1992; Essink-Bot *et al*, 1993). Four different pages were used containing 8 health states on each page. The states 11111 and 33333 were presented on all pages. Combinations of these 4 pages resulted in 4 different questionnaires. The questionnaire was posted to a random selection of 1400 households based on postal area codes on the right bank of the River Maas in Rotterdam. Districts with over 20%

of immigrants were excluded from the sample due to expected language problems. The sample was therefore not representative of the population of the Netherlands. After 2 weeks a reminder card was sent to all people in the sample. After 3 weeks a second questionnaire plus an encouraging letter was sent to all people in the sample who had not yet responded. In the sub-sample of the questionnaire, all non-respondents received a telephone call after 5 weeks. During this call, people were asked to complete the questionnaire. 993 questionnaires were returned, of which 124 were blank. From the resulting 869 responses, 493 respondents (56.7 %) had fully completed the questionnaire. A total of 28 health states was valued, including unconscious, twice the health states 11111 and 33333, and 12 other standard states. The Dutch data set does not include valuations for dead.

Sweden

For the Swedish study (Sweden) a nationwide sample of 1000 Swedish citizens was drawn from an address register (Björk and Norinder, 1999). The ages ranged from 18 to 78 years, the upper limit being the mean life expectancy of men and women in Sweden. In April 1994, the respondents were sent a letter of introduction, together with the questionnaire and a stamped addressed envelope for the reply. A first reminder was sent as a postcard in May, and if required, 2 further reminders including a copy of the questionnaire were sent out later in May and in June. 542 questionnaires were returned. Respondents had to value the 18 states, including unconscious, and twice 11111, 33333, and dead.

6.4 THE EQ-NET TTO DATABASE

The EQ-net TTO database includes data from the UK MVH study, from the German TTO study and the Catalonian Cornellà de Llobregat study. For the UK and the German TTO data there is no difference between the VAS and the TTO data with respect to number of respondents.

The Spanish TTO data consists of the data from the Cornellà de Llobregat study, together with data from a random sample of members of the general population within 1 primary health care district covering 4 different socio-economic areas in Barcelona. Fieldwork was carried out by 11 interviewers over a 6-month period (Badia *et al*, 2001). Individuals were recruited from a primary care database according to age and sex quota sampling so as to be representative of the Catalan general population. Individuals who were illiterate, cognitively impaired, or who had a severe illness or mental disorder, were replaced by others. In order to achieve a final sample size of 1000 respondents, 1930 respondents were initially contacted. 930 individuals did not take part in the study, giving a response rate of 51.8%. 21 questionnaires were subsequently excluded from the analysis due to serious inconsistencies in health state valuations. As a result the Spanish TTO data include 979 respondents.

Respondents first ranked 15 health states and then valued these states. Of these 15 health states, 13 states were randomly chosen from a subset of 43 EQ-5D health states used in the UK MVH study. Every respondent valued the states 11111, 33333, unconscious, and dead.

6.5 BACKGROUND VARIABLES

In this section a description is provided of the background variables in the integrated database. The background variables of the 3 TTO-based studies are the same as those in the EQ-net VAS database and in the EQ-net TTO database because the data on these variables came from the same questionnaires. The background variables can be divided into sample features and respondent characteristics. The sample features refer to attributes of the sample as a whole. These features were added to the database on the basis of the information in the publications on the 11 valuation studies in the EQ-net database. Respondent characteristics describe the attributes of the respondents. Data on these characteristics were elicited from the questionnaires returned in the different samples. The standard EQ-5D questionnaire contains a set of background variables. However, for various reasons, the questionnaires in many valuation studies departed from the standard set. The respondent characteristics also include the variables describing the respondent's scores on the EQ-5D descriptive system and the rating of the respondent's own health on the EQ VAS.

Sample features

The following variables describe the sample features of the EQ-net databases. Table 6.2 summarises the sample features for each study in the database.

Time of data collection: The time of data collection is represented by 2 variables indicating the year and season of the main data collection.

Sample method: This refers to the postal versus interview-based samples.

RIT variable: The ranked, interview-based study protocol was originally developed for the UK MVH study where the respondents carried out VAS and TTO valuations of health states. The respondent ranked the health states before the EQ-5D VAS valuation task. In the VAS and TTO valuation tasks the health states were assumed to have a duration of 10 years, whereas on the standard EQ-5D VAS valuation questionnaire the duration is 1 year. The RIT variable (Ranked, Interview-based, Ten years duration) is a binary variable which indicates whether the data comes from 1 of the 3 interview-based TTO-studies.

Participation of interviewer: When an interviewer was present a distinction was made between an active and a passive interviewer. An active interviewer was an interviewer who was allowed to give assistance with the valuation task. Where ranking took place an active interviewer was assumed.

Table 6.2 presents the sample features of both VAS and TTO EQ-net databases. The number of respondents and the respondent rates differed between the samples, which slightly hinders comparisons of the samples (and countries) in the raw data, since the samples do not weigh equally in the databases. Although the number of health states valued in each sample varies between 18 (e.g. Sweden) and 49 (Finland), the full set of standard states can be found in nearly every sample.

The differences between the postal and interview-based studies were noted. In the interview-based studies the only difference between the RIT and participation of interviewer variables came from the l'Hospitalet del Llobregat sample (see Table 6.2). This sample had an active interviewer, but no ranking took place. Between the sample method and participation of interviewer variables there was a difference only for the Navarra sample. In this study the interviewer had a passive role.

Table 6.2. Sample features in the VAS and TTO databases

	Cat_Cor Cornellà de Llobregat	Cat_Cor Cornellà de Llobregat	Cat_Hos l'Hospitalet del Llobregat	Finland	UK_FR UK Frome	UK_MVH UK MVH	Ger_94 Germany 1994	Ger_97 Germany 1997	Ger_TTO Germany TTO	Navarra	Netherl. Netherlands	Sweden
Database	VAS	TTO	VAS	VAS	VAS	VAS + TTO	VAS	VAS	VAS + TTO	VAS	VAS	VAS
Number of questionnaires	-	1930	682	2530	300	5324	1000	1000	4000	-	1400	1000
Response rate (%)	-	51.8	88	64.4	35.9	63.7	37.0	12.4	8.5	-	70.9	54.2
N	300	1000	600	1630	122	3395	370	124	339	300	993	542
Excluded *a posteriori*	6	21	-	-	-	-	-	-	-	-	-	-
Number of respondents in data collection	294	979	600	1630	122	3395	370	124	339	300	993	542
Number of health states valued	45	43	18	49	18	45 VAS 43 TTO	18	18	36 VAS 35 TTO	18	28	18
Of which VAS values of standard states	15	15	17	18	18	15	17	18	12	17	16	18
Including 11111	1	1	2	2	2	1	2	2	1	2	2	2
33333	1	1	2	2	2	1	2	2	1	2	2	2
Unconcious	1	1	1	1	1	1	1	1	0	1	1	1
Dead	1	1	2	2	2	1	2	2	0	2	0	2
Year/season of the main data collection.	Oct-Dec 4/96		Nov-Dec 4/92	Nov 4/92	Jun–Aug 3/91	Aug-Nov 3/93	Jun 2/94	April 2/97	Oct-Mar 4/97-1/98	Sept 3/95	Jan 1/91	
Sample method. 0 = postal; 1= interview–based.	1	1	1	0	0	1	0	0	1	0	0	0
RIT: no = 0; yes = 1.	1	1	0	0	0	1	0	0	1	0	0	0
Participation of interviewer 0 = passive; 1 = active	1	1	1	0	0	1	0	0	1	0	0	0

Respondent characteristics

The following variables describe the respondent characteristics in the EQ-net databases. The distribution of the variables in the VAS database is shown in Table 6.3 and in the TTO database in Table 6.4.

Age: The studies reported the respondents' ages in years. In the analysis, the ages of the respondents were clustered into age groups. Two aggregated age variables were defined. One variable contains 7 age groups: ≤ 24, 25-34, 35-44, 45-54, 55-64, 65-74 and ≥ 75. The other age variable contains 3 age groups: ≤ 44, 45-64, and ≥ 65.

Experience of illness: Three binary variables were included in the EQ-5D database to describe the respondent's experience of illness:

(i) Experienced serious illness yourself.
(ii) Experienced serious illness in the family.
(iii) Experienced serious illness in caring for others.

Working status: The standard variable concerning daily activities consists of 6 groupings and in most of the study samples this was followed. Data from some samples had to be aggregated into 6 groupings. A binary variable was added to the database in which the 6 groupings were re-coded into 2 groupings, namely employed and not employed.

Level of education: Owing to the differences in the educational systems between countries, different background variables for the level of education were used in the different studies. Two types of questions were used. One was the question from the standard EQ-5D questionnaire. For the second type, the respondent had to classify his or her level of education on the basis of a list of schools (at various levels) or in regard to education he or she had finished. To make data comparable across all the studies it was necessary to re-code the education variables into a new variable describing low, medium and high levels of education.

The education variable from the standard questionnaire consists of 2 questions. The first question asks whether the respondent left school at a minimum age. The second asks whether the respondent has a degree or professional qualification. If a respondent answered "yes" to this latter question he or she was assumed to have a high level of education. A "no" answer together with a "yes" answer to the question of 'left school at minimum age', meant that the respondent was assumed to have a low level of education. If the respondent answered "no" to both questions he or she was assumed to have a medium level of education.

For the re-coding a degree or higher vocational education was deemed equivalent to a high level of education. When a respondent finished education at a minimum age, this was categorised as a low level of education. Other types of schools or education the respondent had finished were classified as medium level education.

Filling in the questionnaire: The standard questionnaire includes a question about the difficulty respondents experienced with filling in the questionnaire, which can be answered by ticking the boxes labelled 'easy', 'fairly difficult' or 'difficult'. The original information was re-coded into a binary variable with the categories 'easy' and 'difficult'. The variable 'difficult' consists of the original categories 'fairly difficult' and 'difficult'.

Own health and EQ VAS: The respondent characteristics also include the variables describing own health of the respondent. These variables are the scores on the EQ-5D descriptive system (mobility, self-care, usual activities, pain/discomfort, anxiety/depression), and the rating of own health on the EQ VAS. A distinction was made between those respondents with a median score of ≥ 85 and those with a score of < 85.

The analysis of the respondent characteristics in the VAS database shows that there were at least some variations in every background variable between the studies (Table 6.3). The same is also true of the TTO database (Table 6.4). The analysis in subsequent chapters handles these variations using a variety of statistical approaches.

Table 6.3. Respondent characteristics in the EQ-net VAS database

		Cat_Cor	Cat_Hos	Finland	UK_FR	UK_MVH	Ger_94	Ger_97	Ger_TTO	Navarra	Netherl.	Sweden	Total
N		294	600	1630	122	3395	370	124	339	300	993	542	8709
Sex (%)	Male	45.9	50.0	48.6	52.5	43.3	64.1	50.0	55.2	48.3	39.4	48.7	46.5
	Female	54.1	50.0	51.4	47.5	56.7	35.1	49.2	44.8	51.7	47.3	50.6	51.9
	Missing	0.0	0.0	0.0	0.0	0.0	0.8	0.8	0.0	0.0	13.3	0.7	1.6
Age (%)	≤ 24	16.0	13.2	12.3	3.3	9.0	8.4	5.6	7.7	15.3	5.6	12.4	10.0
7 groups	25-34	18.4	23.8	16.6	19.7	22.2	10.5	25.8	15.3	20.3	14.4	18.5	19.2
	35-44	16.7	11.7	14.4	16.4	16.5	11.4	12.1	15.6	15.3	13.3	17.2	15.1
	45-54	15.3	19.3	11.5	23.8	14.4	18.6	14.5	16.2	16.7	10.7	19.6	14.6
	55-64	15.0	21.8	9.6	11.5	14.3	26.5	16.9	23.9	12.3	11.4	12.9	14.4
	65-74	17.3	8.8	23.1	17.2	14.4	16.8	12.1	13.6	13.0	15.7	14.8	15.9
	75+	1.4	1.3	12.6	7.4	9.3	7.8	10.5	7.4	7.0	15.2	3.5	9.2
	Missing	0.0	0.0	0.0	0.8	0.0	0.0	2.4	0.3	0.0	13.7	1.3	1.7
Exp. illness yourself (%)	No	83.3	87.5	55.3	64.8	68.0	44.9	54.0	57.5	85.3	-	73.8	59.1
	Yes	16.7	11.7	29.3	27.0	31.7	38.6	33.1	40.1	14.7	-	17.0	24.8
	Missing	0.0	0.8	15.5	8.2	0.3	16.5	12.9	2.4	0.0	100.0	9.2	16.1
Exp. illness family (%)	No	45.2	64.2	37.1	32.0	27.8	23.8	21.8	28.9	50.7	-	45.8	31.2
	Yes	54.8	35.3	34.9	52.5	72.0	53.2	57.3	68.1	49.3	-	48.3	50.1
	Missing	0.0	0.5	28.0	15.6	0.1	23.0	21.0	2.9	0.0	100.0	5.9	18.7
Exp. illness others (%)	No	87.8	89.0	40.7	51.6	-	37.6	43.5	59.0	63.3	34.7	73.2	32.7
	Yes	12.2	10.0	21.3	19.7	-	16.5	18.5	34.5	36.0	8.8	13.8	10.8
	Missing	0.0	1.0	38.0	28.7	100.0	45.9	37.9	6.5	0.7	56.5	12.9	56.6
EQ VAS (%)	EQ VAS ≥ 85	36.4	39.2	42.6	50.0	60.3	38.9	47.6	69.9	26.0	37.5	57.6	49.9
	EQ VAS < 85	63.6	60.8	51.3	47.5	39.3	57.0	47.6	29.2	74.0	38.0	38.4	45.4
	Missing	0.0	0.0	6.1	2.5	0.4	4.1	4.8	0.9	0.0	24.6	4.1	4.7

Table 6.3. Respondent characteristics in the EQ-net VAS database (Continued)

		Cat_Cor	Cat_Hos	Finland	UK_FR	UK_MVH	Ger_94	Ger_97	Ger_TTO	Navarra	Netherl.	Sweden	Total
Smoker (%)	Smoker	31.3	-	21.5	17.2	30.8	9.7	18.5	22.4	-	24.9	25.1	23.3
	Non smoker/ former smoker	68.7	-	76.0	82.8	69.0	72.7	79.8	75.5	-	60.5	73.1	63.2
	Missing	0.0	100.0	2.5	0.0	0.1	17.6	1.6	2.1	100.0	14.6	1.8	13.5
Working status (%)	Employed	41.8	-	37.3	52.5	48.7	42.2	45.2	51.6	-	35.4	58.7	40.2
	Retired	10.9	-	40.3	18.0	22.5	39.5	35.5	30.7	-	24.8	21.6	24.5
	Housework	22.4	-	4.4	14.8	15.5	10.8	6.5	2.7	-	13.3	2.4	10.1
	Student	7.1	-	8.8	0.8	2.4	4.6	6.5	9.1	-	3.1	8.7	4.4
	Unemployed/ Seeking work	10.9	-	5.5	3.3	5.7	2.7	4.8	1.2	-	2.3	5.5	4.5
	Other	6.8	-	2.6	2.5	5.1	0.0	1.6	4.4	-	6.2	1.7	3.8
	Missing	0.0	100.0	1.2	8.2	0.1	0.3	0.0	0.3	100.0	14.8	1.5	12.5
Employed (%)	Not employed	58.2	-	61.5	39.3	51.2	57.6	54.8	48.1	-	49.7	39.9	47.2
	Employed	41.8	-	37.3	52.5	48.7	42.2	45.2	51.6	-	35.4	58.7	40.2
	Missing	0.0	100.0	1.2	8.2	0.1	0.3	0.0	0.3	100.0	14.8	1.5	12.5
Filling in questionnaire (%)	Difficult	25.9	66.3	41.9	32.8	8.6	38.9	42.7	-	32.7	31.3	56.1	27.6
	Easy	74.1	33.5	53.2	66.4	89.7	55.9	54.8	-	67.0	51.8	38.9	64.5
	Missing	0.0	0.2	4.9	0.8	1.6	5.1	2.4	100.0	0.3	16.9	5.0	8.0
Education (%)	Low	56.5	55.8	40.7	27.9	39.8	57.6	11.3	7.1	59.3	33.2	27.1	39.7
	Medium	26.9	25.0	26.6	46.7	40.1	28.1	52.4	59.6	30.3	33.3	40.6	35.5
	High	16.3	18.5	21.7	22.1	20.0	7.0	34.7	33.0	10.0	19.8	26.9	20.4
	Missing	0.3	0.7	11.0	3.3	0.1	7.3	1.6	0.3	0.3	13.6	5.4	4.4

Table 6.4. Respondent characteristics in the TTO database

		UK_MVH	Ger_TTO	Cat_Cor	Total
N		3395	339	979	4713
Age (%)	≤ 24	9.0	7.7	15.8	10.3
7 groups	25-34	22.2	15.3	17.1	20.6
	35-44	16.5	15.6	16.0	16.4
	45-54	14.4	16.2	16.8	15.0
	55-64	14.3	23.9	14.7	15.0
	65-74	14.4	13.6	14.4	14.3
	75+	9.3	7.4	4.6	8.2
	Missing	0.0	0.3	0.6	0.1
Age (%)	≤ 44	47.7	38.6	48.9	47.3
3 groups	45-64	28.6	40.1	31.5	30.0
	65+	23.7	20.9	19.0	22.5
	Missing	0.0	0.3	0.6	0.1
Education (%)	Low	39.8	7.1	61.0	41.8
	Medium	40.1	59.6	25.6	38.5
	High	20.0	33.0	12.2	19.3
	Missing	0.1	0.3	1.2	0.4
EQ VAS (%)	≥ 85	60.3	69.9	30.9	54.9
	< 85	39.3	29.2	68.4	44.6
	Missing	0.4	0.9	0.6	0.5

6.6 EXCLUSIONS AND INCONSISTENCIES

The criteria for exclusions were explained in section 6.2. Table 6.5 shows the number of exclusions and inconsistencies in the EQ-net VAS database. The database consists of records from 8709 respondents spread over 11 different studies. 897 respondents were excluded by applying criteria (i) (all states given the same value) and (ii) (less than 3 states valued). 501 respondents returned questionnaires that contained more than 3 inconsistencies (criterion (iii)). Exclusions were high in the samples from Finland (29.4%), Germany 1994 (51.1%), the Netherlands (40.5%), and Sweden (33.4%). Exclusions were absent in the Catalonian Cat_Cor and the German TTO samples. Exclusions were low in the Catalonian Cat_Hos data (0.5%), the UK MVH data (1.5%), and the Spanish Navarra data (11.0%) These were all interview-based samples. The low number of exclusions in the l'Hospitalet del Llobregat study has to be interpreted with caution, because respondents were selected *a priori*.

Table 6.6 shows the exclusions and inconsistencies in the EQ-net TTO database. Exclusions as a result of incomplete or unreliable data were small. Only 1.3% of the respondents were excluded on this basis. There were no respondents in the German data who valued less than 3 states. Total exclusions in the TTO database were 9.3%. The Catalonian data had the lowest share of total exclusions (5.7%).

Table 6.5. Exclusions and inconsistencies in the EQ-net VAS database: exclusions and inconsistencies calculated on standard states

	Cat_Cor	Cat_Hos	Finland	UK_FR	UK_MVH	Ger_94	Ger_97	Ger_TTO	Navarra	Netherl.	Sweden	Total
Number of respondents	294	600	1630	122	3395	370	124	339	300	993	542	8709
All states valued the same	0	0	42	1	3	12	5	0	0	36	9	108
Less than 3 states valued	0	0	204	1	45	160	19	0	0	320	109	858
Excluded	0	0	217	2	45	162	19	0	0	339	113	897
Not excl.	294	600	1413	120	3350	208	105	339	300	654	429	7812
Inconsistencies (number of respondents)												
0	279	446	680	52	3105	102	47	328	74	431	227	5771
1	15	127	222	24	192	49	28	10	91	93	78	929
2	0	17	149	13	35	20	10	1	70	52	38	405
3	0	7	99	6	12	10	7	0	32	15	18	206
4	0	2	79	2	4	10	3	0	18	13	14	145
5 or more	0	1	184	23	2	17	10	0	15	50	54	356
Inconsistencies (% of total respondents)												
0	94.9	74.3	48.1	43.3	92.7	49.0	44.8	96.8	24.7	65.9	52.9	73.9
1	5.1	21.2	15.7	20.0	5.7	23.6	26.7	2.9	30.3	14.2	18.2	11.9
2	0.0	2.8	10.5	10.8	1.0	9.6	9.5	0.3	23.3	8.0	8.9	5.2
3	0.0	1.2	7.0	5.0	0.4	4.8	6.7	0.0	10.7	2.3	4.2	2.6
4	0.0	0.3	5.6	1.7	0.1	4.8	2.9	0.0	6.0	2.0	3.3	1.9
5 or more	0.0	0.2	13.0	19.2	0.1	8.2	9.5	0.0	5.0	7.6	12.6	4.6

Table 6.5. Exclusions and inconsistencies in the EQ-net VAS database: exclusions and inconsistencies calculated on standard states (Continued)

	Cat_Cor	Cat_Hos	Finland	UK_FR	UK_MVH	Ger_94	Ger_97	Ger_TTO	Navarra	Netherl.	Sweden	Total
Summary:												
Number of respondents	294	600	1630	122	3395	370	124	339	300	993	542	8709
Exclusions:												
Due to incomplete data	0	0	217	2	45	162	19	0	0	339	113	897
Due to incomplete data (%)	0.0	0.0	13.3	1.6	1.3	43.8	15.3	0.0	0.0	34.1	20.8	10.3
Due to more than 3 inconsistencies	0	3	263	25	6	27	13	0	33	63	68	501
Due to more than 3 inconsistencies (%)	0.0	0.5	16.1	20.5	0.2	7.3	10.5	0.0	11.0	6.3	12.5	5.8
Number of respondents in the analyses	294	597	1150	95	3344	181	92	339	267	591	361	7311
Number of respondents in the analyses (%)	100.0	99.5	70.6	77.9	98.5	48.9	74.2	100.0	89.0	59.5	66.6	83.9

Table 6.6. Exclusions and inconsistencies in the EQ-net TTO database

	UK_MVH	Ger_TTO	Cat_Cor	Total
Number of respondents in sample	3395	339	979	4713
Exclusions due to incomplete or unreliable data				
All states the same	24	7	2	33
Less than 3 states valued	28	0	7	35
Total excluded	44	7	9	60
Total excluded (%)	1.3	2.1	0.9	1.3
Not excl.	3351	332	970	4653
Not excl. (%)	98.7	97.9	99.1	98.7
Inconsistencies (number of respondents)				
0	944	64	389	1397
1	1066	89	303	1458
2	715	74	165	954
3	349	53	66	468
4	149	26	29	204
5 or more	128	26	18	172
Inconsistencies (% of total number of respondents)				
0	0	28.2	19.3	40.1
1	31.8	26.8	31.2	31.3
2	21.3	22.3	17.0	20.5
3	10.4	16.0	6.8	10.1
4	4.4	7.8	3.0	4.4
5 or more	3.8	7.8	1.9	3.7
Summary:				
N	3395	339	979	4713
Exclusions:				
Due to incomplete/unreliable data	44	7	9	60
Due to more than 3 inconsistencies	277	52	47	376
Number of respondents not excluded	3074	280	923	4277
% of total number of respondents	90.5	82.6	94.3	90.7

6.7 EFFECT OF EXCLUSIONS ON RESPONDENT CHARACTERISTICS

Table 6.7 presents the effects of the exclusions on the respondent characteristics and on the missing values in the VAS database. For all the respondent characteristics, except the variables smoker, working status and employed, the exclusions were high in the missing values. A Chi-Square test for independence was conducted. For all the background variables, except experience of serious illness in the family (Exp. illness family) independence between the background variables and exclusions had to be rejected ($p < 0.000$). Males, older people, respondents who experienced serious illness themselves or in caring for others, those with an EQ VAS < 85, non-smokers, unemployed respondents, those who found it difficult to fill in the questionnaire and, finally, those respondents with a low level of education, all had a higher share of exclusions.

Table 6.7. Respondent characteristics by exclusions in the EQ-net VAS databases

		N			%	
		Not excl.	Excluded	Total	Not excl.	Excluded
Sex	Male	3352	694	4046	82.8	17.2
	Female	3948	575	4523	87.3	12.7
	Total	7300	1269	8569	85.2	14.8
	Missing	11	129	140	7.9	92.1
Age 7 groups	≤ 24	825	42	867	95.2	4.8
	25-34	1595	76	1671	95.5	4.5
	35-44	1204	111	1315	91.6	8.4
	45-54	1105	165	1270	87.0	13.0
	55-64	1027	223	1250	82.2	17.8
	65-74	1016	371	1387	73.3	26.7
	75+	527	274	801	65.8	34.2
	Total	7299	1262	8561	85.3	14.7
	Missing	12	136	148	8.1	91.9
Exp. illness yourself	No	4713	430	5143	91.6	8.4
	Yes	1771	390	2161	82.0	18.0
	Total	6484	820	7304	88.8	11.2
	Missing	827	578	1405	58.9	41.1
Exp. illness family	No	2451	268	2719	90.1	9.9
	Yes	3965	395	4360	90.9	9.1
	Total	6416	663	7079	90.6	9.4
	Missing	895	735	1630	54.9	45.1

Table 6.7. Respondent characteristics by exclusions in the EQ-net VAS databases (Continued)

		N			%	
		Not excl.	Excluded	Total	Not excl.	Excluded
Exp. illness others	No	2423	421	2844	85.2	14.8
	Yes	747	191	938	79.6	20.4
	Total	3170	612	3782	83.8	16.2
	Missing	4141	786	4927	84.0	16.0
EQ VAS	≥ 85	3972	375	4347	91.4	8.6
	< 85	3269	686	3955	82.7	17.3
	Missing	70	337	407	17.2	82.8
Smoker	Smoker	1784	245	2029	87.9	12.1
	Non-/former smoker	4598	909	5507	83.5	16.5
	Total	6382	1154	7536	84.7	15.3
	Missing	929	244	1173	79.2	20.8
Working status	Employed	3168	337	3505	90.4	9.6
	Retired	1471	660	2131	69.0	31.0
	Housework	784	99	883	88.8	11.2
	Student	355	24	379	93.7	6.3
	Unemployed	347	46	393	88.3	11.7
	Other	294	33	327	89.9	10.1
	Total	6419	1199	7618	84.3	15.7
	Missing	892	199	1091	81.8	18.2
Employed	Not employed	3251	862	4113	79.0	21.0
	Employed	3168	337	3505	90.4	9.6
	Total	6419	1199	7618	84.3	15.7
	Missing	892	199	1091	81.8	18.2
Filling in questionnaire	Difficult	1806	594	2400	75.3	24.8
	Easy	5056	558	5614	90.1	9.9
	Total	6862	1152	8014	85.6	14.4
	Missing	449	246	695	64.6	35.4
Level of education	Low	2713	742	3455	78.5	21.5
	Medium	2823	271	3094	91.2	8.8
	High	1660	113	1773	93.6	6.4
	Total	7196	1126	8322	86.5	13.5
	Missing	115	272	387	29.7	70.3

The effects of exclusions on the background variables in the TTO database are presented in Table 6.8. The Chi Square test for independence indicated that the exclusions were not independent of background variables ($p < 0.001$). Older respondents, respondents with a low level of education, and respondents with an EQ VAS < 85 show more exclusions.

Table 6.8. Respondent characteristics by exclusions in the EQ-net TTO database

		N			%	
		Not excl.	Excluded	Total	Not excl.	Excluded
Total		4277	436	4713	90.7	9.3
Age	≤ 24	452	33	485	93.2	6.8
7 groups	25-34	895	77	972	92.1	7.9
	35-44	710	61	771	92.1	7.9
	45-54	637	70	707	90.1	9.9
	55-64	650	59	709	91.7	8.3
	65-74	601	74	675	89.0	11.0
	75+	325	62	387	84.0	16.0
	Total	4270	436	4706	90.7	9.3
	Missing	7	0	7	100.0	0.0
Age	≤ 44	2057	171	2228	92.3	7.7
3 groups	45-64	1287	129	1416	90.9	9.1
	65+	926	136	1062	87.2	12.8
	Total	4270	436	4706	90.7	9.3
	Missing	7	0	7	100.0	0.0
Level of education	Low	1746	225	1971	88.6	11.4
	Medium	1670	145	1815	92.0	8.0
	High	845	65	910	92.9	7.1
	Total	4261	435	4696	90.7	9.3
	Missing	16	1	17	94.1	5.9
EQ VAS	≥ 85	2376	212	2588	91.8	8.2
	< 85	1883	219	2102	89.6	10.4
	Total	4259	431	4690	90.8	9.2
	Missing	18	5	23	78.3	21.7

6.8 SUMMARY

The construction of the EQ-net databases has been explained in this chapter. Valuation data from 11 studies conducted in 6 countries have been included in the EQ-net databases. Although most studies departed from the standard postal study design in which the EQ-5D questionnaire was used, it was possible to merge the data from the 11 valuation studies into 1 VAS database that included the VAS values, and 1 TTO database in which TTO values from the UK, Catalonian and German TTO studies were included. The EQ-net VAS database has 2 versions. The first version includes only the 18 states (Table 6.1) and the second version contains all the available valuation data from the 11 studies.

To study the effect of background variables on the valuations, information on these variables from the different studies was included in the databases. To make these background variables comparable across studies, the variables regarding working status and education had to be re-coded. The different education variables in the studies reflected the different types of educational systems in the different countries. This had the effect that the education variable in the database could only be expressed in broad categories of education: low, medium and high.

Analysis of respondent characteristics showed that there were some differences between the study populations which were partly influenced by the differences in the sample features, e.g. differences in the methods of collecting valuations. Because the differences may influence analysis of the valuations, forthcoming chapters utilise different kinds of weighting techniques in the analysis of the databases.

Exclusion variables were added to the database. These variables indicated whether the valuations of a respondent should be excluded from analysis on the basis of criteria adopted by the EuroQol Group. Although the number of exclusions and inconsistencies was connected to most of the background variables, old age and low education of the respondent were especially important considerations.

Analysis showed that the number of exclusions and inconsistencies differed between the studies and that these differences were connected to the differences in the study methods used. Basically the quality of the data was much better in the interview-based TTO data sets.

Exclusions and inconsistencies were determined using the different data in the 3 databases. This had the effect that the numbers of exclusions and inconsistencies in the 2 VAS databases were not equal, as different combinations of health states were recorded in the separate databases.

The EQ-net VAS 18 state database is used in Chapter 7 in the analysis of the influence of the background variables on the values for these states. In Chapter 8, the extended EQ-net VAS database is used in the estimation of a European set of weights for the EQ-5D. The EQ-net TTO database is studied in Chapter 9.

7
Comparison of EQ-5D VAS valuations: analysis of background variables

Harri Sintonen, Tom Weijnen, Martin Nieuwenhuizen, Siem Oppe, Xavier Badia, Jan Busschbach, Wolfgang Greiner, Paul Krabbe, Arto Ohinmaa, Montserrat Roset and Frank de Charro

7.1 INTRODUCTION

Preference-based instruments for measuring HRQoL of life have been developed in different countries and applied in empirical research in a much wider range of countries. A major concern in this context has been whether the valuations (values or utility weights) elicited for the instrument in 1 country are applicable in another, that is, whether the valuations in terms of the relative values/utilities of different health states are similar or not. If they are, an instrument that has been valued in country A can be applied in country B without having to carry out a very cumbersome and expensive process of eliciting the valuations in country B. However, if the valuations differ, the use of an instrument with valuations from country A in country B, for example in the evaluation of health interventions, may lead to different results and a different order of preference among the interventions from those should valuations from country B have been available.

One of the main purposes of the EuroQol Group since its inception in 1987 has been to explore the question of whether health state valuations are similar across a number of European countries. To this end, a simple standardised health state descriptive system was created, a set of standard health states was derived from this system, a way of valuing these states in a postal survey (using a VAS "thermometer") of a representative population sample drawn in a standardised way was devised, and a standard set of background variables for each respondent was recorded (The EuroQol Group, 1990). After some experimentation, the first 6-dimensional health state descriptive system was modified in 1991 to produce the present 5-dimensional system (EQ-5D), together with a standard set of health states to be valued, i.e. the present standard EQ-5D questionnaire (Brooks *et al,* 1996).

The early valuation studies in the UK, the Netherlands and Sweden using a set of health states defined by the first 6-dimensional health state descriptive system led the Group to conclude that there is "a striking similarity" in the relative valuations of these states across these countries (The EuroQol Group, 1990). Since then, valuation studies have been carried out with the present standard EQ-5D valuation questionnaire in several European countries. In spite of the aim to standardise the valuation

R. Brooks et al. (eds.),
The Measurement and Valuation of Health Status Using EQ-5D: A European Perspective, 81–101.

studies, in practice the studies have differed in many, potentially important, respects. Hence the 'raw' valuations from different countries may not be directly comparable. At face value valuations appear to be similar across countries, but thus far no rigorous comparison has been made.

The purpose of this chapter is to pool the data from the European VAS-based valuation studies carried out since 1991, and to compare the valuations across studies and countries in a more rigorous way by accounting for measurable differences in methodology, study features and respondent characteristics, i.e. the background variables outlined in Chapter 6. It is evident from the results in Chapter 8 that health state valuations vary mainly because the states are different, i.e. are composed of different levels of different dimensions. Here we keep this source of variance constant and explore the extent to which the variance in the valuations of different health states, when considered separately, can be explained by the background variables. In addition we explore to what extent median VAS valuations differ between the studies.

7.2 MATERIAL AND METHODS

The VAS valuations

The standard valuation method of the EuroQol Group has been a postal questionnaire with the standard health states to be valued (15 different states plus repeated 11111, 33333, and dead). For various reasons, valuation studies have departed from the standard approach. For example, some studies have been interview-based rather than postal surveys. In some studies the health states to be valued have been ranked before valuation and their indicated duration may have departed from the standard 1 year. So not only the set of states to be valued may have departed to some extent from the standard set described above, the treatment of missing and inconsistent valuations may have been different. Finally, the population samples may have been drawn in various ways, resulting in differences in demographic and socio-economic characteristics.

The data sets

The pooled data originated from 11 studies from 6 European countries. These studies have been described in detail in Chapter 6. By using the abbreviations assigned to the studies in Chapter 6 the standard studies are Netherl. (Rotterdam survey in The Netherlands in January 1991); UK_FR (Frome IV study in the UK in June-August 1991); Finland (Finnish national survey in November-December 1992); Cat_Hos (a Catalonian study in l'Hospitalet del Llobregat in November-December 1992); Navarra (a survey in Navarra in September 1995); Sweden (Swedish national survey in April 1994); Ger_94 (a national German survey in June 1994); and Ger_97 (another German survey in April 1997). The non-standard studies are UK_MVH (a national survey conducted in the UK in August-November 1993); Ger_TTO (a national German survey in October 1997-March 1998); and Cat_Cor (a Catalonian study in Cornellà de Llobregat in October-December 1996).

Exclusions and inconsistencies

In January 1999 the Group established a standard set of exclusion criteria. These criteria were discussed in Chapter 6 and are:

(i) The respondent gave all states the same value.
(ii) The respondent valued less than 3 states.
(iii) The respondent had more than 3 inconsistencies in the states valued.

Study features

The pooled data contains a number of common variables describing study features and respondent characteristics. The following study features were considered, *a priori,* to be the most important factors potentially affecting the valuations: whether the health states were ranked before valuation or not; whether the valuation was based on interview rather than self-administration of a postal questionnaire; and whether the duration of states was defined as 10 years, followed by death rather than the standard 1 year (what happens after 1 year is not known and should not be taken into account). Since these features occurred in most cases in the same studies (apart from l'Hospitalet del Llobregat and Navarra), only one variable was defined (RIT, obtains a value of 1, if the study was based on ranking, interview and 10 year duration, 0 otherwise) and included in the analysis.

The features of the studies included in the pooled data and the exclusions from these studies are summarised in Tables 6.2 and 6.5 of Chapter 6. The response rates varied extensively, clearly a result of different study features. The number of observations also varied within a wide range, from 122 to 3395. In about one half of the studies, the data were collected in the standardised way by postal survey, and 3 studies followed the RIT approach.

Respondent characteristics

The information on respondent characteristics is derived from the questionnaires. For age a classification of 7 age groups was used (≤ 24 years, 25-34 years; 35-44 years; 45-54 years, 55-64 years, 65-74 years and 75 years of age and older). The respondent's own rating of his/her health on a 0-100 VAS scale (EQ VAS) was classified so that EQ VAS = 1 if the rating was < 85, and 0 otherwise (≥ 85). For education, 3 levels were defined: low, medium (Edu_med) and high (Edu_high). The 2 education dummies were given a value of 1, if the defined level occurred, otherwise 0. The effect of sex is uncertain, because a weak effect was found in an earlier study and therefore sex was not included (Björk and Norinder 1999).

Methods of comparing valuations

The analysis is based on 18 VAS valuations of EQ-5D states. Only 4 of the 11 studies provide information on all 18 valuations. Mean and median VAS values were computed for each study and over all the studies.

The relationship between mean VAS valuations and key background variables was first examined graphically and separately for each variable. To explore in a more rigorous way whether observed differences in valuations could be explained by study and respondent characteristics, a weighted linear regression analysis was carried out for each state with the valuation of that state as the dependent variable. To correct for the differences in sample sizes, weights (defined as 1/n, where n = the number of respondents in a study after exclusions) were applied. When only 1 set of values for 11111, 33333 and Dead (11111A, 33333A, DeadA) was included, a total of 15 regressions was performed. First, the respondent characteristics and the study feature RIT were entered as explanatory variables. Then the dummies for the standard studies were entered to see whether, after controlling for respondent characteristics and RIT, the different studies had independent explanatory power. Sweden was used in the regression analyses as a comparator or 'norm', because it was closest to the average study.

In order to investigate the similarities in the VAS valuations from the 11 studies, a singular value decomposition (SVD) was carried out on the median VAS scores. This examines to what extent the median scores of the studies can be represented by common scores, except for random error. It is an exploratory technique, looking for the best representation of the median scores for each study, using the common score and a study-specific proportionality constant. This constant shows to what extent (a given percentage) the common scores should be increased or decreased to represent the valuations for a particular study.

If the set of common scores and the study constants do not represent the matrix of scores satisfactorily, the technique shows whether a second component can explain the residuals. This could be the case if participants in some studies (for example, with a particular cultural background) use different valuation strategies than those in other studies (with other cultural backgrounds). In principle, 11 components will always result in a perfect solution. However, it is expected that fewer components will be necessary to represent the data. The first component is, in general, similar to the average values of health state scores (median values averaged over the studies), but not equal to these values. The values on this component are weighted means of the study scores, the weights depending on how well a study is represented by the common component. In this respect the method is related to principal components analysis (sometimes better known as factor analysis). Both techniques can be regarded as examples of smallest space analysis, where the aim is to represent a matrix of scores by another matrix of lower rank (of simpler structure).

A second SVD-analysis was carried out on the regression coefficients for the studies, derived from the regression analyses on the individual health states. In this analysis background variables were added, together with dummy variables for all studies, compared to Sweden. This analysis does not show the overall effects, only the differences in valuations between the studies.

7.3 RESULTS

Description of data and mean and median VAS valuations

From 8709 respondents in the pooled data set 897 respondents were excluded by applying criteria (i) and (ii), and 501 respondents were excluded due to more than 3 inconsistencies, a total of 1398 respondents. The number of exclusions was high in the studies from Finland, Germany 1994, the Netherlands and Sweden. These were all postal surveys. There were significantly less exclusions due to more than 3 inconsistencies from the 2 Catalonian studies, UK_MVH and Ger_TTO (1.8 %) compared to 34.7% in postal surveys ($p < 0.0001$). The 4 studies were all interview-based with ranking of states, apart from Navarra.

Table 7.1 shows the exclusions by respondent characteristics. Older respondents ($p < 0.0005$) and those with low education ($p < 0.0005$) clearly had more exclusions than the others.

Table 7.2 gives an overview of the respondent characteristics in different studies. The age structure varied to some extent across studies. The Catalonian, Ger_94 and Swedish studies had a very low percentage of elderly (75+) respondents, and the youngest age groups were least represented in the UK_MVH, Ger_97, Ger_TTO and Dutch studies. The percentage of respondents with EQ VAS < 85 was clearly highest in the 3 Spanish studies, and the latter also included the highest percentage of respondents with low education.

Table 7.1. Exclusions by respondent characteristics

		Not excl.	Excluded	Total	Excluded (%)
N		7311	1398	8709	16.1
Sex	Male	3352	694	4046	17.2
	Female	3948	575	4523	12.7
	Total	7300	1269	8569	14.8
	Missing	11	129	140	92.1
Age group	Age ≤ 24	825	42	867	4.8
	25-34	1595	76	1671	4.5
	35-44	1204	111	1315	8.4
	45-54	1105	165	1270	13.0
	55-64	1027	223	1250	17.8
	65-74	1016	371	1387	26.7
	75+	527	274	801	34.2
	Total	7299	1262	8561	14.7
	Missing	12	136	148	91.9
Exp. illness yourself	No	4713	430	5143	8.4
	Yes	1771	390	2161	18.0
	Total	6484	820	7304	11.2
	Missing	827	578	1405	41.1
Exp. illness family	No	2451	268	2719	9.9
	Yes	3965	395	4360	9.1
	Total	6416	663	7079	9.4
	Missing	895	735	1630	45.1
Exp. illness others	No	2423	421	2844	14.8
	Yes	747	191	938	20.4
	Total	3170	612	3782	16.2
	Missing	4141	786	4927	16.0
EQ VAS	≥ 85	3972	375	4347	8.6
	< 85	3269	686	3955	17.3
	Missing	70	337	407	82.8
Smoker	Smoker	1784	245	2029	12.1
	Non/former	4598	909	5507	16.5
	Total	6382	1154	7536	15.3
	Missing	929	244	1173	20.8

Table 7.2. The distribution of respondent characteristics by studies after exclusions

		Cat_Cor	Cat_Hos	Finland	UK_FR	UK_MVH	Ger_94	Ger_97	Ger_TTO	Navarra	Netherl.	Sweden	Total
N		294	597	1150	95	3344	181	92	339	267	591	361	7311
Sex (%)	Male	45.9	50.1	46.1	53.7	43.3	61.3	47.8	55.2	45.3	42.5	48.2	45.8
	Female	54.1	49.9	53.9	46.3	56.7	38.1	51.1	44.8	54.7	56.5	51.0	54.0
	Unknown	0.0	0.0	0.0	0.0	0.0	0.6	1.1	0.0	0.0	1.0	0.8	0.2
Age (%)	≤ 24	16.0	13.2	16.4	4.2	9.1	15.5	6.5	7.7	16.1	8.3	14.1	11.3
	25-34	18.4	23.8	21.7	23.2	22.5	18.2	29.3	15.3	21.0	20.8	23.8	21.8
	35-44	16.7	11.6	17.6	17.9	16.6	13.3	13.0	15.6	15.0	19.1	19.7	16.5
	45-54	15.3	19.4	12.3	24.2	14.4	17.7	16.3	16.2	16.1	14.0	19.4	15.1
	55-64	15.0	21.9	8.2	8.4	14.3	19.9	16.3	23.9	12.7	11.8	10.0	14.0
	65-74	17.3	8.7	15.8	16.8	14.2	13.3	10.9	13.6	12.4	15.2	10.5	13.9
	75+	1.4	1.3	8.0	5.3	9.1	2.2	6.5	7.4	6.7	9.6	1.4	7.2
	Unknown	0.0	0.0	0.0	0.0	0.0	0.0	1.1	0.3	0.0	1.0	1.1	0.2
EQ VAS (%)	≥ 85	36.4	39.2	51.0	53.7	60.9	49.2	52.2	69.9	26.6	47.5	64.0	54.3
	< 85	63.6	60.8	46.4	43.2	39.1	48.6	45.7	29.2	73.4	48.4	35.2	44.7
	Unknown	0.0	0.0	2.5	3.2	0.1	2.2	2.2	0.9	0.0	4.1	0.8	1.0
Education (%)	Low	56.5	55.6	32.9	33.7	39.4	43.1	13.0	7.1	59.6	25.2	18.6	37.1
	Medium	26.9	25.1	32.2	38.9	40.4	40.9	50.0	59.6	30.7	45.2	46.0	38.6
	High	16.3	18.6	28.3	25.3	20.2	9.4	35.9	33.0	9.4	29.3	32.4	22.7
	Unknown	0.3	0.7	6.6	2.1	0.1	6.6	1.1	0.3	0.4	0.3	3.0	1.6

Figure 7.1 shows that differences between the total mean and median values emerged at the lower end of the VAS (severe states). The mean VAS values of the moderate health states with 1 or 2 dimensions at level 2 and the other dimensions at level 1 varied considerably across studies. For state 32211 the Cat_Hos study was clearly an outlier

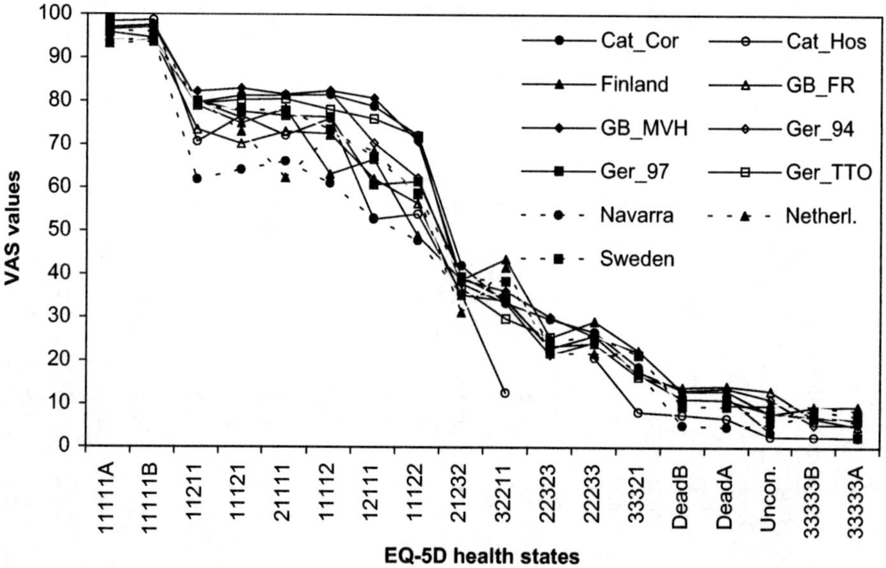

	mean	median	SD		mean	median	SD
11111A	97.1	100	7.4	32211	33.6	30	21.1
11111B	95.3	100	8.9	22323	26.1	25	18.0
11211	77.7	80	15.7	22233	24.9	20	16.5
11121	77.6	80	15.9	33321	18.5	15	15.9
21111	76.4	80	16.1	DeadB	10.3	4	18.0
11112	75	80	18.0	DeadA	10.0	1	18.5
12111	69.1	70	20.0	Uncon.	8.2	2	15.5
11122	59.0	60	18.9	33333B	7.5	3	13.0
21232	37.3	35	18.2	33333A	5.9	2	11.1

Figure 7.1. Mean values of standard states by study and overall

Figure 7.1 does, however, suggest that there was a common pattern in mean valuations across studies, although there were also systematic differences. A large proportion of the variation between studies was evidently due to RIT. The valuations from these studies appeared to be higher, especially for the less serious states. This can be seen clearly from Figure 7.2

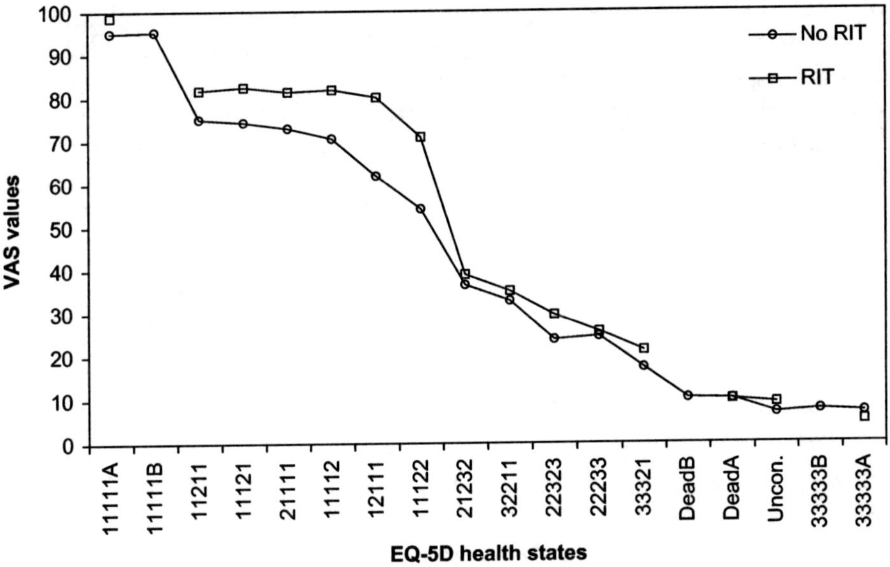

Figure 7.2. Mean VAS valuations from standard studies and those based on RIT

Figure 7.3 shows the relationship between the mean VAS valuations and the age of the respondents. Three age groups were defined: ≤ 44, 45-64 and ≥ 65. For many health states the respondents in age group ≥ 65 had the highest mean values.

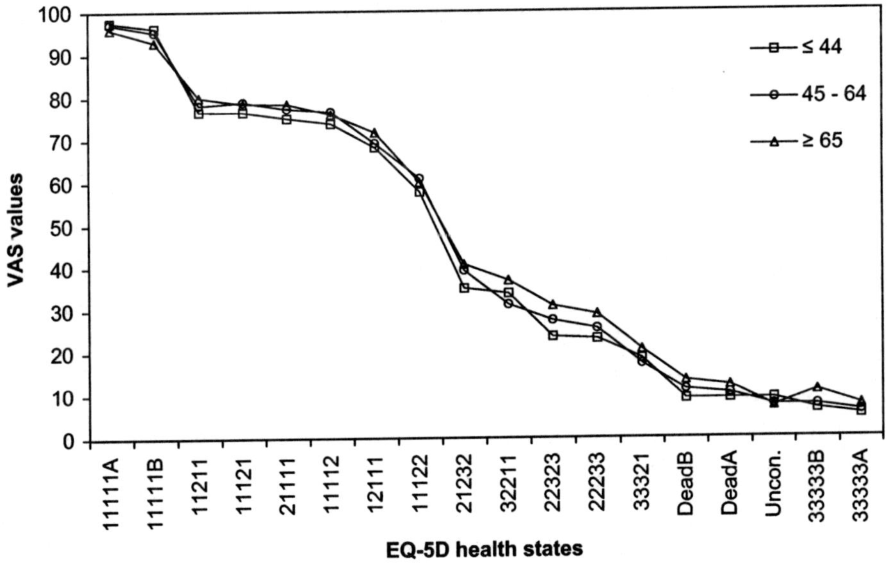

Figure 7.3. Mean EQ VAS valuations by age groups

Figure 7.4 shows the relationship between mean EQ-5D VAS valuations and age and EQ VAS combined. Here a distinction has been made between respondents aged ≤ 44 with EQ VAS ≤ 84 and ≥ 85, and respondents aged ≥ 65 with EQ VAS ≤ 84 and ≥ 85. Here also respondents in the older age group (≥ 65) had the highest mean VAS valuations and respondents aged ≤ 44 had the lowest. In health states with only 1 level 2 the respondents aged ≤ 44 with high EQ VAS had mean VAS valuations which were more or less the same as those of respondents aged ≥ 65 with a low EQ VAS. In health states with at least one level 3 the effect of age appeared to be dominant.

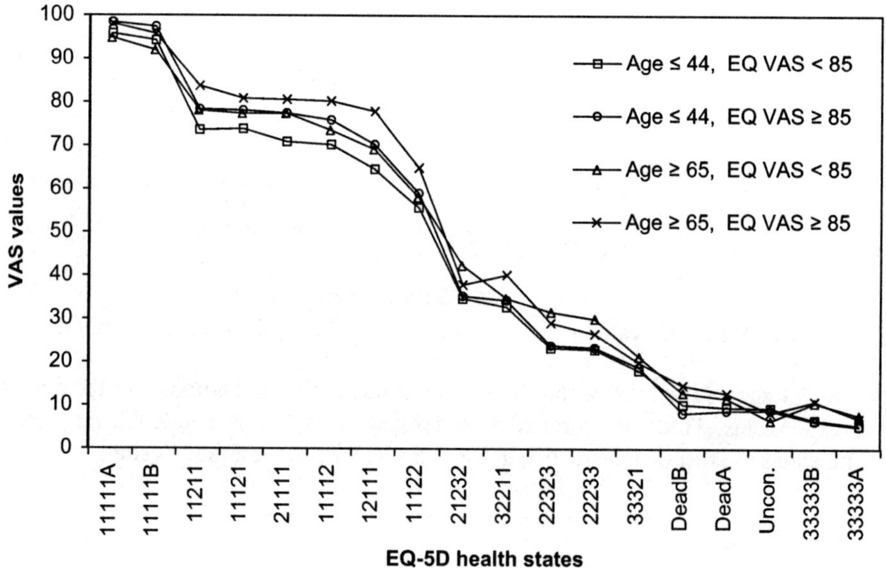

Figure 7.4. Mean EQ-5D VAS valuations by age and EQ VAS combined

Figure 7.5 shows the relationship between mean EQ-5D VAS valuations and education. Respondents with high education tended to have the lowest mean VAS valuations for most states.

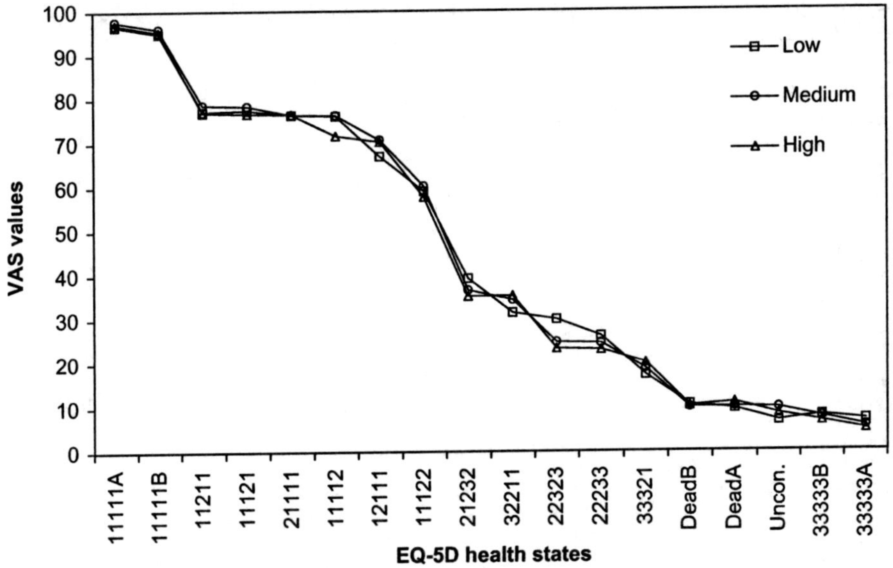

Figure 7.5. Mean VAS valuations by education

Regression analysis of standard states

The results of the linear regressions of the raw VAS values of 15 standard states (i.e. only one valuation for 11111A, 33333A, and DeadA) on the background variables are presented in Table 7.3. Only the coefficients with a significance level of $p < 0.01$ are shown.

Table 7.3. Weighted linear regression of VAS values on background variables for all studies (coefficients with $p < 0.01$ depicted)

	11111A	11211	11121	21111	11112	12111	11122	21232	32211	22323	22233	33321	DeadA	Uncon.	33333A
(Constant)	97.65	72.11	74.03	71.39	73.41	60.68	55.56	35.59	32.72	22.36	21.76	16.85	9.13	8.44	6.05
RIT study	2.82	4.79	7.17	7.72	7.51	16.02	14.88	2.66		5.23					-2.83
Age 25 - 34	-0.96		-2.60												
Age 35 - 44		2.89													
Age 45 - 54		5.26	3.81	6.21	5.03	4.18	4.89							-2.55	
Age 55 - 64		6.60	4.02	4.86	4.42	4.46	5.57	4.91			4.46			-3.00	1.92
Age 65 - 74	-1.14	5.75		4.26	3.44					7.46	5.08			-2.85	2.34
Age ≥ 75	-1.63	6.72									5.42				2.18
EQ VAS < 35	-2.74	-5.08	-4.51	-4.87	-4.96	-5.32	-3.81		-3.02						
Edu_med		3.75	2.18	2.17		3.31	294	597	1150	95	3344	181	92	339	267
Edu_high				2.29	-2.23	3.08			2.62			2.99	1.95		
R^2	0.07	0.06	0.07	0.08	0.07	0.13	0.09	0.02	0.02	0.05	0.02	0.01	0.01	0.02	0.02
Adjusted R^2	0.07	0.06	0.06	0.08	0.07	0.13	0.09	0.02	0.02	0.04	0.02	0.01	0.00	0.01	0.02
F	54.29	24.35	27.52	34.54	31.36	58.15	33.91	7.17	6.66	12.25	6.62	4.61	3.62	9.75	17.83
P	0.00	0.00	0.00	0.00	0.00	0.00	0.00	0.00	0.00	0.00	0.00	0.00	0.00	0.00	0.00

The explanatory power of the regressions is very low with R^2s ranging from 0.01 to 0.13. The RIT approach resulted in higher valuations except for state 33333A. Those who rated their health status on VAS at less than 85 tended to give slightly lower values than those who rated it ≥ 85. The younger respondents (< 45) tended to give lower values than the older ones for states with only one 2 on the descriptive system. The low R^2 values suggest that the main variation was within respondents and not within background variables or studies.

To check this conclusion, dummies for the standard studies were added to the independent variables. The results are shown in Table 7.4. The coefficients indicate a change in comparison with the Swedish respondents, who were younger than 25, with EQ VAS ≥ 85 and a low level of education. Entering the study dummies increases the explanatory power of all models and the range of R^2s is now from 0.03 to 0.21. These values are still very low, given the number of additional dummies. The inclusion of the other study dummies has the effect of reducing the effects of RIT and the coefficients of education have changed predominantly to slightly negative. The coefficients of EQ VAS are hardly affected. The most noteworthy observation is that even after controlling for the factors mentioned above, the coefficients of the Spanish studies (Cat_Hos and Navarra) were clearly and quite consistently negative, suggesting lower valuations for most health states in comparison with other countries. There is no such consistency in the coefficients of other studies, but fewer of them are significant and they tend to be both positive and negative in a less systematic way.

Table 7.4. Weighted linear regression of VAS values on background variables and dummies for the non-ranked studies (coefficients with $p \leq 0.01$ depicted)

	11111A	11211	11121	21111	11112	12111	11122	21232	32211	22323	22233	33321	DeadA	Uncon.	33333A
(Constant)	97.42	78.35	78.88	76.37	75.36	66.40	59.99	39.46	40.33	24.61	24.65	22.02	9.52	8.35	8.27
RIT study	2.91		3.43	3.45	7.02	11.40	12.57		-6.00	3.19					-4.47
Age 25 - 34	-1.06		-2.79											-1.86	
Age 35 - 44														-2.36	
Age 45 - 54		4.22	3.35	5.98	3.66	3.79	3.60							-3.57	
Age 55 - 64		4.70	2.76	4.35		4.28	3.56	4.46			4.48			-3.43	2.00
Age 65 - 74	-0.94	3.65		3.69						7.43	4.65			-4.29	1.85
Age ≥ 75		4.56									4.82				
EQ VAS < 85	-2.73	-3.28	-3.59	-3.97	-3.91	-3.59	-2.51		-1.86						
Edu_med										-2.40				2.02	-0.93
Edu_high		-2.56			-3.28					-2.73					-1.76
Cat_Hos	3.05	-7.82		-4.54	2.81	-13.59	-5.14	-4.92	-25.26	M	-5.74	-12.82	-2.56	-4.02	-5.92
Finland	-1.54				-9.59		-9.34		4.95				3.50		1.78
UK_FR		-6.07	-7.85	-4.72		-4.33		-4.84	-4.39		-3.10	-5.11	5.42	6.74	-2.92
Ger_94	1.18			M	8.17	3.40	3.37		-5.73	-4.81	-2.99	-4.20	3.41	3.73	-3.02
Ger_97	1.32				3.39	-6.48			-3.90			-4.41			
Navarra	-1.21	-16.38	-12.66	-9.87	-11.70	-12.62	-10.41	-5.03		M		-3.53	-4.55		-2.40
Netherl.	-2.36		-4.55	-14.46				-8.02	4.07		-4.80		M	3.09	
R^2	0.11	0.17	-0.12	0.15	0.18	0.21	0.15	0.04	0.19	0.05	0.04	0.08	0.03	0.05	0.05
Adjusted R^2	0.10	0.16	-0.12	0.14	0.17	0.20	0.14	0.03	0.19	0.05	0.03	0.08	0.03	0.05	0.05
F	49.06	46.76	31.44	40.36	49.89	60.97	34.10	7.40	46.33	9.55	7.59	17.46	12.38	18.05	23.89
P	0.00	0.00	0.00	0.00	0.00	0.00	0.00	0.00	0.00	0.00	0.00	0.00	0.00	0.00	0.00

Singular value decomposition of median VAS scores for studies

The application of the SVD technique resulted in a solution with 1 dominant 'eigenvalue', equal to 790.20. This first component represents the bulk (99%) of the variation in health state valuations for studies. The other eigenvalues were significantly smaller. Hence, all studies can be represented reasonably well by the first left and right eigenvector. The results, together with the health state scores for an 'average study' are given in Table 7.5. The absolute differences between the observed median values and those reproduced by the first component are given in Table 7.6..

Table 7.5. Outcomes of the SVD-analysis of 18 health state evaluations for 11 studies

Eigenvalues of X:

790.1965	43.0976	37.5317	17.6197	16.4665	11.0088	9.5112	9.2307
6.9516	4.7496	4.4221					

Cumulative proportion explained variance:

0.9933	0.9962	0.9985	0.9990	0.9994	0.9996	0.9997	0.9999
0.9999	1.0000	1.0000					

Row and column components for first 3 factors:

state:	comp.1	comp.2	comp.3	Mean score comp.1 *)	study:	comp.1	comp.2	comp.3
11111A	0.42	0.36	0.20	99.30	Cat_Cor	0.322	-0.298	-0.022
11111B	0.42	0.36	0.20	99.25	Cat_Hos	0.284	-0.065	0.842
11211	0.33	-0.14	-0.14	78.38	Finland	0.296	0.276	-0.246
11121	0.33	-0.11	0.12	78.59	UK_FR	0.293	0.076	0.014
21111	0.33	0.00	0.09	78.58	UK_MVH	0.326	-0.351	-0.261
11112	0.33	-0.30	0.21	77.90	Ger_94	0.306	-0.064	0.028
12111	0.29	-0.35	-0.53	68.52	Ger_97	0.303	0.042	0.207
11122	0.26	-0.32	-0.06	62.26	Ger_TTO	0.319	-0.338	-0.067
21232	0.16	0.16	0.06	37.39	Navarra	0.267	0.757	0.027
32211	0.14	0.37	-0.61	32.90	Netherl.	0.291	0.040	-0.291
22323	0.09	-0.41	0.06	21.19	Sweden	0.306	0.085	-0.167
22233	0.10	0.20	-0.02	22.67	Average	0.301	0.015	0.006
33321	0.07	0.08	-0.32	16.02				
DeadA	0.01	-0.02	0.17	3.43				
DeadB	0.02	-0.07	0.15	4.09				
Uncon.	0.01	-0.05	-0.05	1.30				
33333B	0.01	0.08	-0.09	3.47		comp.1	comp.2	comp.3
33333A	0.01	0.03	-0.09	1.31	Eigenvalues:	790.20	43.10	37.53

*) Equal to state score x eigenvalue x average study score For the first health state this value is: 0.42 x 790.20 x 0.301 = 99.30 etc.

Table 7.6 shows that a representation using only the first comman component does not show consistent deviations between the studies: only some isolated states have a substantial deviation from the value predicted by the first left and right eigenvector

Table 7.6. Absolute differences between the original scores and the representation by the first component

Study	Cat_Cor	Cat_Hos	Finland	UK_FR	UK_MVH	Ger_94	Ger_97	Ger_TTO	Navarra	Netherl.	Sweden	Mean State
11211	1.21	3.92	3.00	1.65	0.22	0.23	1.21	0.11	9.44	4.32	0.46	2.34
11111A	6.15	6.35	1.45	2.27	7.41	1.05	0.19	5.29	12.03	1.63	0.77	4.05
21232	5.03	0.26	2.27	1.42	2.45	3.05	2.42	4.65	6.87	6.10	2.05	3.32
11122	3.44	3.72	11.17	0.65	7.65	7.86	2.42	8.98	5.16	0.11	3.19	4.30
11121	0.98	5.88	1.79	6.56	0.02	0.01	1.00	1.66	4.63	0.88	0.24	2.15
22233	0.76	1.38	5.73	2.09	0.52	2.57	2.21	4.04	7.91	1.89	3.01	2.92
33333A	1.40	1.23	3.72	0.77	0.59	1.33	1.31	1.39	1.16	3.74	0.67	1.57
33321	2.13	10.11	4.26	0.61	2.67	1.31	0.11	1.99	0.80	4.53	3.74	2.93
21111	1.00	0.89	2.80	2.45	0.00	0.03	1.01	1.68	0.38	10.87	0.26	1.94
11111B	6.10	6.40	1.49	2.31	7.36	1.01	0.23	5.24	12.07	1.17	0.72	4.01
Uncon.	1.39	1.22	1.28	3.73	3.60	1.32	1.31	0.62	1.15	0.75	1.32	1.61
12111	6.76	14.62	2.69	1.75	10.88	0.27	8.87	7.35	10.70	3.85	0.47	6.20
11112	1.72	6.53	11.54	0.89	2.73	5.72	1.69	1.89	9.02	0.22	0.06	3.82
32211	5.17	21.03	7.68	1.95	0.59	0.52	3.07	4.88	10.85	8.24	6.61	6.42
33333B	0.71	3.27	1.59	1.12	0.75	3.53	1.51	0.68	1.93	1.65	1.48	1.66
22323	7.34	5.01	0.82	0.65	5.07	1.57	1.30	2.53	16.28	0.46	1.51	3.87
DeadA	1.34	4.77	0.37	4.66	3.71	1.51	1.56	2.63	3.04	2.31	1.48	2.49
DeadB	0.37	5.14	1.02	1.02	0.42	1.66	3.39	0.34	3.62	0.05	2.15	1.74
Mean	2.94	5.65	3.59	2.03	3.15	3.15	1.93	3.11	6.50	2.93	1.68	3.19

Figure 7.6 gives a representation of the average median values resulting from this first component. The study-specific proportional constants for this component are given in Figure 7.7. The RIT studies (UK_MVH, Cat-Cor and Ger_TTO) have the highest values for the constant, Navarra and Cat_Hos the lowest.

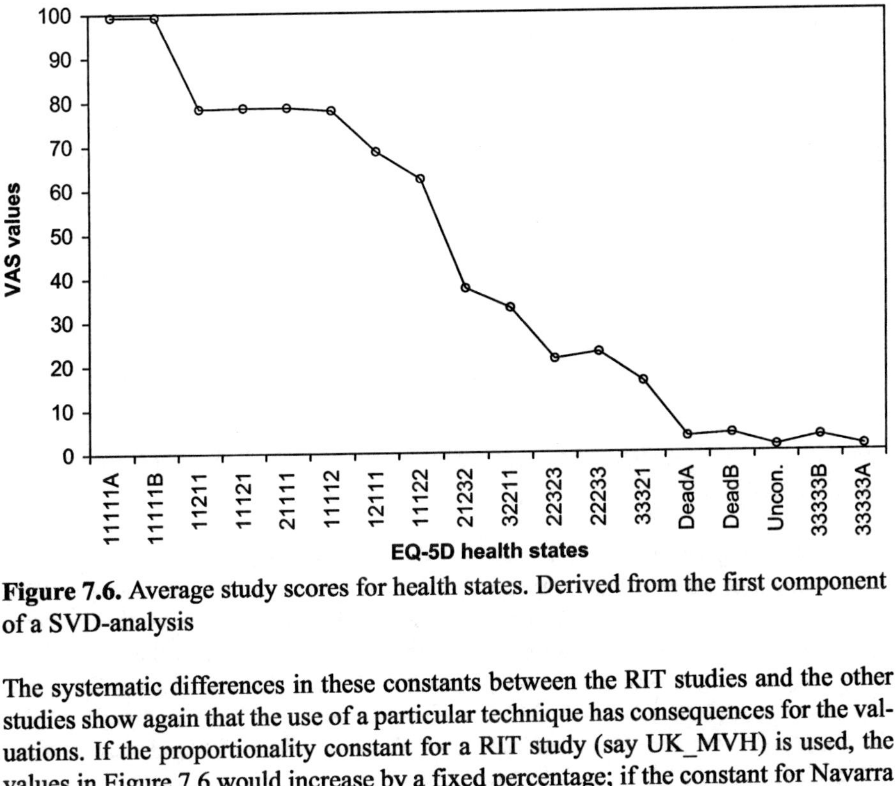

Figure 7.6. Average study scores for health states. Derived from the first component of a SVD-analysis

The systematic differences in these constants between the RIT studies and the other studies show again that the use of a particular technique has consequences for the valuations. If the proportionality constant for a RIT study (say UK_MVH) is used, the values in Figure 7.6 would increase by a fixed percentage; if the constant for Navarra is used, all values would decrease by a fixed percentage. The trend, however, would be the same in both cases. The values for each study can be found by dividing the mean scores for the first component given in Table 7.5 by 0.301 and multiplying them by the study-specific proportionality constant (e.g. 0.326 for UK_MVH and 0.267 for Navarra).

The fact that there was no special component to distinguish between RIT and the other studies shows that the difference in technique merely affects the level of the scores and not the scale itself.

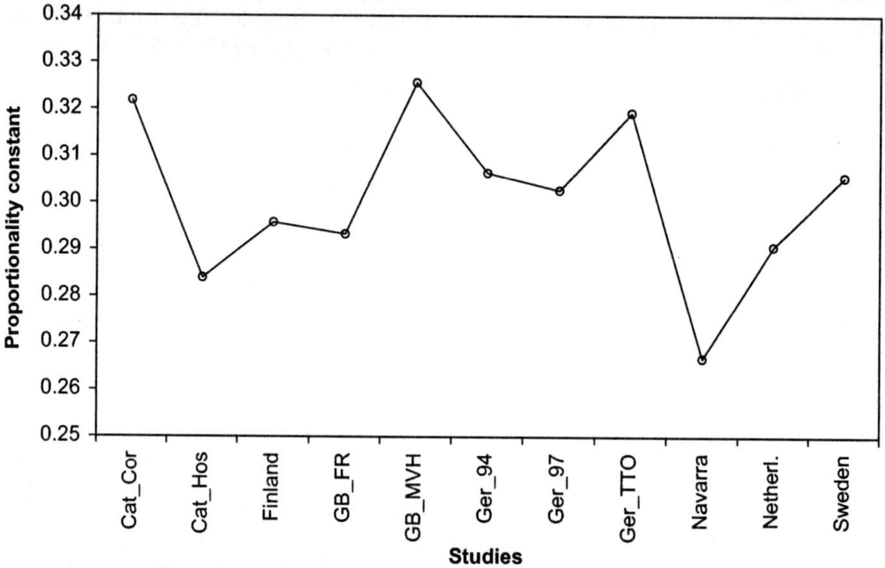

Figure 7.7. Proportionality constants for studies. Derived from the first component of a SVD-analysis

The second component is mainly related to the deviations for Navarra: the value on the column component for this study is 0.76, connected to the row components that correspond to the largest deviations in the table of differences. But the contribution of this factor, which is a combination of the column component and the eigenvalue (0.76 x 43.10 = 32.62), is still low, compared to the contribution of Navarra to the first component (0.27 x 790.20 = 210.76). This second component represents deviations in states 11111A, 11111B and 32211, which are relatively high and states 11112, 12111, 11122 and 22323, which are relatively low.

The third component is mainly related to Cat_Hos: the value on the column component for this study is 0.84. It represents states 11111A and 11111B, with relatively high scores and states 12111, 32211 and 33321, with relatively low scores. Moreover, for this study the contribution to the first component is considerably larger than to the third one.

The fact that the deviations from the first component for Navarra and Cat_Hos are represented by different components means that they do not have a common background. With the exception of the states 11111A and 11111B, the deviations for the 2 studies are for different states and/or in different directions.

In the SVD-analysis on the regression coefficients the main common factor again shows the differences in weights between RIT and other studies. Compared to Sweden, the RIT studies have positive values. Navarra and Cat_Hos have very low row values. These values pertain mainly to the health states with a value 2 on one dimension and a value 1 on all other dimensions. The second factor primarily represents the deviation of the state 32211 for Cat_Hos, while the third factor shows a deviation for the Dutch study, mainly due to the coefficient for the health state 21111. Compared to Sweden, the Dutch score, especially for health state 21111, is low. The fourth factor shows the deviations for Navarra concerning health states 11211, 11112, 12111 and 22322.

Except for the third factor, the picture is very much in agreement with the results from the SVD analysis on the median values. This supports the idea that the median values for the health states of the studies can be interpreted as stable outcomes, even when the background variables are taken into account, as is the case in the regression analyses on the individual health states.

7.4 DISCUSSION

This study set out to analyse the relationship between European VAS-based health state valuations from different studies and countries, where there are measurable differences in the methods employed, in study features, and in respondent characteristics. We have been able to draw important conclusions about whether or not these valuations are similar across studies and countries.

A striking difference between the studies was in sample sizes. To prevent the larger studies from dominating the results (e.g. 46 % of the respondents in the pooled data came from a single study, the UK_MVH study) the analyses were carried out with weighted data. The 11 different studies were weighted by the reciprocal of the number of respondents per study after exclusions. This weighting procedure has the effect that the potential differences in study features and respondent characteristics across studies (and countries) had a fair chance of becoming standardising factors in comparing valuations between studies and countries.

The studies did differ in study features and respondent characteristics. A typical feature of the Spanish studies in comparison with the other studies was a very high response rate and hardly any exclusions on the basis of the standard exclusion criteria. It is not known from the Spanish studies how many people were approached and how many were excluded, and for what reasons, before the final samples were reached. It is likely, though, that the processes in arriving at the final samples analysed here may have been different in the Spanish studies from the other studies.

Our analyses show that the study features and respondent characteristics, as they were measured, had an effect on valuations, although the proportion of variation they explain remains very low. This suggests that we may not have been able to measure these characteristics properly, there may be important omitted explanatory variables, and/or that there is a large proportion of random variation. Many studies included a wider range of potential explanatory variables, but the set used was common to all studies. More stringent exclusion criteria than those applied would reduce the random variation and thus increase the proportion of variation explained, but maximising this proportion is not of primary importance in itself.

From the variables considered, the study characteristic referred to, as 'RIT' appears to have had the clearest and most consistent effect on valuations. This feature resulted in generally higher valuations than the standard approach. With respect to respondent characteristics, the respondent's own health status as rated on the EQ VAS exhibited a rather consistent effect so that poorer health status tended to be associated with lower valuations, other things being equal, especially where less serious health states are concerned. Age and education also seemed to have some effect: higher age tended to be associated with higher valuations, but for education there was no systematic pattern.

After controlling for these factors the origin of the study did not have a consistent effect on valuations with the exception of the studies from Spain (Cat_Hos and Navarra), which produced significantly lower valuations. This raises the question whether the Spanish values really differ or whether the results can be explained by some subtle features of Spanish studies (e.g. respondent selection) that are not reflected in our variables. One feature that might explain, at least partially, the results from Cat_Hos is related to an earlier translation of the questionnaire from the UK English used in the study. This indicates the importance of checking the translations carefully for international comparisons.

The SVD analyses show how similar the median valuations of the studies for the standard states are if the EQ-5D model restrictions described in Chapter 8 are omitted. These analyses suggest that all studies are rather well represented by the solution of the first component. However, the median values for studies differ in the multiplicative constant. For some studies, especially the RIT studies (UK_MVH, Cat_Cor and Ger_TTO), the common scores must be increased by a given percentage. For other studies (especially Navarra and Cat_Hos) the overall values must be reduced by a given percentage. For Navarra and Cat_Hos it was also found that there were (minor) inconsistencies, expressed by different factors. However, there was no indication that these differences were related to specific response strategies, nor were they of the same kind.

The trend as represented by the first component represents the majority of the variation in health state ratings for all studies. Hence this trend can indeed be interpreted as the representation of the health state value on the VAS scale as seen by all studies. However, the systematic differences in the multiplicative constants between the RIT and the other studies show that the use of a particular technique has consequences for the level of valuations. The fact that there was no special SVD-component to distinguish between the RIT and the other studies shows that the difference in technique merely affects the range of the scale values used; the relative valuations, given the range, were the same.

The main conclusion is that there appears to be a considerable degree of agreement between health state valuations in studies from several European countries, with the exception of Spain. The valuations from 3 RIT-based studies from 3 European countries appear to be even more similar. We are therefore left with the impression that the differences found in Spain in standard studies may be explained by some subtle methodological and/or linguistic differences that we were not able to measure and account for, rather than cultural differences. A recent paper (briefly described in Chapter 13) comparing Finnish and US valuations of a common set of health states concluded on the basis of a thorough analysis that there were small and inconsistent differences in valuations between these 2 countries, but that these differences in valuations are generally unlikely to affect EQ-5D valuations in international studies (Johnson *et al*, 2000a). Thus the evidence so far seems to suggest that the Western industrialised countries at least may share a similar value climate. Hence in this cultural area it appears unnecessary to replicate expensive and detailed valuation studies in each country in order to arrive at valid preference-based HRQoL instruments.

8
A European EQ-5D VAS valuation set

Wolfgang Greiner and the Rotterdam Analysis Team: Tom Weijnen, Martin Nieuwenhuizen, Siem Oppe and Frank de Charro

8.1 INTRODUCTION

One of the objectives of the EQ-net project was to find out whether there were differences in the relative valuations of health states across countries. It has been shown in chapter 7 that there is a considerable degree of agreement between health state valuations across European countries, and it was concluded that expensive and cumbersome valuation studies do not necessarily have to be carried out in each country in order to elicit VAS-based valuations for HRQoL instruments.

The development of an international set of values that could be used for a variety of purposes, derived from the existing European data, was viewed as an important step. By pooling the data from 11 studies in 6 countries, it is possible to include a wider range of health states than in previous studies. This chapter investigates whether it is possible to describe the joint data sets of VAS valuations in the EQ-net database by 1 model. The model should assign a unique HRQoL value to each possible health state as defined by EQ-5D. Hence a multi-level regression model was applied to a database that contains the VAS scores from the 11 studies.

Socio-economic or cultural (regional or countrywide) differences in valuation are not tested extensively in this study: chapter 7 provided some commentary. Only the effect of 2 types of study design will be studied in addition to the effects of the values on the 5-dimensional classification of the EQ-5D descriptive system. In addition, the distribution of the sample by various background variables is presented.

8.2 MATERIAL AND METHODS

The data

The analysis for this chapter has been carried out on the data set of the extended EQ-net VAS database, which contains all the available data from the 11 valuation studies. A description of this database and of the studies included was given in Chapter 6.

The pooled data from the 11 studies resulted in a total of 124077 EQ-5D VAS valuations from 8709 respondents. In most studies, the health states 11111, 33333 and dead were valued twice. Per respondent, the mean value was calculated from the 2 valua-

R. Brooks et al. (eds.),
The Measurement and Valuation of Health Status Using EQ-5D: A European Perspective, 103–142.

tions of the same health state. Only these mean values were used in the analysis. As a result the analyses were performed on 114220 valuations.

Exclusions

The exclusion criteria used were discussed in chapter 6. They were:

(i) The respondent gave all states the same value.
(ii) The respondent valued less than 3 states.
(iii) The respondent had more than 3 inconsistencies in the states valued.

Transformation

Because of the restriction of the range of the raw VAS values to between 0 and 100, skewed response distributions were expected, and found, at the ends of the scale. This limits linear regression analysis, because the values to be included in that kind of analysis are assumed to be normally distributed. In order to solve this problem, a logistic transformation was applied, similar to that applied in a logit-analysis on frequencies or probabilities. Such a transformation will, in general, solve the problem of skewed response distributions, however it also changes the nature of the linear additive model into a multiplicative model. Hence it is necessary to investigate the effects of the transformation on the model.

The following transformation rule was used:

$$T_x = Ln\left(\frac{x - Min}{Max - x}\right) \quad (1)$$

where x is the original value, Min is the lower limit and Max is the upper limit.

The reverse transformation is:

$$x = \left(\frac{Max \cdot e^{T_x} + Min}{1 + e^{T_x}}\right) \quad (2)$$

where T_x is the value on the logistic scale and e the natural number.

The raw VAS values have been transformed, with 100.5 and – 0.5 as the upper and lower limits in the transformation procedure. These values produced the lowest skewness.

Table 8.1 presents the results from the transformation for the standard states based on linear regressions. The mean and median of the transformed values have been re-transformed using formula (2) for the reverse of the transformations. Transformation and re-transformation does not affect the median values, because the rank order between them does not change. The transformation is effective in reducing the skewness of the health states at both ends of the scale. For these health states the absolute differences between the mean and the median values become smaller. For dead and unconscious the transformed mean approaches the median values.

Table 8.1. Effects of the transformation procedures on the mean, median and measure for skewness (0 : a normal distribution; > 1 and < -1 : a skewed distribution) Standard states only

	Raw values				Re-transformed values			
	Mean	Median	Difference mean-median	Skewness	Mean	Median	Difference Mean-median	Skewness
11111	97.5	100.0	-2.5	-4.3	99.4	100.0	-0.6	-1.4
11211	78.0	80.0	-2.0	-1.2	82.1	80.0	2.1	0.3
11121	77.8	80.0	-2.2	-1.3	81.7	80.0	1.7	-0.1
21111	76.7	80.0	-3.3	-1.4	80.2	80.0	0.2	-0.5
11112	75.3	80.0	-4.7	-1.2	79.5	80.0	-0.5	-0.3
12111	69.4	71.0	-1.6	-0.8	73.2	71.0	2.2	-0.6
11122	59.3	60.0	-0.7	-0.3	60.8	60.0	0.8	-0.3
21232	36.9	35.0	1.9	0.4	34.0	35.0	-1.0	-0.8
32211	32.9	30.0	2.9	0.4	27.4	30.0	-2.6	-0.8
22323	25.3	23.0	2.3	0.9	19.5	23.0	-3.5	-0.9
22233	24.3	20.0	4.3	1.0	19.4	20.0	-0.6	-1.1
33321	17.9	15.0	2.9	1.4	12.3	15.0	-2.7	-0.6
33333	5.3	2.0	3.3	4.1	1.8	2.0	-0.2	0.5
Dead	10.0	2.0	8.0	2.9	2.6	2.0	0.6	1.1
Uncon.	8.0	2.0	6.0	3.2	2.3	2.0	0.3	0.9
Total (absolute values)			48.6	24.8			19.7	10.3

Rescaling

For applications where scenarios about quality of life questions are considered, the value set should be anchored on full health and dead. Usually, VAS values will be rescaled in such a way that the value for dead is set at zero and the value for full health (11111) at 1 or 100. Rescaling can take place either for each individual respondent, using his/her scores for full health and dead, or at the end of the analysis on the estimated VAS values which result from regression analysis. Individual rescaling is then used to make the response scales of individuals comparable. Preliminary OLS analyses showed that individual rescaling resulted in a much lower R^2 for the regression analyses. In Tables 8.7 and 8.8 the results of the regressions are shown. The R^2s of the regressions on the raw values are 0.72-0.74. The R^2s of the regressions on the rescaled values are 0.57-0.63. A possible explanation is that 'dead' as an individual anchor point is ambivalent. Hence no individual rescaling was applied in the final analyses.

In this chapter, the rescaling procedure was performed on the estimated VAS values in order to elicit a value for the health states on a scale with full health equal to 100 and dead equal to 0. Two versions were explored, 1 using the mean value for dead, the other the median value for dead.

The formula for rescaling is:

$$X_{res} = 100\left(\frac{X_{est} - dead_{\text{mean or median}}}{11111_{est} - dead_{\text{mean or median}}}\right)$$

X_{res}	rescaled estimated VAS value for health state X
X_{est}	estimated VAS value for health state X
$dead_{\text{mean or median}}$	mean or median value for dead
11111_{est}	estimated value for full health

The mean value for dead was 10.0 and the median value 2.0. Application of the formula implies that the rescaled health state 11111 has a value of 100 and the rescaled value for dead is 0.

Modelling

The regression was performed on all the original individual values of the non-excluded respondents from all studies. The assumption that individuals use the response scale equally is rather strong. However, as stated in the previous section, the results of an analysis on individually rescaled data caused a deterioration in the explanatory power of the model.

Another way of dealing with individual effects, avoiding the extension of the model with a parameter for each individual, is using a multi-level (random effects) model. In a multi-level analysis, it is assumed that the data is hierarchically structured. In the VAS data, 3 levels were distinguished. The valuations of the health states constitute the lowest level. Nesting these valuations within respondents gives the second level. Then respondents are nested within studies to form the third and highest level. The multi-level model differs from the ordinary OLS-regression model in estimating fixed effects as well as random effects. The error variance is decomposed into 3 components: random error, error due to individual differences in the constant, and error due to study differences in the constant. If individual and study differences exist, and are systematic, more precise estimation of the fixed parameters results.

The multi-level regression technique was applied using the MlwiN 1.02 software. A first series of models contains 2 dummy variables for each of the EQ-5D dimensions, and 2 extra dummies N2 and N3.

Five dummies for the EQ-5D descriptive system represent health states scored with either 2 or 3 on a dimension (Mob2, Self2, Act2, Pain2 and Anx2), as are 5 dummies representing health states scored with 3 on a dimension (Mob3, Self3, Act3, Pain3 and Anx3). Dummy N2 represents health states with a score of 2 or 3 on any dimension. This means that only 'full health' (state 11111) receives a value of 0 and all other states a value of 1. Dummy N3 represents health states that scored 3 on any dimension. The N2 and N3 dummies were added because they measure overall aspects, not expressed by the scores on the individual dimensions.

In a second series of models dummies are added for RIT-effects. In these models, interaction is allowed between the RIT variable and the N2 and N3 variables. This interaction is represented by the RN2 and RN3 dummies, which form a combination of the RIT variable and the N2 and N3 variables. Table 8.2 summarises the dummy variables and their scores.

Table 8.2. The dummy variables and their scores in the model

Dummy for	EQ-5D dimension rated on		
	Level 1	Level 2	Level 3
Study methodology			
Ranked, interview-based studies with MVH protocol	RIT = 0 or 1	RIT = 0 or 1	RIT = 0 or 1
Ratings on at least one EQ-5D dimension			
At least one dimension = 2 or 3	N2 = 0	N2 = 1	N2 = 1
Al least one dimension = 3	N3 = 0	N3 = 0	N3 = 1
Interaction			
RIT studies + N2	RN2 = 0	RN2 = 1	RN2 =1
RIT studies + N3	RN3 = 0	RN3 = 0	RN2 = 1
Ratings on the EQ-5D descriptive system			
Mobility	Mo2 = 0 Mo3 = 0	Mo2 = 1 Mo3 = 0	Mo2 = 0 Mo3 = 1
Self-Care	Se2 = 0 Se3 = 0	Se2 = 1 Se3 = 0	Se2 = 0 Se3 = 1
Usual Activities	Ua2 = 0 Ua3 = 0	Ua2 = 1 Ua3 = 0	Ua2 = 0 Ua3 = 1
Pain/Discomfort	Pd2 = 0 Pd3 = 0	Pd2 = 1 Pd3 = 0	Pd2 = 0 Pd3 = 1
Anxiety/Depression	Ad2 = 0 Ad3 = 0	Ad2 = 1 Ad3 = 0	Ad2 = 0 Ad3 = 1

The full fixed model can be expressed by the following equation:

$$VAS_{\text{health state x}} = C + c_1.RIT + c_2.N2 + c_3.N3 + c_4.RN2 + c_5.RN3 + c_6.Mo2 + c_7.Mo3 + c_8.Se2 + c_9.Se3 + c_{10}.Ua2 + c_{11}.Ua3 + c_{12}.Pd2 + c_{13}.Pd3 + c_{14}.\ Ad2 + c_{15}.\ Ad3$$

$VAS_{\text{health state x}}$ = the estimated VAS value for health state x

C: constant

To calculate the estimated VAS value, this model can be simplified. The coefficient for RIT studies and the constant can be added together. In calculating the estimated

VAS value for a particular health state, the RIT dummy variable always has the value of 1. In addition the coefficients expressing the interaction can be added to the coefficients of the N2 and N3 variables. Per health state, the dummies for N2 or N3 and their interaction dummies have the same value of 0 or 1.

If the estimated VAS value of, for example, the health state 12113 is calculated, the dummies in the model will have the following scores:

$$VAS_{12113} = (C + c_1.1) + (c_2.1 + c_4.1) + (c_3.1 + c_5.1) + c_6.0 + c_7.0 + c_8.1 + c_9.0 + c_{10}.0 + c_{11}.0 + c_{12}.0 + c_{13}.0 + c_{14}.0 + c_{15}.1$$

8.3 RESULTS

Influence of number of inconsistencies

Table 8.3 shows the number of health states per number of inconsistencies. When the maximum possible inconsistencies per respondent of 14 are allowed, the data consists of a total of 101583 health states. When no inconsistencies per respondent are allowed, 49% of the health states will be included. Beyond a level of 5 inconsistencies per respondent, the influence on the number of health states becomes small. The exclusion criterion of no more than 3 inconsistencies leads to the exclusion of 12.2% of the health states.

Table 8.3. Number of health states by number of inconsistencies

Number of inconsistencies	Number of health states	%
0	49764	49.0
1	72001	70.9
2	82948	81.7
3	89146	87.8
4	92689	91.2
5	95224	93.7
6	96800	95.3
7	98153	96.6
8	99312	97.8
9	100248	98.7
10	100844	99.3
11	101317	99.7
12	101477	99.9
13	101570	100.0
14	101583	100.0

Table 8.4 shows the results of the separate regressions on the health states with different inconsistencies from no inconsistencies to 14 inconsistencies. This latter figure includes all respondents. The 95% confidence intervals for the regression parameters have also been presented. The parameters are all significant ($p < 0.001$). The regression on the data with no inconsistencies has the highest R^2 (0.78); the regression on the data on all respondents with the maximum number of 14 inconsistencies has the lowest R^2 (0.64). The confidence intervals of the parameter scores are small. This has the consequence that the confidence interval for the constant of the regression with 3 inconsistencies overlaps with the interval for the constant from the regression with no inconsistencies. However with 4 inconsistencies the confidence interval of the constant falls outside the same interval for the regression with 0 inconsistencies The conclusion could be that regressions on data of respondents with more than 3 inconsistencies give different results compared to a regression on data of respondents with 0 inconsistencies.

Table 8.4. Influence of the number of inconsistencies on the regression results (coefficient from the regression and 95% confidence interval)

	Inconsistencies = 0			Inconsistencies = 3			Inconsistencies ≥ 4			All respondents		
	Coeff.	95% CI		Coeff.	95% CI		Coeff.	95% CI		Coeff.	95% CI	
Constant	98.32	97.84	98.80	97.50	97.11	97.90	97.26	96.87	97.66	95.70	95.28	96.12
At least one 2 or 3	-16.02	-16.60	-15.43	-17.48	-17.96	-17.01	-17.53	-18.00	-17.05	-16.65	-17.16	-16.14
At least one 3	-17.26	-17.76	-16.76	-15.34	-15.74	-14.93	-15.00	-15.41	-14.59	-13.82	-14.26	-13.39
Mobility = 2	-5.65	-6.02	-5.29	-5.57	-5.87	-5.27	-5.54	-5.84	-5.24	-5.44	-5.76	-5.12
Mobility = 3	-17.32	-17.79	-16.85	-16.68	-17.07	-16.29	-16.61	-17.00	-16.22	-15.70	-16.12	-15.28
Self-Care = 2	-9.14	-9.50	-8.78	-8.60	-8.89	-8.31	-8.54	-8.83	-8.25	-8.29	-8.60	-7.98
Self-Care = 3	-13.04	-13.54	-12.55	-12.61	-13.01	-12.20	-12.57	-12.98	-12.17	-12.57	-13.01	-12.13
Usual Activities = 2	-3.41	-3.83	-3.00	-2.97	-3.30	-2.63	-2.96	-3.29	-2.63	-2.70	-3.05	-2.35
Usual Activities = 3	-7.56	-8.09	-7.02	-7.44	-7.88	-7.00	-7.45	-7.89	-7.01	-7.36	-7.83	-6.88
Pain/Discomfort = 2	-7.72	-8.06	-7.37	-7.22	-7.50	-6.94	-7.13	-7.41	-6.85	-6.70	-7.01	-6.40
Pain/Discomfort = 3	-13.53	-13.95	-13.12	-12.59	-12.94	-12.24	-12.38	-12.73	-12.03	-11.41	-11.79	-11.03
Anxiety/Depression = 2	-6.34	-6.69	-5.99	-6.61	-6.89	-6.32	-6.66	-6.95	-6.37	-6.59	-6.89	-6.28
Anxiety/Depression = 3	-10.37	-10.78	-9.95	-10.16	-10.50	-9.82	-10.12	-10.46	-9.78	-9.53	-0.13	-51.03
R^2	0.776			0.725			0.713			0.640		
Adjusted R^2	0.776			0.725			0.713			0.640		
F	14215.78			19468.28			19092.26			14973.41		
P	0.000			0.000			0.000			0.000		

Exclusions and number of valuations

Table 8.5 shows the number of exclusions and inconsistencies that result from the application of the criteria listed earlier.

The EQ-5D database consists of data from 8709 respondents from 11 different studies. 873 respondents were excluded because they gave all states the same value or valued less than 3 states. 966 respondents were excluded because they returned questionnaires that contained more than 3 inconsistencies. Thus 1839 respondents were excluded before the analysis was performed, leaving 6870 respondents in the analysis.

Total exclusions were high in the sample from Finland, the German 1994 sample, and in the samples from the Netherlands and Sweden. Exclusions due to more than 3 inconsistencies were especially high in the Finnish and Dutch data. Exclusions were low in the 2 Catalonian samples, the UK MVH data and the German TTO sample, which were all interview-based samples.

After exclusions, there were a total of 100068 valuations from 6870 respondents. The scores for dead and unconscious could not be taken into account in the regression model because these states are not defined in terms of the EQ-5D descriptive system. Valuations of health states from the Catalonian l'Hospitalet del Llobregat (Cat_Hos) study were not used in the analysis. This was to avoid a study-related bias on the overall results, there being some evidence of a translation problem for the wording of level 3 on the mobility dimension. Hence the valuations of 2 health states with level 3 on mobility from this sample have been excluded.

Consequently the regression analysis reported in this chapter was performed on 82910 valuations. Annex 8.1 gives an overview of these valuations by health state and sample.

Table 8.5. Exclusions and inconsistencies

	Cat_Cor	Cat_Hos	Finland	UK_FR	UK_MVH	Ger_94
	Cornellà de Llobregat	L'Hospitalet del Llobregat		UK Frome	UK MVH	Germany 1994
N	294	600	1630	122	3395	370
Exclusions due to incomplete data	-	-	207 (12.7%)	2 (1.5%)	40 (1.2%)	161 (43.5%)
Due to more than 3 inconsistencies	7 (2.4%)	3 (0.5%)	485 (29.8%)	24 (19.7%)	180 (5.3%)	25 (6.8%)
Number of respondents not excluded	287 (97.6%)	597 (99.5%)	938 (57.5%)	96 (78.7%)	3175 (93.5%)	184 (49.7%)

Table 8.5. Exclusions and inconsistencies (Continued)

	Ger_97	Ger_TTO	Navarra	Netherl.	Sweden
	Germany 1997	Germany TTO		Netherlands	
N	124	339	300	993	542
Exclusions due to incomplete data	19 (15.3%)	-	-	330 (33.2 %)	114 (21.0 %)
Due to more than 3 inconsistencies	11 (8.9%)	6 (1.8 %)	34 (11.3 %)	132 (13.3 %)	59 (10.9 %)
Number of respondents not excluded	94 (75.8%)	333 (98.2%)	266 (88.7%)	531 (53.5%)	369 (68.1%)

Background variables

Chapter 7 showed that some background variables have considerable influence on the VAS valuations. The sample characteristic 'RIT design study', and the respondent characteristics 'VAS score < 85', 'Age ≥ 65', 'Education medium and Education high', which had an influence on the VAS valuations, were tested for their impact on the regression results.

Table 8.6 shows the distribution of these respondent characteristics in the regressions. The table consists of 2 parts. The lower part describes the distribution of the background variables after exclusions. There was a clear effect of the exclusions on the distribution of background variables. The largest effects can be found in the data sets where exclusions were high. These were the samples from Finland, the German 1994 and 1997 samples, the Netherlands sample and the sample from Sweden. In the Finnish data, the effect of exclusions was especially high on the variable 'Age ≥ 65': the percentage of respondents older than 64 dropped from 35.64% to 21.00%. The same effect could be found in the other samples with a high number of exclusions. The percentages for 'VAS score < 85' also went down in the samples from Finland, Germany 1994, Germany 1997, the Netherlands, and Sweden. However, the percentages for medium level of education and high level of education rose in these samples due to the exclusions. The overall effects of the exclusions were that respondents were healthier and more educated, which may have been caused by the higher exclusions of respondents older than 64.

In Chapter 7 we reported the outcome of an OLS regression analysis with only the background variables as explanatory factors for the VAS valuations. We now report the outcomes of OLS analysis in which the EQ-5D dimensions and background variables are included. Results are given for the transformed, rescaled and transformed-rescaled VAS values.

The results of the OLS regression analyses with and without the background variables in the model are presented in Tables 8.7 and 8.8. Compared to the regressions which include the background variables there are no big changes in the values of the constant or the values of the coefficients for the scores on the descriptive system. Moreover, the coefficients for the 2 variables which describe the effects of any deviation from full health (N2 and N3) show a large influence on the predicted VAS values. The coefficients for N3 are higher compared to these coefficients in the regressions with the background variables. The R^2s are of the same magnitude as for the regressions with the background variables.

The R^2 for the analysis on the (individually) rescaled VAS values is 0.58. This is considerably lower than the R^2 for the analysis on the original values. This result may have been caused by the fact that 'dead', used as an anchor in the rescaling, is ambivalent. Furthermore, the fact that health states may be sampled over different ranges of the severity scale for different individuals may result in non-comparable rescaling effects.

Moreover, the R^2 for the analysis of the transformed (0.73) and rescaled-transformed (0.63) values is lower than in the analysis of the original ones. This implies that, although the transformation results in a much smaller skewness of the distributions of values, use of this transformation worsens the model outcomes. A possible explanation is that the linear model indeed holds for the original values and that this model is destroyed by the logistic transformation: the error assumptions are improved, but the model assumptions are worsened. It was therefore decided to carry out a non-linear analysis on the data, to find out which transformation of the VAS values results in the best linear prediction.

Table 8.6. Share of respondents with a background characteristic in the different studies. Before and after exclusions

	Cat_Cor	Cat_Hos	Finland	UK_FR	UK_MVH	Ger_94
N	294	600	1630	122	3395	370
Distribution of the background variables before exclusions. In percentages of valid responses.						
VAS score < 85	63.61	60.83	54.64	48.74	39.43	59.44
Age ≥ 65	18.71	10.17	35.64	24.79	23.71	24.59
Edu_med	26.96	25.17	29.84	48.31	40.17	30.32
Edu_high	16.38	18.62	24.40	22.88	20.02	7.58
Number of respondents after exclusions	287	597	908	95	3175	180
Distribution of the background variables after exclusions. In percentages of valid responses.						
VAS score < 85	64.11	60.80	45.07	45.16	38.28	50.28
Age ≥ 65	18.12	10.05	21.00	21.88	22.90	15.76
Edu_med	27.62	25.30	36.69	39.36	41.05	43.60
Edu_high	16.43	18.72	32.94	26.60	20.87	9.88

	Ger_97	Ger_TTO	Navarra	Netherl.	Sweden	Total
N	124	339	300	993	542	8709
Distribution of the background variables before exclusions. In percentages of valid responses.						
VAS score < 85	50.00	29.46	74.00	50.33	40.00	47.64
Age ≥ 65	23.14	21.01	20.00	35.82	18.50	25.56
Edu_med	53.28	59.76	30.43	38.58	42.88	37.18
Edu_high	35.25	33.14	10.03	22.96	28.46	21.30
Number of respondents after exclusions.	92	333	252	512	361	6792
Distribution of the background variables after exclusions. In percentages of valid responses.						
VAS score < 85	46.74	28.79	73.68	48.82	35.52	44.34
Age ≥ 65	17.20	21.02	19.17	23.76	13.15	20.35
Edu_med	50.54	59.64	30.19	44.42	46.37	39.74
Edu_high	36.56	33.43	10.19	31.19	33.80	23.64

Table 8.7. Results from OLS regression on the VAS values. Model with background variables (linear regression)

(Adjusted)		Raw VAS		Transformed VAS		Rescaled VAS		Transformed Rescaled VAS	
Constant		97.11	***	4.31	***	100	***	3.71	***
RIT study		2.90	***	0.82	***	ns		ns	
VAS score < 85		-1.86	***	-0.32	***	ns		ns	
Age ≥ 65		ns		-0.13	**	ns		ns	
Edu-med		ns		ns		ns		ns	
Edu-high		ns		-0.19	***	ns		ns	
N2: At least 1, 2 or 3		-19.83	***	-2.92	***	-23.30	***	-1.72	***
N3: At least one 3		-10.75	***	-0.12	***	-12.30	***	-0.38	***
Mobility = 2		-6.21	***	-0.30	***	-6.36	***	-0.19	***
Mobility = 3		-16.71	***	-1.23	***	-18.90	***	-0.44	***
Self-Care = 2		-10.01	***	-0.50	***	-11.86	***	-0.39	***
Self-Care = 3		-13.75	***	-0.99	***	-15.73	***	-0.43	***
Usual Activities = 2		-3.16	***	-0.16	***	-3.06	***	-0.08	***
Usual Activities = 3		-7.44	***	-0.66	***	-8.18	***	-0.19	***
Pain/Discomfort = 2		-7.82	***	-0.35	***	-9.13	***	-0.28	***
Pain/Discomfort = 3		-12.84	***	-1.00	***	-14.98	***	-0.38	***
Anxiety/Depression = 2		-7.10	***	-0.41	***	-7.98	***	-0.27	***
Anxiety/Depression = 3		-10.24	***	-0.92	***	-11.72	***	-0.29	***
RIT study	At least one 2 or 3	8.45	***	-0.21	***	10.10	***	0.34	***
	At least one 3	-10.49	***	-0.48	***	-10.28	***	-0.39	***
VAS score < 85	At least one 2 or 3	-0.96	*	0.14	***	-2.23	**	-0.09	***
	At least one 3	2.29	***	0.15	***	1.35	**	0.07	***
Age ≥ 65	At least one 2 or 3	2.33	***	0.21	***	ns		ns	
	At least one 3	ns		0.05		-1.36	*	-0.07	***
Edu-med	At least one 2 or 3	ns		ns		ns		ns	
	At lest one 3	ns		ns		-1.25	*	-0.04	*
Edu-high	At least one 2 or 3	ns		ns		-2.51	*	-0.08	*
	At least one 3	ns		ns		-2.59	***	-0.05	**
R^2		0.742		0.734		0.580		0.632	
Adjusted R^2		0.742		0.734		0.580		0.632	

* $p < 0.05$ ** $p < 0.01$ *** $p < 0.001$

Table 8.8. Results from OLS regression on the VAS values. Model without background variables (linear regression)

(Adjusted)	Raw VAS		Transformed VAS		Rescaled VAS		Transformed Rescaled VAS	
Constant	97.50	***	4.54	***	100	***	3.71	***
At least one 2 or 3	-17.48	***	-3.01	***	-21.00	***	-1.65	***
At least one 3	-15.33	***	-0.26	***	-19.15	***	-0.63	***
Mobility = 2	-5.57	***	-0.28	***	-5.58	***	-0.16	***
Mobility = 3	-16.69	***	-1.25	***	-18.72	***	-0.43	***
Self-Care = 2	-8.60	***	-0.43	***	-10.74	***	-0.35	***
Self-Care = 3	-12.61	***	-0.92	***	-14.87	***	-0.41	***
Usual Activities = 2	-2.97	***	-0.16	***	-2.49	***	-0.06	***
Usual Activities = 3	-7.44	***	-0.67	***	-7.87	***	-0.18	***
Pain/Discomfort = 2	-7.22	***	-0.33	***	-8.63	***	-0.26	***
Pain/Discomfort = 3	-12.60	***	-1.00	***	-14.72	***	-0.37	***
Anxiety/Depression = 2	-6.61	***	-0.38	***	-7.66	***	-0.27	***
Anxiety/Depression = 3	-10.17	***	-0.90	***	-11.74	***	-0.29	***
R^2	0.725		0.719		0.572		0.623	
Adjusted R^2	0.725		0.719		0.572		0.623	

*: p < 0,05. **: p < 0,01. ***: p < 0,001

Non-linear regression analysis

The 'CANALS' model (Gifi, 1990) from the SAS-programme 'TRANSREG' was used for the non-linear regression analysis In CANALS it is assumed that the nature of all variables is categorical, i.e. the 'score' on a particular variable is regarded as a classification into a category of that variable. This implies that the score is just a category name. Further restrictions can be added: the underlying measurement scale can be regarded as purely nominal (just a name, without any order between the categories), ordered, or metric (no transformation).

The essential feature of CANALS is that in one and the same analysis optimal transformations (with regard to the linear model) are found for the dependent and independent variables, together with the best fitting linear regression model on the transformed variables. The outcome is a solution of optimally transformed variables (independent as well as dependent) together with regression weights for the variables. Given the optimal transformations, the model is an ordinary (multiple) linear regression model.

Conceptually the CANALS solution of the regression on the categorised variables can be compared with the method of using dummy variables for the categories of independent variables in a linear regression. The scores of these dummy variables resulting from the regression weights can be interpreted as transformed values for the categories within a variable.

An advantage of assuming an ordinal scale for the dependent variables is the possibility to check whether a log-linear or logistic model is preferable to a linear model. If the transformation turns out to be a logarithmic one, then the regression outcomes should be interpreted as the results of a log-linear model instead of a linear one.

Table 8.9 shows the outcomes of an OLS regression model in column 2 compared with several CANALS outcomes. The results in columns 3, 5, and 7 are from a CANALS analysis with a linear restriction on the VAS values and using the dummies as independent variables. The CANALS results in column 3 are from an analysis which used the same regression model as was used in the OLS regression of column 2. It can be seen that the outcomes of the CANALS analysis in column 3 were identical to the results from the OLS regression model in column 2.

Column 7 shows CANALS analysis results from a model in which the EQ-5D levels per dimension are represented by 1,2,3. Dummies were only used for the variables RIT, N2, N3, and the 2 interaction variables RIT * N2 and RIT * N3. This approach assumes nominal scales for each EQ-5D dimension. From column 7 it can be seen that the R^2, the parameters for RIT, N2, N3, RIT * N2 and RIT * N3 are identical with the values from column 3. The difference compared with the models from column 2 and 3 is that this model results in 1 regression weight instead of 2 for each EQ-5D dimension. The regression weights for the dimensions in order of magnitude are: -7.81 for mobility, -7.52 for self care, -7.23 for pain/discomfort, -5.96 for anxiety/ depression, and finally -3.75 for usual activities.

Moreover, the intercept value appears from column 7 to be different. However this difference is caused by the fact that the solution in column 7 does not start from a value of 0 for level 1 of each EQ-5D dimension, but from the value 1. In the CANALS analysis on the original variables the value is equal to the intercept plus the weighted scale values for level 1 on each dimension. In Table 8.10 it is shown that, by subtracting the weighted scale values from the intercept, this results in the same value of 95.75 for state 11111 compared to the solution using dummies. It is also shown in Table 8.10 that the regression weights for the EQ 5D dimensions from the models using dummies can be reconstructed from the regression weights and the level transformations from the model in column 7 (see the rows 'product2 - product1' and 'product3 - product1').

Table 8.9. Results of CANALS solutions compared with results from OLS regression

	Parameter and R^2 values						
	With N2 and N3			Without N2 and N3		With N2 and N3	
	OLS	CANALS on dummies		CANALS on dummies		CANALS on levels represented by 1,2,3	
1	2	3	4	5	6	7	8
		linear	monotonic	linear	monotonic	linear[a]	monotonic[a]
Intercept	95.75	95.75	117.02	83.30	81.60	127.76	136.50
Mob2	-5.67	-5.67	-4.01	-7.15	-6.07	-7.81	-4.61
Mob3	-15.88	-15.88	-9.33	-18.81	-20.03		
Self2	-10.21	-10.21	-7.71	-11.12	-9.50	-7.52	-5.26
Self3	-13.72	-13.72	-9.10	-15.18	-15.62		
Act2	-2.46	-2.46	-1.19	-8.62	-6.97	-3.75	-2.01
Act3	-7.50	-7.50	-4.01	-17.15	-16.17		
Pain2	-8.22	-8.22	-5.80	-8.93	-7.87	-7.23	-4.49
Pain3	-14.27	-14.27	-8.62	-19.17	-19.64		
Anx2	-7.84	-7.84	-5.97	-10.94	-9.41	-5.96	-3.87
Anx3	-11.33	-11.32	-6.79	-16.55	-17.27		
N2	-19.50	-19.50	-53.55			-19.50	-53.57
N3	-8.72	-8.72	-7.18			-8.72	-7.17
RIT	3.17	3.17	18.69	4.30	4.23	3.17	18.70
RIT*N2	-8.11	8.11	-11.08			8.11	-11.09
RIT*N3	-11.14	-11.14	-8.00			-11.14	-8.00
R^2	0.75	0.75	0.79	0.70	0.72	0.75	0.79

a. The scores for intercept and EQ-5D dimensions relate to level 1=1 and not to level 1=0

Table 8.10. Reconstructed dummy-weights from the CANALS transformation and regression

		EQ-5D dimensions					
		Mobility	Self-Care	Usual Activities	Pain/ Discomfort	Anxiety/ Depression	intercept
level 1	Transformation value	1.08	0.92	1.10	0.97	0.93	127.76
	Regression weight	-7.81	-7.52	-3.75	-7.23	-5.96	
	Product1[a]	-8.42	-6.92	-4.14	-6.99	-5.55	-32.02
						corrected intercept:	95.75
level 2	Transformation value	1.80	2.28	1.76	2.10	2.25	
	Regression weight	-7.81	-7.52	-3.75	-7.23	-5.96	
	Product2[a]	-14.09	-17.13	-6.60	-15.21	-13.38	
	Product2-product1	-5.67	-10.21	-2.46	-8.22	-7.84	
level 3	Transformation value	3.11	2.74	3.10	2.94	2.83	
	Regression weight	-7.81	-7.52	-3.75	-7.23	-5.96	
	Product3[a]	-24.31	-20.64	-11.64	-21.26	-16.87	
	Product3-product1	-15.88	-13.72	-7.50	-14.27	-11.33	

a. transformation scores multiplied by regression weights

Figure 8.1 displays the transformed values for the EQ-5D dimensions. The response scales for all 5 dimensions are almost linear. This means that the VAS values can be reproduced quite well by weighing the dimensions with the CANALS weights, applied to the level scores 1 to 3 directly. This relatively simple model predicts the VAS values surprisingly well.

Another CANALS analysis was conducted using the same model as before with, however, a monotonic instead of a linear transformation of the VAS values. The regression weights and R^2 are given in columns 4 and 6 of Table 8.9 for the dummy models and in column 8 for the dimension level models. It can be noted that the R^2 improves considerably from 0.75 to 0.79 in column 4. However, this seems to be due only to the effect on the N2 parameter, decreasing from -19.50 to -53.57, now becoming the dominant factor. The EQ-5D parameters as well as the N3 parameter become less important.

It can be seen from Figure 8.2 that the transformation is almost linear over the full range, except for the highest values on the scale. There the scale is dramatically changed. This all suggests a rather artificial solution related to N2: at the higher end of the scale almost all values are with respect to state 11111.

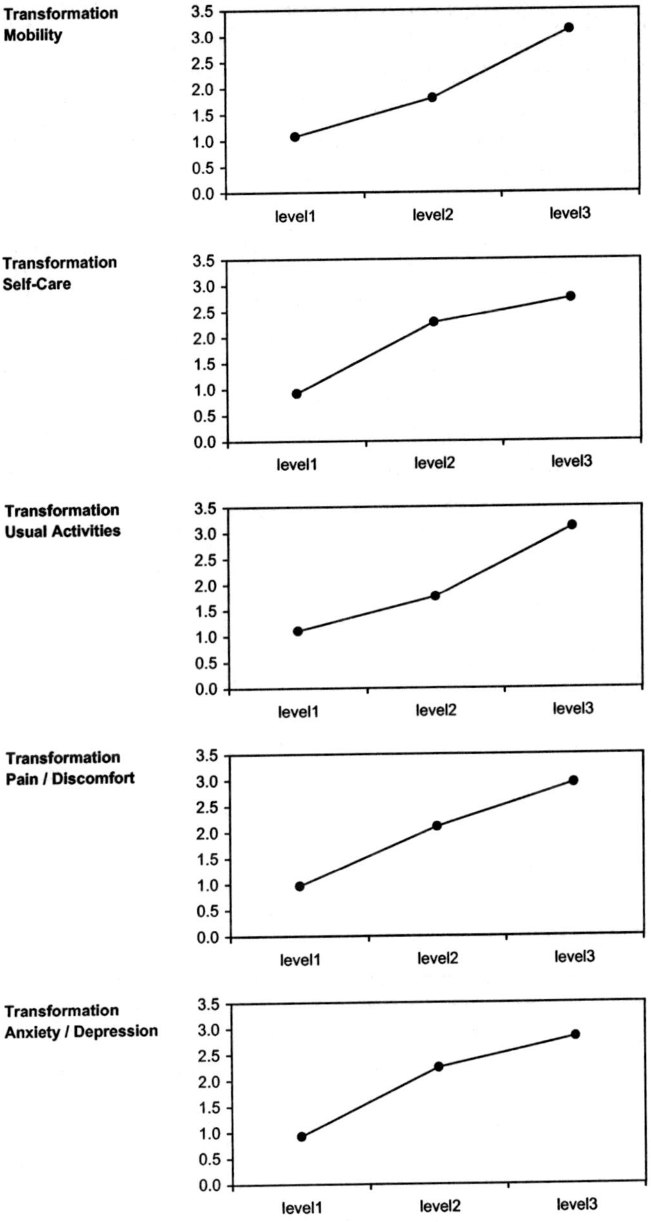

Figure 8.1. Transformations of the categories on the EQ-5D dimensions from CANALS analysis with linear restriction on the VAS values

Hence a new analysis was undertaken without N2, N3, and the 2 interaction parameters with RIT. The solutions, again with a linear restriction and a monotonic restriction on the transformation of the VAS values are given in columns 5 and 6 of Table 8.9. Now we find a much greater similarity in outcomes for the EQ-5D parameters for the linear and monotonic transformations, with an improvement of the R^2 from 0.70 to 0.72 for the monotonic transformation. The transformation is shown in Figure 8.3. It can be seen again that the transformation is linear over most of the scale. At both ends we see a deviation from linearity, as expected from the skewness of the response distributions, which seems not to be an artefact. The difference from the logistic transformation used before appears to be that the mid-range is linear. This suggests that respondents do indeed use a linear scale which is slightly distorted at the 2 anchor points. The transformation from this analysis could be used (with a linear restriction) for further research, e.g. to include the N2 and N3 variables again, and to include other independent (background) variables. Because of the rather small improvement in the model (from $R^2 = 0.70$ to $R^2 = 0.72$) this transformation was not applied in the final multilevel model.

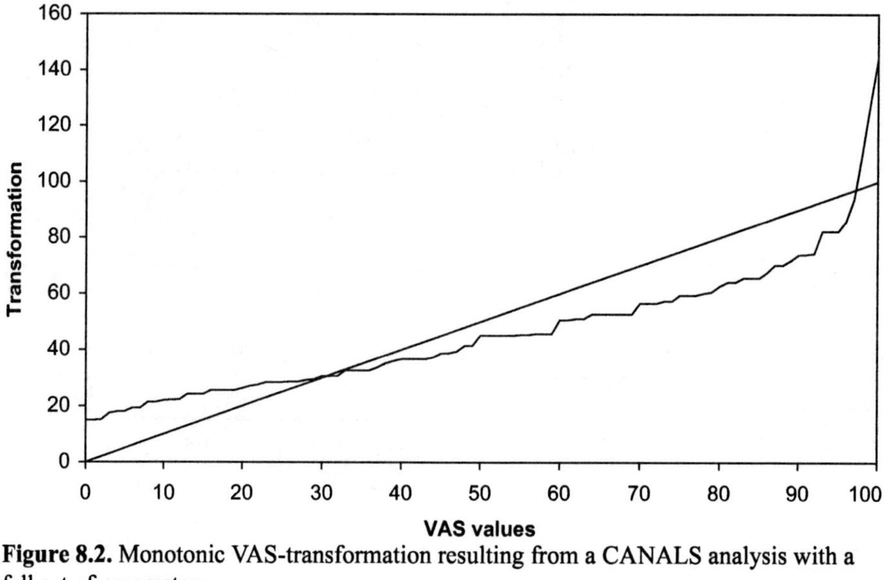

Figure 8.2. Monotonic VAS-transformation resulting from a CANALS analysis with a full set of parameters

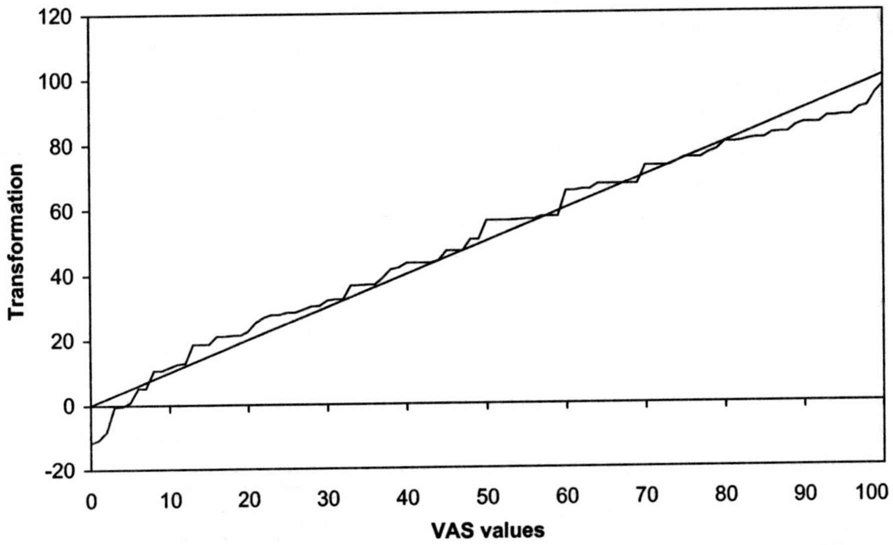

Figure 8.3. Monotonic VAS-transformation resulting from a CANALS analysis with a reduced set of parameters, including the EQ-5D dimensions and the RIT dummy

Multilevel regression analysis

A number of analyses have been carried out with and without RIT-effects. In the first analysis only fixed effects (referred to as 'level I') were defined, with the data measured at the health state level. The variance component is therefore denoted by 'error' referring to the usual error term in ordinary regression. The second analysis included random effects at level II for individual respondents ('level I+II'). The variance term is denoted by 'individual'. The third analysis contains random effects both at level II and level III ('level I+II+III'). with variance terms for individuals and studies respectively, and the error term. These levels should be clearly distinguished from the levels on EQ-5D dimensions (levels 1,2,3).

It should be realised that the random effects are only included for the constant and not for the slopes of the dummies. Given the large number of slope parameters for all dummies an extension of the model with random effects for the slopes would be rather complicated and difficult to interpret.

The results are summarised in Table 8.11. It can be seen from the table that the model improves considerably if random effects are used. If only the random effect at level II is added, the difference between the –2LogL scores (a Chi^2 statistic with 1 degree of freedom) is highly significant (Chi^2 = 17075.5, df=1). The addition of a random effect at level III results in a further significant but much smaller improvement in the model (Chi^2 = 564.80, df = 1).

Clearly the level of significance is considerably influenced by the large number of observations. A more relevant insight can be found from a comparison of the residuals (not shown here) and from the percentage of variance addressed to the variance components. From the estimates of the variance components in the model at levels II and III it can be seen that the variance component for the studies (7.01) is considerably smaller than the variance component for individuals (70.76).

From the parameter estimates of the fixed effects only the parameter for the constant is considerably lower in the level I+II+III analysis. The other estimates show only minor changes.

Table 8.11. Analysis with dummies for EQ-5D dimensions only. Multilevel analysis on 82910 health states valued in more than 1 study

	Without RIT dummy			With RIT dummy			Aggregated coefficients
Parameters	Level I	Level I+II	Level I+II+III	Level I	Level I+II	Level I+II+III	for RIT
Constant	97.576	97.529	95.786	95.781	95.792	95.709	97.66
Mob2	-4.726	-4.581	-4.536	-5.669	-5.777	-5.775	-5.78
Mob3	-15.699	-15.321	-15.198	-15.885	-16.04	-16.027	-16.03
Self2	-8.603	-9.113	-9.215	-10.207	-10.273	-10.281	-10.28
Self3	-12.466	-13.374	-13.573	-13.714	-13.659	-13.674	-13.67
Act2	-1.755	-1.374	-1.336	-2.469	-2.303	-2.309	-2.31
Act3	-7.076	-6.747	-6.685	-7.509	-7.533	-7.542	-7.54
Pain2	-7.719	-7.55	-7.526	-8.224	-8.149	-8.147	-8.15
Pain3	-14.034	-13.704	-13.612	-14.282	-14.355	-14.349	-14.35
Anx2	-7.229	-7.63	-7.693	-7.836	-7.822	-7.813	-7.81
Anx3	-11.149	-11.377	-11.43	-11.321	-11.295	-11.313	-11.31
N2	-17.073	-16.568	-16.509	-19.535	-19.517	-19.518	-11.21
N3	-15.407	-16.253	-16.419	-8.707	-8.581	-8.579	-20.06
RIT				3.092	3.116	1.955	
RIT*N2				8.189	8.301	8.304	
RIT*N3				-11.143	-11.483	-11.477	
Variance components							Percentage
Study			7.011			4.132	1.6%
Individual		78.769	70.764		73.935	71.719	28.3%
Error	262.915	184.346	184.368	251.475	177.607	177.63	70.08%
-2*LogL	697252.8	680177.2	679612.5	693559.7	676941.5	676804.1	
Difference		-17075.6	-564.7		-16618.2	-137.4	
R^2	0.734	0.734	0.734	0.746	0.746	0.745	
Adjusted R^2	0.734	0.734	0.734	0.746	0.746	0.745	

In the second series of analyses, a dummy for the RIT-effect was added, together with 2 dummies for the interaction of RIT with the N2 and N3 effects. In previous analyses it was found that the addition of the interaction terms improved the regression solution significantly: the RIT effect in the higher region of VAS values was larger than in the lower region.

From the 3 analyses including the RIT-effects the constant fell in all analyses to the value found in the previous solution for level I+II+III, including the study effect. The variance component for studies fell considerably (from 7.01 to 4.13), indicating that the major difference between studies was with respect to the RIT-effect.

From the fixed effects RIT-parameters it can be seen that there was a general but moderate RIT-effect (1.96): RIT values were on average higher. The RIT*N2-effect shows that a considerable extra increase (8.30) is necessary if at least one 2 or 3 is scored on 1 dimension, but that an even bigger figure should be subtracted (-11.48) if a 3 is scored on at least 1 dimension. These effects combined suggest that the difference in constants is indeed multiplicative as found in the SVD-analysis reported in Chapter 7, instead of additive as assumed in an ordinary regression analysis.

If the first and second series of analyses are compared, the parameters for the EQ-5D dimensions are only slightly different. However, the parameters for N2 and N3 are much more influenced by the addition of RIT-effects. This can be explained by the addition of the interaction parameters for RIT and N2 and N3. The column with the aggregated coefficients presents the simplified I+II+III level model for RIT-studies, in which the coefficients for RIT and the constant were added together, and in which the coefficients expressing the interactions were added to the coefficients of the N2 and N3 variables.

The goodness-of-fit, as measured by R^2 was 0.745. All regression weights were significant at $p < 0.001$. For all the dimensions of EQ-5D, the weights for a score on level 2 are smaller than the weights for a score on level 3. The largest effect in the non-aggregated model is found for any deviation from full health, indicated by the N2 variable (-19.52). For the aggregated coefficients the N3 variable, which indicates at least one 3 on the descriptive system, together with the variable which indicates interaction of N3 with RIT, showed the largest influence (-20.06). When the first 3 appears on the descriptive system the predicted VAS value goes down by 33 points regardless of the scores on each different dimension.

Figure 8.4 and Annex 8.2 show the estimated VAS values for the observed health states, compared to the mean and the median values of these health states. The health states have been ordered according to the mean VAS values. For the mild health states the estimated values are very close to the median values and higher than the mean values; for the worst health states the estimated values are lower than the mean values. Figure 8.5 shows the difference between the observed mean and median values and the estimated values. However, the estimation procedure was based on the minimisation of the differences with regard to the mean and not the median values. In this figure the health states which show differences of less than minus 6 or greater than 6 have been indicated.

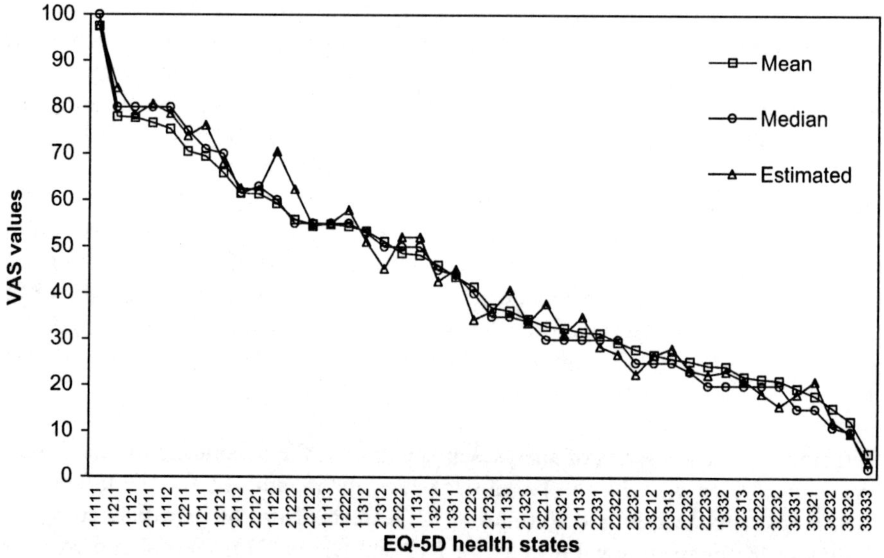

Figure 8.4. EQ-5D health states ranked according to mean, median and estimated VAS values

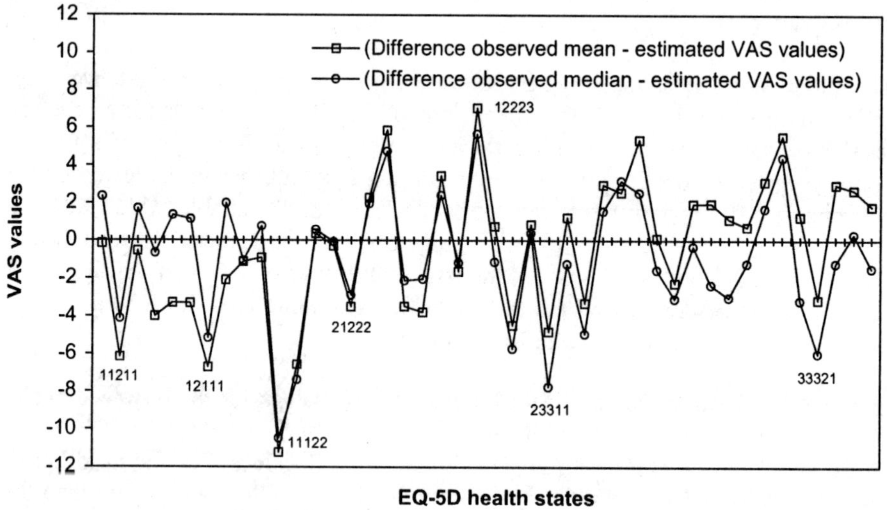

Figure 8.5. EQ-5D health states ranked according to difference between mean and median observed values and estimated VAS values

Rescaling

The estimated VAS values have been rescaled using the mean and the median values for dead. The estimates that are rescaled with the mean value of dead (10.0) have 5 health states with negative values. These states are 33333 and all the states with 1, 2 and 4 threes, except 23333. As there are no estimated scores lower than 6.5 (for 33333), rescaling with the median value of dead (2.0) does not result in negative estimated values.

Table 8.12 shows the results of the rescaling operation. The estimated value of 97.7 for 11111 is very close to the rescaled value fixed at 100 in the rescaling procedure. When using the mean value for dead in the rescaling procedure, the effect is considerable for values under 50. The values which have been rescaled with the median value for dead are all close to the original values.

Table 8.12 and Figure 8.6 also show the differences between the observed mean and rescaled estimated values and the observed median and estimated values that are rescaled using the median value of dead for a linear regression. The sum of absolute differences of the rescaled values is lowest for the values that have been rescaled using the median value for dead. Figure 8.6 and Annex 8.3 show the estimated and rescaled estimated values for all the 243 EQ-5D health states.

Table 8.12. Observed mean and median values (linear regression); estimated and rescaled estimated values and differences between the observed mean and estimated values. The standard states

Observed and estimated VAS values				Rescaled estimated values rescaled with		Differences between observed mean and			Median and rescaled estimated values rescaled with median dead
							Rescaled estimated values rescaled with		
state	mean	median	estimated	mean dead	median dead	estimated scores	mean dead	median dead	
11111	97.5	100.0	97.7	100.0	100.0	-0.2	-2.5	-2.5	0.0
11211	78.0	80.0	84.1	84.6	85.9	-6.2	-6.6	-7.9	-5.9
11121	77.8	80.0	78.3	77.9	79.8	-0.5	-0.2	-2.0	0.2
21111	76.7	80.0	80.7	80.6	82.2	-4.0	-4.0	-5.6	-2.2
11112	75.3	80.0	78.6	78.3	80.1	-3.3	-3.0	-4.8	-0.1
12111	69.4	71.0	76.2	75.5	77.5	-6.7	-6.0	-8.1	-6.5
11122	59.3	60.0	70.5	69.0	71.6	-11.2	-9.7	-12.3	-11.6
21232	36.9	35.0	36.1	29.8	35.7	0.8	7.1	1.2	-0.7
32211	32.9	30.0	37.8	31.7	37.4	-4.8	1.3	-4.5	-7.4
22323	25.3	23.0	23.3	15.2	22.3	1.9	10.1	3.0	0.7
22233	24.3	20.0	22.4	14.1	21.3	2.0	10.2	3.0	-1.3
33321	17.9	15.0	21.0	12.5	19.9	-3.1	5.3	-2.0	-4.9
33333	5.3	2.0	3.5	-7.4	1.6	1.8	12.7	3.8	0.4
Sum of absolute differences						46.6	78.6	60.6	42.0
Mean sum of absolute differences						3.6	6.0	4.7	3.2

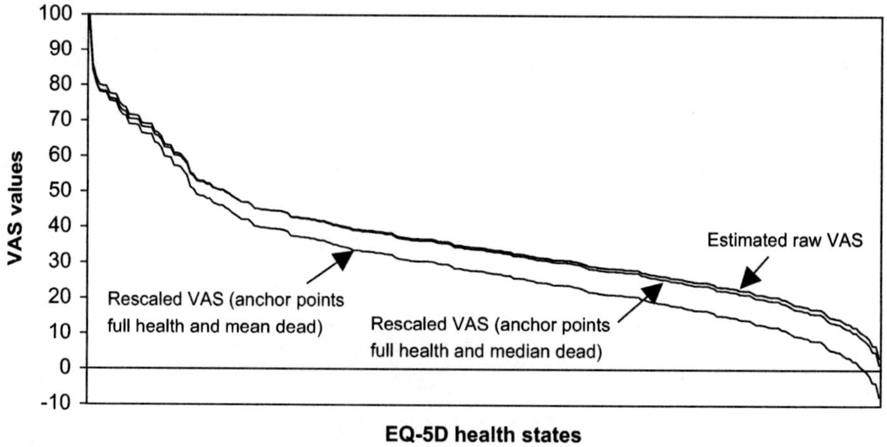

Figure 8.6. Estimated and estimated rescaled values. Rescaled with mean and median value for dead. All 243 EQ-5D health states

8.4 DISCUSSION

Data from respondents who valued all the health states the same or who valued less than 3 states were excluded from the analysis. These exclusions had an effect on the distribution of the background variables. Respondents aged over 65 had a higher probability of being excluded, as did respondents with a VAS value of less than 85, and respondents with low education. This had the effect that the data on which the regressions were performed was from respondents who were younger, healthier, and more educated. In the data from Finland and the Netherlands, 36 % of the respondents were older than 64. After exclusions, the share of respondents older than 65 dropped to 21 % for Finland and 24 % for the Netherlands. These shares were more in line with the overall share in the database of respondents aged over 65.

Because of the restriction of the range of the raw VAS values to between 0 and 100, skewed response distributions were expected, and found, at the end of the scale. This was expected to limit linear regression analysis because the values to be included in this kind of analysis are assumed to be normally distributed. In order to solve this problem, a logistic transformation was applied. The raw VAS values were transformed, with 100.5 and minus 0.5 as the upper and lower limits in the transformation procedure. These produced the lowest skewness. This transformation was effective in reducing the skewness of the values for the health states at both ends of the scale. For these health states the absolute difference between the mean and the median values became smaller. In particular, for dead and unconscious the transformed mean approached the median values. The regression on the transformed values, however, resulted in a much lower R^2 compared to the regression on the non-transformed data. The explanation is that although the transformation solved the problem of skewed response distributions, it also changed the nature of the linear additive model into a kind of multiplicative model. So it can be assumed that the underlying structure of the VAS values is indeed additive and that the transformation applied made the situation worse. It was therefore decided to apply a non-linear regression analysis in order to check this assumption. It emerged that the best transformation was linear over most of the scale, with exceptions at the ends of the scale. The improvement in the model (in terms of the R^2) was, however, small. Thus it was decided to maintain the use of the linear regression model.

In order to take individual and study differences other than the RIT-model into account, a multi-level (random effects) model was used. This revealed that 28.3% of the total error variance was due to individual differences and 1.6% was due to study differences. However, this had only a small effect on the parameter estimates in the model. The fixed parameters can be compared directly with the OLS-parameters. A weighted OLS model was used in which the weights expressed the differences in the total number of valuations per study. This revealed that the estimated values of the health states, calculated with the fixed parameters, did not deviate much from those calculated with the parameters of the weighted OLS regression. The average absolute difference between the estimated values was 1.2 points on a scale of 98 to 4. This observation, that the differences between OLS and multilevel models is small, is in accordance with the findings of Busschbach *et al,* 1999, who concluded that one could rely on the well-known fixed effects model.

The aims of this study were to find out to what extent the observations could be reproduced solely on the basis of EQ-5D characteristics and the impact of differences in study methodology used (i.e. the 'ranking effect'). This difference in methodology contains more factors than mere ranking. The 3 studies referred to as 'RIT studies' were interviewer-based TTO studies in which a VAS valuation task took place after the health states were ranked by the respondents, and thus not postal studies. However, we found that the major effect of the difference in methodology concerned the level of scoring, rather than the scores on the separate EQ-5D dimensions. In particular, the very mild, and to a lesser extent, the less serious health states were rated higher. For evaluation studies comparing different forms of treatment the absolute value is less important than its relative weight. Thus the constant term of the value set to calculate the index is less consequential than the values of the other regression coefficients.

It was shown in Chapters 6 and 7 that background variables such as age and own health were relevant factors in valuation, although to a much lesser extent than EQ-5D dimensions. Although the composition of the samples from the various studies differed considerably, no indications were found for regional or cultural differences between studies, apart from the ranking effect. Analyses were carried out on those health states that were valued in more than 1 study. Approximately half of the valuations in the database came from the more structured studies (that included TTO), with a low share of more than 3 inconsistencies. A characteristic of the 3 studies (that included TTO) is that they are interview-based and that ranking of the health states took place prior to the VAS valuation task. From the low share of inconsistencies in these studies it can be concluded that ranking before valuation enhances the quality of the data. Chapter 6 also indicated that there was a considerable influence of study design on the valuations. To account for this influence, a dummy variable was included in the model that described the influence of the interview-based, ranked studies that included TTO. As we have pointed out, this variable confirmed the influence of study design on the level of VAS values, but not the weighting of the EQ-5D dimensions. For future valuation studies, it should be kept in mind that VAS values differ between RIT and non-RIT studies and that the RIT-methodology produces more consistent outcomes. Future VAS valuation studies therefore should be designed to incorporate the ranking task.

From a theoretical point of view rescaling (e.g. 'perfect health' = 100 and dead = 0) is necessary for a data set to be used in economic evaluation studies. Rescaling can take place on the individual valuations, using the individual values for perfect health and dead, or it can take place at the end of the analysis on the estimated VAS valuations. A problem with the rescaling procedure on the individual valuations is that this procedure sometimes results in rescaled values of greater than 1 and less than minus 1. The rescaled values of less than minus 1 can be extremely negative, causing standard deviations to double in the mild health states, and to increase by more than a factor of 2 in the more severe states. All the rescaled health states had a high negative skewness. To counter these effects. the negative values were truncated at minus 1, which is an arbitrary cut-off point.

Another side effect of rescaling on the individual valuations was that the data from the Dutch and German studies (that included TTO) were excluded because in these studies respondents did not value the state of dead. Preliminary analyses showed, however, that individual rescaling resulted in a much lower R^2 for the regression analyses. A possible explanation for this is that dead as an individual anchor point is ambivalent for raters, especially perhaps for those who might be concerned about religious or ethical issues.

A rescaling procedure was therefore carried out on the estimated values where the estimated value for 11111 was the upper anchor and a measure of central tendency for dead was the lower anchor. The mean (10.0) and median (2.0) value for dead were the measures applied. When rescaled with the mean value for dead the estimates, especially at the lower end of the spectrum of health states, were clearly lower.

Given the high value for the R^2 in the regression analyses the overall conclusion is that there is strong evidence that it is possible to describe the joint VAS data set gathered by the EuroQol Group by one common model which could be used in economic evaluation studies. The results from the multilevel regression do not contradict the expected characteristics of the value set derived from the EQ-5D. All the coefficients have the right signs, while the values all differ from zero producing values that are plausible. For all the dimensions of the EQ-5D a 3 on the descriptive system has a stronger negative effect on the estimated VAS scores than a 2.

The results of this study on the basis of pooled data from 11 European studies (some with differences in study design, e.g. ranking or selection of hypothetical health states) should be compared with valuation data from a future study with a uniform European or even world-wide approach. The results of the current study suggest that valuation studies need not be confined to national borders. There is scope for widening the context of research on VAS-based instruments such as EQ-5D and finding scores or valuations that can be generalised, at least for Western European industrialised countries.

Annex 8.1. Number of valuations per sample in the analysis

After exclusions have been carried out (subtotal: the total of the standard states in the analysis)

	Cat_Cor	Cat_Hos	Finland	UK_FR	UK_MVH	Ger_94	Ger_97	Ger_TTO	Navarra	Netherl.	Sweden	Total
11111	287	597	908	95	3174	183	93	331	266	524	369	6827
11112	121	597	509	92	1241	170	93	146	266	275	357	3867
11121	119	597	495	94	1279	170	92	166	266	272	362	3912
11122	69	596	493	93	787	172	92	91	266	271	364	3294
11211	112	597	500	94	1286	171	91	162	266	270	366	3915
12111	113	595	513	94	1252	164	92	151	266	274	352	3866
21111	109	596	519	92	1268		94	147	266	266	355	3712
21232	83	596	494	94	797	171	92	87	264	270	359	3307
22233	76	596	483	93	792	165	94		266	271	359	3195
22323	70		515	92	777	165	93	97		276	349	2434
32211	66		512	92	781	166	92	135	266	274	353	2737
33321	72		486	93	783	171	94	100	266	270	358	2693
33333	286	597	890	93	3160	173	94	333	266	515	361	6768
Subtotal	1583	5964	7317	1211	17377	2041	1206	1946	3190	4028	4664	50527

	Cat_Cor	Cat_Hos	Finland	UK_FR	UK_MVH	Ger_94	Ger_97	Ger_TTO	Navarra	Netherl.	Sweden	Total
11113	59				787			143				989
11131	76				773			109				958
11133	75				801			90				966
11312	61		174		791			155				1181
12121	69		136		795	172		96				1268
12211	88		175		797			94				1154
12222	68		173		801			81				1123
12223	66		136		789			96				1087

Annex 8.1. Number of valuations per sample in the analysis (Continued)

	Cat_Cor	Cat_Hos	Finland	UK_FR	UK_MVH	Ger_94	Ger_97	Ger_TTO	Navarra	Netherl.	Sweden	Total
13212	66				789			97				952
13311	75				780							855
13332	91		162		780							1033
21133	77		132		796			79				1084
21222	68		158		785			100				1111
21312	67				785							852
21323	71				785			86				942
22112	80		159		785			92				1116
22121	71		172		794							1037
22122	69		161		775			91				1096
22222	86		157		787			142				1172
22322		594							265			859
22331	73		173		789			83				1118
23232	69		160		782			140				1151
23313	62				791							853
23321	74		158		790			86				1108
32223	72		161		793			146				1172
32232	73		162		799			96				1130
32313	73		157		812							1042
32331	65				793			93				951
33212	63				789			95				947
33232	64				791			93				948
33323	75		158		813			82				1128
Total	3729	6558	10341	1211	41094	2213	1206	4411	3455	4028	4664	82910

Annex 8.2. Mean, median, estimates and difference between mean or median and estimates

(VAS values of health states valued in more than 1 study)

State	Observed VAS values		Estimated VAS values	Difference observed mean - estimation	Difference observed median - estimation
	Mean	Median			
11111	97.5	100.0	97.7	-0.16	2.34
11211	78.0	80.0	84.1	-6.17	-4.14
11121	77.8	80.0	78.3	-0.54	1.70
21111	76.7	80.0	80.7	-4.01	-0.67
11112	75.3	80.0	78.6	-3.29	1.36
12211	70.5	75.0	73.9	-3.32	1.14
12111	69.4	71.0	76.2	-6.72	-5.17
12121	65.9	70.0	68.0	-2.10	1.98
22112	61.5	61.5	62.6	-1.13	-1.08
22121	61.3	63.0	62.2	-0.92	0.76
11122	59.3	60.0	70.5	-11.23	-10.49
21222	55.8	55.0	62.4	-6.58	-7.40
22122	54.8	55.0	54.4	0.37	0.57
11113	54.8	55.0	55.1	-0.30	-0.08
12222	54.4	55.0	57.9	-3.50	-2.90
11312	53.3	53.0	51.0	2.28	1.96
21312	51.1	50.0	45.3	5.86	4.74
22222	48.6	50.0	52.1	-3.48	-2.12
11131	48.2	50.0	52.0	-3.80	-2.04
13212	46.0	45.0	42.6	3.45	2.40
13311	43.5	44.0	45.2	-1.63	-1.18
12223	41.4	40.0	34.3	7.04	5.66
21232	36.9	35.0	36.1	0.76	-1.14
11133	36.2	35.0	40.7	-4.49	-5.73
21323	34.5	34.0	33.6	0.86	0.39

Annex 8.2. Mean, median, estimates and difference between mean or median and estimates (Continued)

(VAS values of health states valued in more than 1 study)

State	Observed VAS values		Estimated VAS values	Difference observed mean - estimation	Difference observed median - estimation
	Mean	Median			
32211	32.9	30.0	37.8	-4.83	-7.77
23321	32.5	30.0	31.3	1.24	-1.25
21133	31.6	30.0	35.0	-3.32	-4.95
22331	31.4	30.0	28.4	2.97	1.56
22322	29.4	30.0	26.8	2.56	3.17
23232	27.8	25.0	22.5	5.35	2.53
33212	26.7	25.0	26.6	0.12	-1.57
23313	25.8	25.0	28.1	-2.26	-3.09
22323	25.3	23.0	23.3	1.95	-0.33
22233	24.3	20.0	22.4	1.97	-2.36
13332	24.2	20.0	23.0	1.13	-3.02
32313	22.0	20.0	21.2	0.73	-1.23
32223	21.4	20.0	18.3	3.12	1.69
32232	21.1	20.0	15.6	5.53	4.39
32331	19.5	15.0	18.2	1.27	-3.19
33321	17.9	15.0	21.0	-3.14	-6.00
33232	15.2	11.0	12.2	2.97	-1.22
33323	12.4	10.0	9.7	2.68	0.31
33333	5.3	2.0	3.5	1.82	-1.49
Sum of absolute differences				132.95	120.26
Mean absolute difference				3.02	2.73

Annex 8.3. Estimated and rescaled estimated values for all 243 EQ-5D health states

EQ-5D health state	Estimated values	Rescaled with mean value for dead (10.0)	Rescaled with median value for dead (2.0)
11111	97.66	100.00	100.00
11112	78.64	78.30	80.12
11113	55.08	51.43	55.49
11121	78.30	77.91	79.76
11122	70.49	69.01	71.60
11123	46.93	42.13	46.97
11131	52.04	47.96	52.31
11132	44.23	39.05	44.15
11133	40.73	35.06	40.49
11211	84.14	84.58	85.87
11212	76.33	75.67	77.70
11223	44.62	39.49	44.55
11231	49.73	45.32	49.90
11232	41.92	36.41	41.73
11233	38.42	32.42	38.07
11311	58.85	55.73	59.43
11312	51.04	46.82	51.26
11313	47.54	42.82	47.61
11321	50.70	46.43	50.91
11322	42.89	37.52	42.75
11323	39.39	33.53	39.09
11331	44.50	39.36	44.43
11332	36.69	30.45	36.26
11333	33.19	26.45	32.61
12111	76.17	75.48	77.54
12112	68.36	66.58	69.37
12113	44.80	39.70	44.74
12121	68.02	66.19	69.02
12122	60.21	57.28	60.85
12123	36.65	30.40	36.22
12131	41.76	36.23	41.56
12132	33.95	27.32	33.40
12133	30.45	23.33	29.74
12211	73.86	72.85	75.12

Annex 8.3. Estimated and rescaled estimated values for all 243 EQ-5D health states (Continued)

EQ-5D health state	Estimated values	Rescaled with mean value for dead (10.0)	Rescaled with median value for dead (2.0)
12212	66.05	63.94	66.96
12213	42.49	37.06	42.33
12221	65.71	63.55	66.60
12222	57.90	54.64	58.44
12223	34.34	27.77	33.81
12231	39.45	33.60	39.15
12232	31.64	24.69	30.98
12233	28.14	20.69	27.33
12311	48.57	44.00	48.68
12312	40.76	35.09	40.52
12313	37.26	31.10	36.86
12321	40.42	34.70	40.16
12322	32.61	25.79	32.00
12323	29.11	21.80	28.34
12331	34.22	27.63	33.68
12332	26.41	18.72	25.52
12333	22.91	14.73	21.86
13111	52.72	48.73	53.02
13112	44.91	39.82	44.86
13113	41.41	35.83	41.20
13121	44.57	39.44	44.50
13122	36.76	30.53	36.34
13123	33.26	26.53	32.68
13131	38.37	32.36	38.02
13132	30.56	23.45	29.86
13133	27.06	19.46	26.20
13211	50.41	46.10	50.61
13212	42.60	37.19	42.44
13213	39.10	33.20	38.78
13221	42.26	36.80	42.09
13222	34.45	27.89	33.92
13223	30.95	23.90	30.26
13231	36.06	29.73	35.61
13232	28.25	20.82	27.44

Annex 8.3. Estimated and rescaled estimated values for all 243 EQ-5D health states (Continued)

EQ-5D health state	Estimated values	Rescaled with mean value for dead (10.0)	Rescaled with median value for dead (2.0)
13233	24.75	16.83	23.78
13311	45.18	40.13	45.14
13312	37.37	31.22	36.97
13313	33.87	27.23	33.32
13321	37.03	30.84	36.62
13322	29.22	21.93	28.45
13323	25.72	17.93	24.80
13331	30.83	23.76	30.14
13332	23.02	14.85	21.97
13333	19.52	10.86	18.31
21111	80.67	80.62	82.24
21112	72.86	71.71	74.07
21113	49.30	44.83	49.45
21121	72.52	71.32	73.72
21122	64.71	62.41	65.56
21123	41.15	35.54	40.93
21131	46.26	41.36	46.27
21132	38.45	32.45	38.10
21133	34.95	28.46	34.44
21221	70.21	68.69	71.30
21222	62.40	59.78	63.14
21223	38.84	32.90	38.51
21231	43.95	38.73	43.85
21232	36.14	29.82	35.69
21233	32.64	25.83	32.03
21311	53.07	49.13	53.39
21312	45.26	40.22	45.22
21313	41.76	36.23	41.56
21321	44.92	39.84	44.87
21322	37.11	30.93	36.70
21323	33.61	26.93	33.04
21331	38.72	32.76	38.39
21332	30.91	23.85	30.22
21333	27.41	19.86	26.56

Annex 8.3. Estimated and rescaled estimated values for all 243 EQ-5D health states (Continued)

EQ-5D health state	Estimated values	Rescaled with mean value for dead (10.0)	Rescaled with median value for dead (2.0)
22111	70.39	68.89	71.49
22112	62.58	59.98	63.33
22113	39.02	33.11	38.70
22121	62.24	59.59	62.97
22122	54.43	50.68	54.81
22123	30.87	23.81	30.18
22131	35.98	29.64	35.52
22132	28.17	20.73	27.36
22133	24.67	16.74	23.70
22211	68.08	66.26	69.08
22212	60.27	57.35	60.91
22213	36.71	30.47	36.28
22221	59.93	56.96	60.56
22222	52.12	48.05	52.39
22223	28.56	21.17	27.77
22231	33.67	27.00	33.11
22232	25.86	18.09	24.94
22233	22.36	14.10	21.28
22311	42.79	37.41	42.64
22312	34.98	28.50	34.48
22313	31.48	24.50	30.82
22321	34.64	28.11	34.12
22322	26.83	19.20	25.96
22333	17.13	8.13	15.82
23111	46.94	42.14	46.98
23112	39.13	33.23	38.81
23113	35.63	29.24	35.16
23121	38.79	32.84	38.46
23122	30.98	23.93	30.29
23123	27.48	19.94	26.64
23131	32.59	25.77	31.98
23132	24.78	16.86	23.81
23133	21.28	12.87	20.15
23211	44.63	39.50	44.56

Annex 8.3. Estimated and rescaled estimated values for all 243 EQ-5D health states (Continued)

EQ-5D health state	Estimated values	Rescaled with mean value for dead (10.0)	Rescaled with median value for dead (2.0)
23212	36.82	30.60	36.40
23213	33.32	26.60	32.74
23221	36.48	30.21	36.04
23222	28.67	21.30	27.88
23223	25.17	17.31	24.22
23231	30.28	23.13	29.56
23232	22.47	14.23	21.40
23233	18.97	10.23	17.74
23311	39.40	33.54	39.10
23312	31.59	24.63	30.93
23313	28.09	20.64	27.27
23321	31.25	24.24	30.58
23322	23.44	15.33	22.41
23323	19.94	11.34	18.75
23331	25.05	17.17	24.10
23332	17.24	8.26	15.93
23333	13.74	4.27	12.27
31111	50.36	46.04	50.55
31112	42.55	37.13	42.39
31113	39.05	33.14	38.73
31121	42.21	36.74	42.03
31122	34.40	27.83	33.87
31123	30.90	23.84	30.21
31131	36.01	29.67	35.55
31132	28.20	20.76	27.39
31133	24.70	16.77	23.73
31211	48.05	43.41	48.14
31222	32.09	25.20	31.46
31223	28.59	21.21	27.80
31231	33.70	27.04	33.14
31232	25.89	18.13	24.97
31233	22.39	14.13	21.32
31311	42.82	37.44	42.67
31312	35.01	28.53	34.51

Annex 8.3. Estimated and rescaled estimated values for all 243 EQ-5D health states (Continued)

EQ-5D health state	Estimated values	Rescaled with mean value for dead (10.0)	Rescaled with median value for dead (2.0)
31313	31.51	24.54	30.85
31321	34.67	28.14	34.15
31322	26.86	19.23	25.99
31323	23.36	15.24	22.33
31331	28.47	21.07	27.67
31332	20.66	12.16	19.51
31333	17.16	8.17	15.85
32111	40.08	34.31	39.81
32112	32.27	25.40	31.64
32113	28.77	21.41	27.98
32121	31.93	25.02	31.29
32122	24.12	16.11	23.12
32123	20.62	12.11	19.46
32131	25.73	17.94	24.81
32132	17.92	9.03	16.64
32133	14.42	5.04	12.98
32211	37.77	31.68	37.39
32212	29.96	22.77	29.23
32213	26.46	18.78	25.57
32221	29.62	22.38	28.87
32222	21.81	13.47	20.71
32223	18.31	9.48	17.05
32231	23.42	15.31	22.39
32232	15.61	6.40	14.23
32233	12.11	2.41	10.57
32311	32.54	25.71	31.93
32312	24.73	16.80	23.76
32313	21.23	12.81	20.10
32321	24.39	16.42	23.41
32322	16.58	7.51	15.24
32323	13.08	3.51	11.58
33111	36.69	30.45	36.26
33112	28.88	21.54	28.10
33113	25.38	17.55	24.44

Annex 8.3. Estimated and rescaled estimated values for all 243 EQ-5D health states (Continued)

EQ-5D health state	Estimated values	Rescaled with mean value for dead (10.0)	Rescaled with median value for dead (2.0)
33121	28.54	21.15	27.74
33122	20.73	12.24	19.58
33123	17.23	8.25	15.92
33131	22.34	14.08	21.26
33132	14.53	5.17	13.10
33133	11.03	1.17	9.44
33211	34.38	27.81	33.85
33212	26.57	18.90	25.68
33213	23.07	14.91	22.03
33221	26.23	18.51	25.33
33222	18.42	9.61	17.16
33223	14.92	5.61	13.51
33231	20.03	11.44	18.85
33232	12.22	2.53	10.68
33233	8.72	-1.46	7.02
33311	29.15	21.85	28.38
33312	21.34	12.94	20.22
33313	17.84	8.94	16.56
33321	21.00	12.55	19.86
33322	13.19	3.64	11.70
33323	9.69	-0.35	8.04
33331	14.80	5.48	13.38
33332	6.99	-3.43	5.22
33333	3.49	-7.43	1.56

9
A comparison of EQ-5D time trade-off values obtained in Germany, The United Kingdom and Spain

Jan Busschbach, Tom Weijnen, Martin Nieuwenhuizen, Siem Oppe, Xavier Badia, Paul Dolan, Wolfgang Greiner, Paul Kind, Paul Krabbe, Arto Ohinmaa, Montserrat Roset, Harri Sintonen, Aki Tsuchiya, Alan Williams, John Yfantopoulos and Frank De Charro

9.1 INTRODUCTION

EQ-5D has been valued using a standardised TTO by general population samples in 3 different European countries: Spain, Germany and the United Kingdom (Badia *et al*, 2001; Claes *et al*, 1999; Dolan, 1997). This has created an opportunity to compare TTO values for health states between countries. These types of comparisons are rare and those submitted or publicised are bilateral (Badia *et al*, 2001; Claes *et al*, 1999). Moreover, such comparisons do not usually involve the general public (Bleichrodt & Johannesson 1997) and tend to use VAS instead of TTO. For this reason, little is known about variations in health state valuations between countries using TTO. Hence it is not known if the results of decision analyses and cost-effectiveness analyses involving utility measurement in 1 country can be generalised to other countries. It would thus be helpful if more were known about international differences in TTO values. In this chapter, we report on the mutual efforts of several research groups within the EuroQol Group to make an international comparison of TTO values. On the basis of this comparison, general guidelines are formulated for the exchangeability of TTO value sets between different countries.

One of the key aims of the EQ-net project was to create compatible sets of general population valuations of health states in different European countries. One of the primary purposes of the Group has been to develop a standardised non-disease-specific instrument for describing and valuing HRQoL over a number of different European countries (Brooks, 1996). The first analyses within the EQ-net project were carried out on VAS-based values of EQ-5D health states elicited in a number of European countries. This Group effort suggested that most national differences could be attributed to differences in sampling methods or in research protocols. After controlling for these differences, there seemed to be little variation in the VAS values that could be attributed to a 'national' effect (see Chapters 7 and 8) This was a surprising conclusion given the common notion that the value of health is, to a large extent, culturally determined. Consequently the Group has presented a European set of health state valuations based on the VAS method (Chapter 8). Such a European value set will considerably facilitate investigations, because it reduces the need for further national

R. Brooks et al. (eds.),
The Measurement and Valuation of Health Status Using EQ-5D: A European Perspective, 143–165.

valuation studies to be carried out in Western European countries. It makes it possible to use 1 European value set in international trials, where several national value sets would otherwise be required. Whether the conclusions also hold for TTO values cannot be confirmed without further research, reported upon in this chapter.

In the early 1990s, the Centre for Health Economics in York, UK undertook a large population study (the MVH study) in more than 3000 households which included the valuation of 43 EQ-5D health states using TTO. Soon afterwards, the Catalan Institute of Public Health at the University of Barcelona in Spain and the Institute for Insurance at the University of Hannover in Germany, replicated the MVH-study using the same research protocol. Comparison of the results of these 3 investigations provides an opportunity to test differences in TTO values for health states between these countries.

If differences were to be found between the three investigations, 4 competing explanations can be offered.

Different nationalities value health states differently. According to this hypothesis, the 'national nature' of the inhabitants of specific countries drives the differences in TTO values: the value for health is therefore culturally determined.

Differences in the distribution of the respondents' background variables, other than nationality, cause the values to deviate. For instance, assume that older respondents value health states differently from young respondents. This would mean that differences in the distribution of age in the 3 samples would generate differences in the TTO values of the health states. This second hypothesis can be distinguished from the first by introducing a regression model that controls for differences in the distribution of background variables. If in such a regression model, the differences between the samples disappear, the second hypothesis is likely to be true. If differences still remain, the first hypothesis is more likely. Note that differences in the distribution of the background variables could be both the result of differences in sampling or the result of differences in demographics between countries. In the latter case it can still be argued that there is a 'national effect', although this effect is then not caused by the 'national nature' of the inhabitants.

Background variables have a different impact in the different countries. For instance age could be important in Spain but have no effect on the responses in Germany. Such effects must of course be interpreted as national effects. This hypothesis can be tested with a regression model where the background variables are allowed to interact with nationality.

Small differences in the operationalisation of the TTO task cause differences in the value of the health states. Such an explanation was found to be the most likely in the analysis of the VAS-based values (Chapters 7 and 8). Because nationality is linked with the investigator group, we cannot distinguish empirically this fourth hypothesis from the other 3.

9.2 METHODS

The MVH-protocol has already been described in detail (Dolan 1997; Gudex *et al*, 1997; MVH Group, 1995; Gudex, 1994). The report on the Spanish results has been published recently (Badia *et al*, 2001). Publication of the German research is underway and has been documented in the EuroQol proceedings (Claes *et al, 1999).*

The MVH-protocol

The MVH-protocol describes a face-to-face interview that can be separated into several sections. First, the respondents were asked to describe their own health using the EQ-5D descriptive system. Then the respondents ranked 15 health states. This set of 15 health states always included the best health state (11111) and immediate death. The respondents had to assume that the duration of the health state was 10 years, followed by death. After the ranking exercise, the subjects were asked to place the health states on the EQ-5D VAS. Results for these VAS valuations are reported elsewhere in Chapters 7 and 8. After the VAS valuation task had been completed, 13 health states were valued using the TTO method. States 11111 and immediate death cannot be valued directly using standard TTO. A TTO board that visualised the difference in life years between the health states was used to help the respondent make a balanced choice. For states "better-than-death", respondents were lead by a process of 'bracketing' to select a length of time in state 11111 that they regarded as equivalent to 10 years in the target state, where both states would be followed by death (Dolan, 1997; Gudex *et al*, 1997; MVH Group, 1995). In the bracketing process, respondents were first asked whether they would be prepared to spend 5 years in state 11111 to avoid the target state, then 4 or 6 years depending on the answer given, up to a maximum of 9 years and a minimum of 1 year. The trade-off was first presented in steps of 1 year and then refined into steps of 3 months. In order to allow an even finer differentiation between relatively good states, trade-offs smaller than 1 year were measured in weeks.

Health states could also be valued below the value of death. If the respondent preferred death over the health state presented, the interviewer proceeded by asking if the respondent preferred 5 years in the restricted state followed by 5 years in 11111, or still preferred death. If the respondent still preferred death, the period in the restricted health state was reduced to the point where the respondent opted for the short period in the restricted health state followed by the disease-free health state. In the reverse case, the period in the restricted health state was extended, up to 9.75 years. The absolute value of the negative health states can be very large compared to the positive values: the minimal value is minus 39. These large negative values could easily dominate the much smaller positive values. For this reason, negative values were rescaled to a scale from 0 to minus 1 (Dolan, 1997).

The valuation of negative values has a long and controversial history. The main issue in the debate is not so much the existence of negative values *per se*, as most researchers appear to be convinced that negative values for health states exist and should be accounted for. The topic of the debate is centred on how to measure negative values and how to deal with the issue of large negative values. Torrance (1986) described the difficulties that arise as negative utilities can have infinitely low values. He suggested truncation of these large negative values at minus 1. Smith and Dobson (1993) stated that Torrance had not provided a theoretical foundation for such truncation. Despite such a foundation still being lacking, many researchers dealing with infinitely low values have followed the suggestions of Torrance. Their motivation is based on practical arguments and they usually refer to minus 1 as an appealing mirror image of plus 1, the almost-always-applied and less controversial upper limit (Patrick *et al*, 1994; Dolan, 1997). This pragmatic approach creates a workable solution that evidently appeals, but it does not resolve the debate. In this investigation, we have tried to contribute to the debate by examining positive and negative values separately.

The UK data

Researchers at York used the MVH protocol in a representative sample of the non-institutionalised adult population of England, Scotland and Wales. They selected 6080 addresses from a postcode address file. Of these, 756 were outside the scope of the survey, being non-residential, empty / derelict, untraceable or were addresses of houses not yet built, leaving a total of 5324 in-scope addresses. 3395 interviews were completed: a response rate of 63.7%. Trained interviewers collected values of 43 EQ-5D health states plus the health state unconscious and dead (Dolan *et al,* 1996a; Dolan, 1997; MVH Group, 1995).

The Spanish data

The Spanish study, which also used the MVH protocol, is usually referred to as the Cornellà de Llobregat study (Badia *et al*, 2001). In this study, a random sample of members of the general population from different socio-economic areas in Barcelona was included. Individuals were recruited from a primary care database according to age and sex quota sampling so as to be representative of the Catalan general population. Individuals who were illiterate, cognitively impaired, or who had a severe illness or mental disorder were replaced by others. Fieldwork was carried out by 11 interviewers, and the final sample constituted 979 respondents. The 43 EQ-5D health states included in the Cornellà de Llobregat study were the same as those used in the MVH-study. A small difference was that the refinement of the trade-off was restricted to 3 months. In the original protocol a trade-off of less than a year could be refined down to 1 week (for positive values only).

The German data

In Germany in 1997, a random sample of 4000 addresses was selected from the telephone directory of the German telephone company Telekom (Claes *et al,* 1999). In order to represent urban and rural regions equally, the selection process was based on postal zip code areas in Northern Germany. The selection procedure also ensured that half of the selected persons were female. Upon selection, potential participants were informed in writing about the study and were asked about their willingness to participate using a reply card. The response rate was 9.5 %, or 380 addresses. No reminder was sent out. The interviewers agreed to an interview date with the participants by a phone call. If it was not possible to find a mutual date for a meeting or after 3 fruitless attempts to contact the person, the interview was cancelled. The German researchers were able to interview 339 subjects. Five interviews had to be aborted prematurely because the participants could not master the task.

The German investigators did not include the states 'unconscious', 13332, 21312, 13311, 22233, 32313, 22121 and 23313 in the investigation. This decision was taken because modelling practices on the other 2 data sets had suggested that a sample of less than 43 health states could be used to validly estimate all 243 EQ-5D health states. A departure from the MVH-protocol was that for trade-offs larger than 1 year, there was no fine-tuning of the trade-off in steps of 3 months, as in the original MVH-protocol. Fine-tuning for the relatively good health states with a trade-off of less than 1 year was undertaken in steps of 4 weeks, instead of steps of 1 week.

Exclusions and inconsistencies

The data for the present investigation comprises the merged raw data files of the 3 national investigations, but not all raw data was used. The exclusion criteria applied were:

(i) A respondent gave all states the same value.
(ii) A respondent valued less than 3 states.
(iii) A respondent gave more than 3 inconsistent responses.

This last exclusion criterion was used because earlier research had shown that value models built on responses of subjects "... who had 4 or more inconsistencies did not produce logically consistent data for modelling" (Ohinmaa & Sintonen, 1999). These 3 exclusion criteria are close to the exclusion criteria that were used in the presentation of the results of the individual studies, but not exactly the same. This explains small differences between the presentation of the average values of health states in the present study and the presentation of average values in the reports of the individual studies elsewhere.

The regression models

In this study we used multi-level models, because these models can handle the nested structure of the data (health states nested within respondent, respondents nested within nations) better than ordinary least squares regression (Busschbach *et al*, 1999; Dolan, 1997). Four multi-level models where used. In the first multi-level model, the explanatory variables were the dimensions and levels of the EQ-5D descriptive system, including the N3 parameter. This parameter was introduced by Dolan (1997) in order to account for some interaction between the health dimensions, when at least 1 of the EQ-5D dimensions was at its worst level. Thus the N3 parameter was "0" for states such as 11222, 21111, and "1" for the states 31111 and 13331.

In a second model, dummies were added for the 3 studies in order to control for possible differences between the studies. In the third model, dummies were added to control for the influence of different distributions of the background variables such as age and sex. Possible differences in the influence of these background variables by country were studied by allowing for interaction between the background variables and the dummies indicating the studies: the fourth model. This last model gives answers to questions such as: has age a different effect in Germany than in Spain?

In the fourth model, differences between countries were treated as constants over the whole range of health. It could be that differences between countries are not well expressed by such single constants because differences only occur in specific dimensions of health, such as mobility or pain, or even at specific levels of those dimensions. For this reason, a fifth analysis was undertaken in which the countries' parameters were allowed to interact with the specific dimensions and levels of the EQ-5D descriptive system. Because differences between countries are now expressed in 20 instead of 2 parameters, interactions with the background variables (discussed below) become extremely complex to interpret. For this reason, these interactions were left out.

Background variables

From the numerous background variables registered, a limited number were chosen for inclusion in the analysis. A selection was made because the interpretation of the effects becomes more difficult when the number of variables increases. This is especially the case when interactions are allowed, as in the fourth model. The selection of background variables was made on the basis on their availability in all 3 samples, their influence on the TTO values or VAS values, differences in the distribution of the variables between the 3 samples and the relationship of the variables to the background variables already included. On the basis of these considerations, 4 background variables were chosen: age, sex, level of education and own health state as shown by the EQ-5D VAS score given by the respondent.

It was anticipated that age and own health would not have a linear relationship with the values given to the health states. For this reason the continuous background variables EQ VAS score and age were split into 2 levels. Division of age into more than 2 categories was considered. However, it was felt appropriate to account for an interaction between age and education, so only 2 categories of age groups, namely less than or equal to 64, and greater than 64 years, were constructed in order to maintain transparency in the interpretation of the interaction effects.

The scores for own health states were the values given by respondents on the EQ VAS. People without health problems often do not rate their own health at 100, but somewhere between 100 and 80. In this investigation we tried to make a distinction between those who valued their health relatively highly and those who did not. To do so, a distinction was made on the basis of the median value of the VAS scores given in the 3 samples. This median value was 85. Using this value, 2 groups have been distinguished: respondents with an EQ VAS score equal or higher than 85 and respondents with a score lower than 85.

Considerable efforts were made to ensure that the classification of education could be made comparable over the 3 countries. The variable describing the level of education was eventually divided into a low, a medium, and a high level. A low level indicates that the respondent left school at some minimum age, a high level indicates that the respondent had a degree or professional qualification, while a medium level indicates that the respondent did not leave school at some minimum age, but did not have a degree or professional education.

Additional analysis

Several additional analyses were performed to analyse the validity of the methodological choices made. For example the influences of the categorisation of the 2 continuous variables age and own health were studied by comparing the results of the categorised variables with the results of the inclusion of the variables in their original continuous form. The influence of the large differences between the number of respondents involved in the 3 studies was studied by performing a weighted analysis. The weighting was undertaken by dividing the input of the multi-level analysis by the number of respondents in the 3 studies. Issues surrounding negative values were investigated by analysing both negative and positive values separately.

9.3 RESULTS

Raw TTO and VAS values compared between studies

Table 9.1 presents the raw data from the 3 studies. Figure 9.1 shows that if a comparison is made, small but consistent differences between the samples are present. In particular, the values for the German sample were consistently higher than those of the studies from the UK and Spain. The Spanish values were also slightly higher than the UK ones, but the differences between the German values and the other 2 sets are more noticeable. In order to get an idea of the magnitude of the differences, it is helpful to look at Figure 9.2, which represents the differences found in comparisons of the raw VAS values that were also collected on the basis of the MVH protocol. The differences between the raw TTO values in the different countries were larger than the differences between the VAS values. Also of interest is that the German VAS values seemed to be lower than those of the other countries, while the German TTO values seemed higher. Clearly the conclusions arising from the comparison of the VAS studies cannot be extended to the TTO studies.

Table 9.1. Mean TTO values, SD and number of observations after exclusions

	UK			Germany			Spain		
	Mean	SD	N	Mean	SD	N	Mean	SD	N
21111	0.88	0.23	1212	0.93	0.21	128	0.88	0.22	397
11211	0.88	0.22	1243	0.92	0.15	136	0.87	0.23	367
11121	0.86	0.24	1207	0.91	0.22	143	0.90	0.17	354
11112	0.85	0.26	1181	0.92	0.14	126	0.89	0.24	351
12111	0.85	0.27	1205	0.93	0.12	131	0.86	0.25	375
12211	0.78	0.31	758	0.85	0.29	84	0.77	0.34	248
11122	0.74	0.36	754	0.89	0.17	73	0.83	0.26	230
12121	0.75	0.30	756	0.83	0.23	77	0.73	0.39	234
22112	0.66	0.37	778	0.74	0.31	76	0.70	0.38	232
22121	0.64	0.42	768				0.66	0.43	219
21222	0.55	0.47	750	0.77	0.24	81	0.62	0.44	211
12222	0.55	0.46	755	0.75	0.32	66	0.60	0.50	203
22122	0.53	0.48	745	0.72	0.33	73	0.64	0.40	222
11312	0.56	0.48	750	0.68	0.34	132	0.44	0.56	231
22222	0.50	0.48	753	0.66	0.40	123	0.57	0.47	239
21312	0.51	0.49	754				0.42	0.54	234
11113	0.41	0.54	762	0.61	0.47	119	0.64	0.46	221
13212	0.39	0.52	748	0.52	0.40	83	0.24	0.61	222
13311	0.33	0.56	748				0.21	0.59	230

Table 9.1. Mean TTO values, SD and number of observations after exclusions (Continued)

	UK			Germany			Spain		
	Mean	SD	N	Mean	SD	N	Mean	SD	N
11131	0.24	0.60	735	0.33	0.49	80	0.40	0.59	227
12223	0.20	0.56	755	0.50	0.45	76	0.36	0.55	234
21323	0.14	0.60	758	0.32	0.46	75	0.11	0.62	227
21232	0.06	0.61	760	0.36	0.51	71	0.23	0.63	241
23321	0.13	0.61	771	0.40	0.49	70	-0.03	0.62	242
32211	0.13	0.60	778	0.29	0.48	117	-0.04	0.63	225
22323	0.02	0.59	738	0.27	0.56	82	0.06	0.60	224
11133	-0.07	0.61	777	0.27	0.52	80	0.21	0.63	221
21133	-0.07	0.59	757	0.18	0.52	64	0.19	0.59	244
22331	-0.02	0.60	741	0.28	0.50	72	-0.04	0.60	238
33212	-0.04	0.59	760	0.16	0.51	84	-0.21	0.60	212
23232	-0.12	0.59	750	0.02	0.51	119	-0.12	0.61	213
23313	-0.08	0.59	771				-0.19	0.60	221
22233	-0.17	0.57	759				-0.07	0.61	213
33321	-0.14	0.57	751	0.08	0.47	84	-0.34	0.52	255
32223	-0.19	0.56	761	0.07	0.49	120	-0.25	0.56	216
32313	-0.17	0.56	773				-0.26	0.57	244
32232	-0.24	0.56	759	-0.03	0.45	82	-0.28	0.55	231
13332	-0.24	0.55	760				-0.28	0.57	272
32331	-0.29	0.55	779	0.05	0.43	78	-0.32	0.56	218
33232	-0.34	0.50	758	-0.10	0.47	77	-0.39	0.52	206
33323	-0.40	0.49	766	-0.07	0.49	64	-0.55	0.43	225
Uncon.	-0.41	0.38	3032				-0.52	0.38	913
33333	-0.56	0.41	3029	-0.22	0.38	278	-0.61	0.39	914

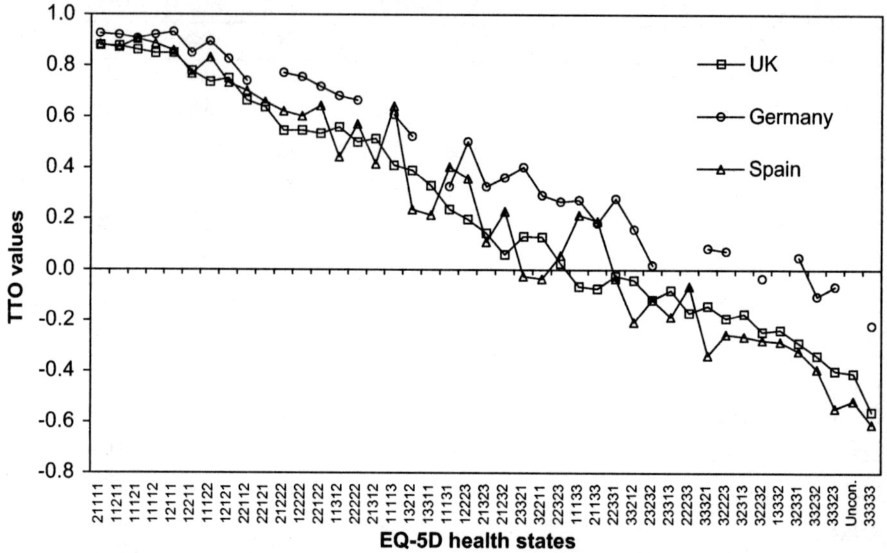

Figure 9.1. EQ-5D health states ranked according to mean TTO values after exclusions

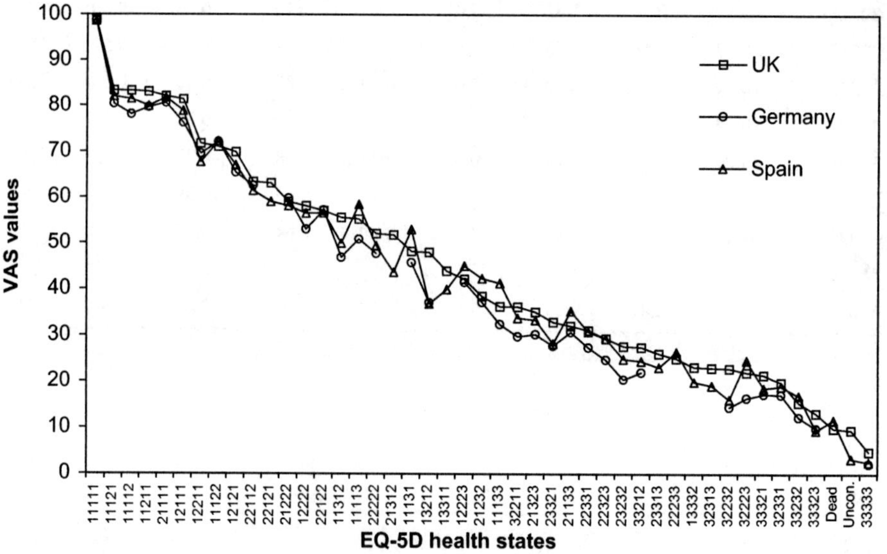

Figure 9.2. EQ-5D health states ranked according to mean VAS values

Table 9.2 presents the distribution of background variables in the 3 studies. It can be seen that the distribution of the background variables differs between the samples.

The most noticeable of these differences are that the German sample was older and had a higher level of education. Furthermore, the Spanish respondents seemed to value their own health states (EQ VAS scores) lower and have on average lower education.

Table 9.2. Background variables

		UK		Spain		Germany		Total
Total N		3074	(%)	923	(%)	280	(%)	3997
Sex	Male	1344	44	420	46	163	58	1927
	Female	1730	56	497	54	117	42	2344
	Data missing	0		6		0		6
Age	≤ 44	1489	48	457	50	111	40	2057
	45-64	880	29	289	32	118	42	1287
	≥ 65	705	23	171	19	50	18	926
	Data missing	0		6		1		7
Own health*	EQ VAS < 85	1175	38	628	68	80	29	1883
	EQ VAS ≥ 85	1889	62	289	32	198	71	2376
	Data missing	10		6		2		18
Education	Low	1174	38	556	61	16	6	1746
	Medium	1264	41	241	26	165	59	1670
	High	632	21	115	13	98	35	845
	Data missing	4		11		1		16

* value of own health as measured with the EQ VAS

9.4 MULTI-LEVEL ANALYSES

Table 9.3 shows the results of the multi-level analyses. The dummies of the national studies in model 2 show the influence of the German study and of the Spanish study compared to the UK study. In line with the observations in Figure 9.1, the results of model 2 indicate that, on average, the German values were 0.189 higher than the UK values. The Spanish coefficient does not differ significantly from the UK study. The parameters of model 3 suggest that older respondents gave lower TTO valuations than young respondents and women gave lower values then men. Furthermore, respondents with lower and medium education gave lower TTO values than higher-educated respondents. In model 3, the coefficient for own health, indicated by an own EQ VAS score of less than 85, is not significant. This is also true for the interaction between education and age.

The inclusion in model 3 of the dummies for these background variables had only a small effect on the coefficient that represents the deviation of the German study. This coefficient only goes down from 0.189 to 0.172. This means that, even after correction for differences in the distribution of background variables, the German respondents appeared to give higher values in the TTO exercise than their Spanish and UK counterparts.

The inclusion in model 3 of the dummies for the background variables is illustrated in Figure 9.3, which is based on the most important aggregated coefficients from model 3 (EQ VAS scores held constant). The Spanish and UK parameters converged, but the German parameters still deviate from the Spanish and UK ones.

Furthermore it can be seen that older responders had lower coefficients than the young. The education effect appeared to be different in the young and the old, but the interaction between these 2 background variables in model 3 is not statistically significant (see Table 9.3).

Table 9.3. Multi-level parameter estimates of the 4 model specifications. If the parameters are twice as large as the standard error of the mean, results are statistically significant at a p-level of less than 5% (2-sided)

	Model 1		Model 2		Model 3		Model 4	
	PE	SE	PE	SE	PE	SE	PE	SE
Constant	0.996	0.051	0.935	0.007	0.929	0.013	0.928	0.015
N3	-0.280	0.006	-0.280	0.006	-0.279	0.006	-0.279	0.006
Mobility = 2	-0.085	0.004	-0.085	0.004	-0.085	0.004	-0.085	0.004
Mobility = 3	-0.343	0.005	-0.343	0.005	-0.344	0.005	-0.344	0.005
Self-Care = 2	-0.112	0.004	-0.112	0.004	-0.112	0.004	-0.112	0.004
Self-Care = 3	-0.239	0.005	-0.239	0.005	-0.238	0.006	-0.238	0.006
Usual Activities = 2	-0.050	0.005	-0.050	0.005	-0.050	0.005	-0.050	0.005
Usual Activities = 3	-0.120	0.006	-0.120	0.006	-0.120	0.006	-0.120	0.006
Pain/Discomfort = 2	-0.113	0.004	-0.113	0.004	-0.112	0.004	-0.112	0.004
Pain/Discomfort = 3	-0.352	0.005	-0.352	0.005	-0.352	0.005	-0.352	0.005
Anxiety/Depression = 2	-0.066	0.004	-0.066	0.004	-0.066	0.004	-0.066	0.004
Anxiety/Depression = 3	-0.212	0.005	-0.212	0.005	-0.213	0.005	-0.213	0.005
German study			0.189	0.021	0.172	0.021	0.113	0.104
Spanish study			-0.001	0.012	0.000	0.013	0.005	0.029
Sex (male = 1)					0.043	0.010		
EQ VAS < 85					0.003	0.011		
Age > 64					-0.124	0.016		
Education medium					0.013	0.013		
Education high					0.044	0.016		
Education medium + age > 64					0.003	0.030		
Education high + age > 64					-0.067	0.041		

Table 9.3. Multi-level parameter estimates of the 4 model specifications. If the parameters are twice as large as the standard error of the mean, results are statistically significant at a p-level of less than 5% (2-sided) (Continued)

	Model 1		Model 2		Model 3		Model 4	
	PE	SE	PE	SE	PE	SE	PE	SE
UK study + sex							0.051	0.012
UK study + EQ VAS < 85							0.001	0.013
UK study + age > 64							-0.115	0.020
UK study + education medium							0.016	0.016
UK study + education high							0.030	0.019
UK + education medium + Age > 64							-0.022	0.034
UK + education high + Age > 64							-0.097	0.046
Spanish study + sex							0.032	0.022
Spanish study + EQ VAS < 85							0.006	0.024
Spanish study + age > 64							-0.156	0.031
Spanish study + education medium							0.004	0.027
Spanish study + education high							0.093	0.035
Spain + education medium + Age > 64							0.061	0.121
Spain + education high + Age > 64							0.015	0.153
German study + sex							0.015	0.040
German study + EQ VAS < 85							0.032	0.044
German study + age > 64							-0.009	0.176
German study + education medium							0.053	0.103
German study + education high							0.127	0.105
Germany + education medium + Age > 64							-0.047	0.188
Germany + education high + Age > 64							-0.045	0.206
Variance components								
Country level	0.008		0.000		0.000		0.000	
Individual level	0.099		0.099		0.095		0.095	
Error	0.136		0.136		0.135		0.135	
R2	0.471		0.476		0.486		0.487	

* For an explanation of the N3 parameter see Dolan, 1997 and the text.

In model 4, the background variables are related to the origin of the data, by allowing an interaction between background dummies and the dummies which represent the differences in the 3 national studies. None of the German interaction parameters reached satisfactory levels of statistical significance. In the Spanish and UK data, the interaction dummy for the value of own health state remained small, unlike the interaction of study origin with age, sex and education. Figure 9.4 is based on the aggregated coefficients from model 4 as presented in Table 9.3. As in Figure 9.3, the aggregated coefficients for the parameters of Germany in Figure 9.4 were also higher than the coefficients for Spain and the UK. The important difference from Figure 9.3 is that Figure 9.4 shows that in the UK data older respondents with a high level of education had lower valuations than respondents with low and medium levels of education. This interaction between education and age was absent in the other data sets. Adding these country-specific background parameters to the model had the effect that the coefficient representing the German differences decreased from 0.189 to 0.113, and was no longer statistically significant. This implies that differences in the specific way education and age interact with the value of health in the 3 different studies explain approximately half of the difference between the German, Spanish and UK TTO valuations. The remaining statistically non-significant German differences further implies that within this data set and within these model specifications, the German respondents can no longer be distinguished from the average respondent.

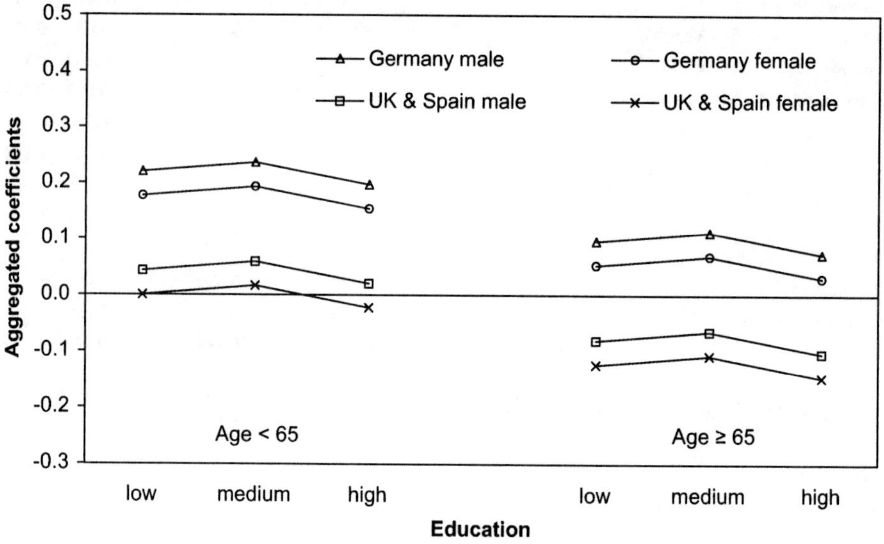

Figure 9.3. Aggregated background coefficients model 3 (Own VAS ≥ 85)

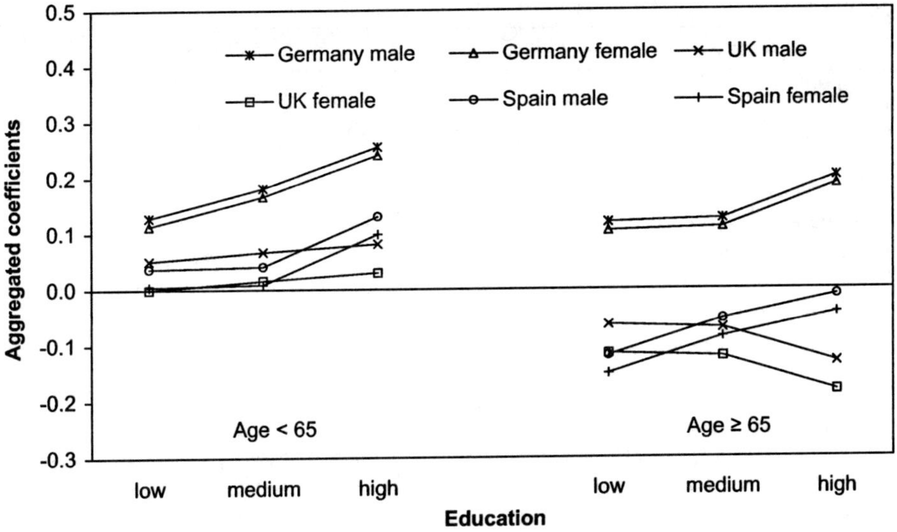

Figure 9.4. The values of the German, Spanish and UK dummies for different background variables form model 4

Table 9.4 presents the differences between countries on the individual dimensions and levels of the descriptive system of the EQ-5D. The coefficients of German and Spanish respondents represent differences from the UK parameters. All German coefficients are positive as could be expected from Figure 9.1. The Spanish coefficients are more complex to interpret: some are negative (mobility, self-care, usual activities and some are positive (pain/discomfort and anxiety/depression). Similar differences between the Spanish and UK data sets were found in the bilateral comparison of the Spanish and the UK data made by Badia *et al* (2001).

Table 9.4. Differences between countries on the individual dimensions and levels of the EQ-5D

	UK	Germany	Spain
Constant	0.955		
N3	-0.280	ns	ns
Mobility level 2	-0.080	ns	-0.024
Mobility level 3	-0.322	ns	-0.107
Self-Care level 2	-0.111	0.049	ns
Self-Care level 3	-0.221	ns	-0.090
Usual Activities level 2	-0.044	ns	-0.034
Usual Activities level 3	-0.102	0.081	-0.096
Pain / Discomfort level 2	-0.127	0.050	0.045
Pain / Discomfort level 3	-0.385	0.096	0.126
Anxiety / Depression level 2	-0.072	0.038	ns
Anxiety / Depression level 3	-0.238	0.102	0.096
Variance components			
Country level	0.000		
Individual level	0.099		
Error	0.134		
R^2	0.481		

ns = not statistically significant $P > 0.05$

Additional analyses

Table 9.5 shows the same model 3 as presented in Table 9.3, but now with the variables age and own health (EQ VAS score) as continuous variables. As can be seen, the country parameters do not converge 0.172 (Germany) and 0.000 (Spain) becomes 0.182 and minus 0.003. Thus the differences between the data sets are not an artefact of the way age and own health is dichotomised. Similar negative results were obtained when all analyses were re-run on weighted samples: the country parameters hardly changed.

Table 9.5. Model 3 with continuous variables for EQ VAS and age

	PE	SE
(Constant)	1.020	0.036
N3	-0.279	0.279
Mobility = 2	-0.085	0.004
Mobility = 3	-0.344	0.005
Self-Care = 2	-0.112	0.004
Self-Care = 3	-0.238	0.006
Usual Activities = 2	-0.050	0.005
Usual Activities = 3	-0.120	0.006
Pain/Discomfort = 2	-0.112	0.004
Pain/Discomfort = 3	-0.352	0.005
Anxiety/Depression = 2	-0.066	0.004
Anxiety/Depression = 3	-0.213	0.005
German study	0.182	0.021
Spanish study	-0.003	0.013
Sex	0.045	0.010
EQ VAS < 85	0.000	0.000
Age	-0.002	0.000
Education medium	0.021	0.014
Education high	0.058	0.016
Education medium + age > 64	-0.055	0.028
Education high + age > 64	-0.130	0.039
Variance components		
Country level	0.000	
Individual level	0.096	
Error	0.135	
R^2	0.484	

Figures 9.5 and 9.6 shed light on the differences between the positive and negative values involved in the analyses. These figures represent the average values based only on negative and positive values. Note that it is no longer possible to study the distributions of these data sets by means of a normal regression or multi-level analysis: the distribution of the background variables of the subjects over the values of health is disturbed by the selection of the health state values.

In Figure 9.5 it can be seen that the positive values from the UK, Germany and Spain differ less than in Figure 9.1. Figure 9.5 resembles the VAS data as presented in Figure 9.2. It seems that when negative values are excluded from the analysis the diversity between the 3 investigations is reduced.

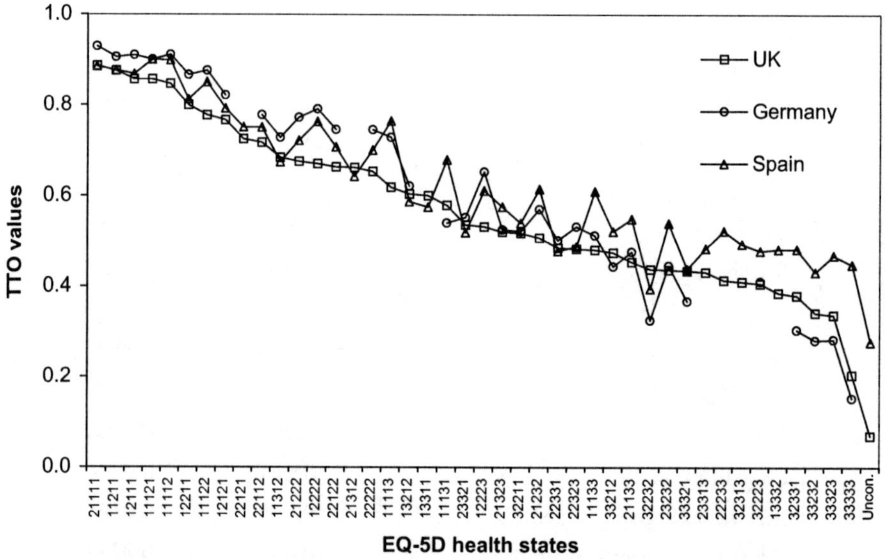

Figure 9.5. EQ-5D health states ranked according to mean positive TTO values

Figure 9.6 reveals in the selection of negative values considerably more differences between the 3 investigations than in the selection of positive values as presented in Figure 9.5. In particular, the German negative values appear to be higher than those found in the other 2 investigations. The proportion of negative values given also differed. On average, 35% of the Spanish and UK responses were negative, and 23% in the German sample. Thus the German responders gave less and higher (closer to zero) negative values. Given the small variance in positive values in Figure 9.5, the variance found in the negative values seems to drive the differences between the German and the other 2 samples.

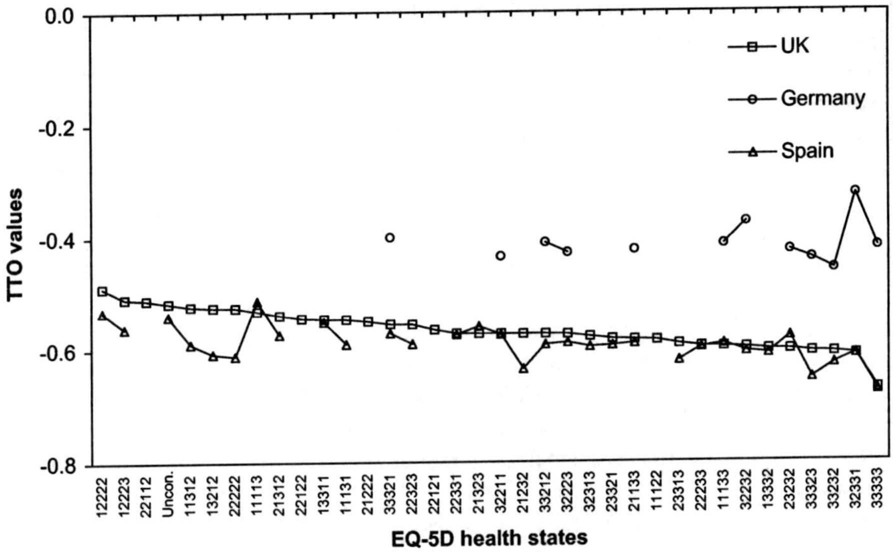

Figure 9.6. EQ-5D health states ranked according to mean negative TTO values

Another striking aspect when comparing Figures 9.5 and 9.6 is the differences in which the positive and negative values can be differentiated between the health states. The negative values differentiate much less than the positive values. Clearly it was much easier for respondents to differentiate health states in terms of positive values than in terms of negative ones.

9.5 DISCUSSION

This study shows that there were differences in EQ-5D TTO valuations from 3 different European countries: the Spanish values resembled the UK values, but the German values were higher. The differences were small but larger than the differences found in the VAS values. The differences found in the TTO values cannot be explained by differences in the distribution of background variables. These results suggest that health is valued systematically differently in different countries, when measured using TTO. At least a part of this variance could be attributed to the way education interacted with age differently in each country. The differences found seemed to be driven by differences in the proportion and the magnitude of the negative TTO valuations of health states.

When the data is tested with an emphasis on the dimensions of the EQ-5D, this investigation confirms the analysis of Badia *et al* (2001) who found that the Spanish coefficients for the dimensions mobility, self-care, and usual activities were more negative and the coefficients for pain/discomfort and anxiety/depression were more positive. They noted that Spanish subjects also attached more importance to mobility than American subjects when choosing weights for the Sickness Impact Profile (Badia and Alonso, 1995b). These authors suggested that there were cultural explanations for the differences found.

Can the small differences found in this analysis indeed be attributed to cultural, that is to say, national differences, or are they the result of small differences in the operationalisation of the TTO task? Both the German and Spanish groups devoted considerable time and effort into replicating the MVH protocol. For instance, both used the same visual aids and translated the MVH protocol literally. Furthermore, both groups of investigators consulted members of the York group during the design of the replication studies. Nevertheless, small differences in the operationalisation of the 3 investigations can be noted. For example, the German investigators used steps of 1 year instead of 3 months for trade-offs bigger than 1 year. The German researchers tried to correct for this difference, but the correction only resulted in small changes of the absolute values of the health states (Claes *et al*, 1999). Hence it seems unlikely that these small differences in protocol were responsible for the differences between the 3 data sets. This lends weight to the conclusion that the differences found were indeed real differences between the countries.

On the other hand, there are also some arguments that the small differences found were the results of subtle differences in the administration of the TTO task. First, the national differences seemed to be driven by differences in the negative values, clearly the most difficult and complex part of the TTO interview to administer. Indeed the differences found seem to be related to education and age, which points to the cognitive aspects of the TTO task. Furthermore, differences in values could not be found when the same respondents valued the health states with the much more easily administered VAS. The final answer cannot be given in this chapter. In the data used here, nationality and investigator teams are linked: a different team of investigators is also a different nationality. Therefore this investigation cannot provide 'hard evidence' that the differences found were indeed 'national differences', or just differences between the operating procedures used by the investigator teams. The final answer has to come from other replication studies within the UK, Spain or Germany. For the present, investigators should anticipate the possibility of small national differences in TTO values between countries.

It should be stressed that the conclusion drawn above is independent of differences in the sampling strategies of the 3 investigating teams. By using multi-level models that incorporate the most important background variables, any differences in the distribution of these background variables have been accounted for.

It could also be hypothesised that the differences found do not represent differences in the value of health, but differences in the translation of the health states. Indeed, if the translations were not precise, one would expect to find different values attached to these health states even when different nationalities share the same values for health. This explanation seems unlikely for 2 reasons. First, the development of compatible national questionnaires was, and remains, one of the primary aims of the EuroQol Group and the EQ-net project. The translation process used by the EuroQol Group is a standardised procedure reflecting recommendations in the international literature (see Chapter 11). The second reason is that if there had been semantic differences between the 3 versions, they would also have had a systematic influence on the VAS values. This was not the case.

The different results in VAS and TTO comparisons between the 3 countries could imply the following. First, it could mean that the VAS technique is in some way less influenced by cultural differences. Second, it could mean that the VAS is much easier to replicate, resulting in less variation between studies.

In model 3, the coefficient for own health, indicated by an EQ VAS score of less than 0.85, was not significant. Hence in this model, the VAS values of own health state do not influence the TTO values given to the EQ-5D health states. Similar results were found elsewhere (Dolan *et al*, 1996b). Note that this remark is made in the presence of significant effects on age and education, which are both related to the EQ VAS score.

It is important to remember, however, that the variations found in the TTO values appeared to be mainly driven by the variations in the negative values. Figure 9.5, based on positive values, presents a much more consistent picture. Clearly the way negative values are perceived and measured deserves more attention.

The approach followed in this investigation has interesting features for other TTO valuation studies of EQ-5D. It might not be necessary to value all, or almost all, of the 43 health states, as was the case in the 3 studies presented here. It might also not be necessary to draw a precise representative sample from the general public. Instead, it might be possible to value a more limited number of health states, say 10. On the basis of national statistics of the background variables, it should then be possible to model a representative value set, using a constant for the absolute level of the new study. It should be noted, however, that although in this case the sample does not necessarily have to be representative of the general population, the different groups in the population do have to be sampled in sufficient numbers to allow parameter estimations. This approach has two major advantages. First, it will be much cheaper and easier to collect the necessary data. Second, the investigation will be less vulnerable to non-response in the sample, as the values are modelled afterwards for national characteristics. Furthermore, the linked data sets will improve in power when more data is added.

An important finding of this investigation is that background variables, including nationality, seemed to influence TTO values, but this conclusion must be viewed within the perspective that the influence of background variables was small and often interrelated. For instance, the influence of sex and the EQ VAS score diminish when age and education are incorporated in the models. Furthermore, although age and education did have statistically significant parameters, their absolute size was only 11% or lower. The only notable exception was the value of the German national parameter with a value of 18%. However, when controlling for specific education and age effects, the differences between Germany and the other countries were no longer statistically significant. Thus the conclusion must be that there are indeed systematic differences between populations in the value of health, but these systematic differences are likely to be small. Note that this statement does not include individual variance. Indeed, as usual in this kind of investigation, the unsystematic individual difference was large.

In this study we used multi-level models, because these models can handle the nested structure of the data (health states nested in respondent, respondents nested in nations) better than ordinary least squares regression. We also tested the hypotheses with ordinary least square regression. In line with previous empirical findings, we did not find different results, as the observations at the second level of the analysis, the respondents, were numerous (Busschbach *et al*, 1999).

What are the practical implications of this investigation for the choice of the TTO value set for a particular investigation? Economic evaluation is carried out for a variety of reasons, including reimbursement issues in respect of health sector resource provision. Given that it cannot be ruled out that there are national differences in TTO values, choice of a particular TTO value set has best to anticipate these national differences. Clearly, such a choice is more straightforward in Germany, Spain and the UK because for these countries national TTO value sets for the EQ-5D are available (Claes *et al*, 1999; Badia *et al*, 2001; Dolan, 1997). The choice for other countries will most likely be based on demographic considerations, the size of the valuation sample and the quality of the publications. The UK MVH-study is based on the largest sample size and is well documented, so may be considered for use in other countries. On the other hand, it might be expected that an investigator in Portugal might prefer to use the Spanish TTO values, given that this set of values is based on a sample of inhabitants of the Iberian Peninsula. For similar reasons, an Austrian investigator might prefer to use the German TTO values.

Within international trials, it might be considered appropriate to use 1 TTO-based value set for reasons of compatibility within the trial data. Again the sensible choice for this single set will most likely be based on demographic considerations, the size of the valuation sample, and the quality of the published studies. For these reasons the original UK MVH study has so far been chosen most often to fulfil this roll. An alternative might be to use model 1 presented in Table 9.3, but note that state 11111 was not used in the estimation and should be put at its theoretical value of 1.00. By using model 1, the maximal power of the combined data sets is being employed, as the estimates are based on the values of 3997 respondents.

Although a single value set could be used in an international trial, in particular to sum up the trial results, it is recommended that the best local value set be used in, for example, reimbursement discussions. In such cases it would not be appropriate to use UK values, say, with German authorities, as a German value set is available. This is similar to the argument for presenting national cost estimates from international trial results, by adjusting the international trial results with national cost data.

Note that these recommendations apply to TTO values, and specifically in the context of cost-utility analysis, where QALYs may be calculated. VAS-values may be more appropriate in other valuation contexts, especially those not involving formal economic analyses.

10
What concepts does the EQ-5D measure? Intentions and interpretations

Julia Fox-Rushby and Caroline Selai

10.1 INTRODUCTION

The EQ-5D is a generic instrument for describing, measuring and valuing HRQoL. Its descriptive system is based on 5 dimensions of health (mobility, self-care, usual activities, pain/discomfort and anxiety/depression), each with 3 levels of severity. This simple design reflected a variety of desires, including the creation of a preference-based health index, the ability to create a common data set across countries, and use as a self-completed postal survey questionnaire.

The dimensions of EQ-5D were selected on the basis of a review of other generic HRQoL measures at that time (EuroQol Group, 1990) and the experiences of the EuroQol Group members. There was general agreement that the following dimensions be included: mobility, daily activities and self-care, psychological functioning, social and role performance, and pain or other health problems (Gudex, 1996). The selection of levels took place during Group discussions and involved on-the-spot translations by the developers for key words in all 5 languages of development (English, Dutch, Swedish, Finnish and Norwegian). The levels were designed with the aim of covering a wide range of severity and to ensure ordinality (Gudex, 1996). The first descriptive system emerged in 1988 with 6 dimensions. Following initial experimentation, a large survey of lay concepts in the UK, and further deliberation about the impact of dimensions and levels on the number of potential health states (and hence requirements for valuation), the current EQ-5D was developed (Gudex, 1996).

The EQ-5D has been used in a range of studies including population surveys, as a measure of change in patient health over time and as a measure of the impact of health interventions for use in economic analysis. In addition to the 5 countries in which it was developed, the EQ-5D is also being used extensively in the US and Canada as well as in a variety of countries in Europe, Asia, Latin America, Australasia and Africa. Its use in an increasing number of settings has led to greater questioning about what the EQ-5D is measuring in each setting. For example, translators of new language versions of the EQ-5D have asked which of a variety of words in the target language would most reflect the intention of the original EQ-5D. Users of the EQ-5D have also suggested that different groups of patients may interpret questions differently given the context of their disease (Selai, 1998a).

R. Brooks et al. (eds.),
The Measurement and Valuation of Health Status Using EQ-5D: A European Perspective, 167–182.

That an instrument like the EQ-5D may be interpreted differently is not new knowledge. However, as this may affect what is measured and valued, it is important to begin to unravel the issues of how and why meanings vary and when meanings may be shared. The aim of this chapter is to indicate the range of interpretations given to the EQ-5D using the available evidence. As issues of quantification have dominated the work of the EuroQol Group to date, the evidence is based on a disparate collection of studies, none of which had the specific aim of accessing either individuals' or groups' cognitive understanding of the whole questionnaire. However, the collection of work built up not only helps to show the range of possible interpretations and potential hypotheses for future investigation, but also serves as a useful reminder of the fluidity of language and meaning.

The chapter is structured around 3 main areas of research. The first section outlines the range of shared and differing meanings amongst EuroQol Group members. This represents a unique attempt to draw out the intended meanings of the survey questions by the original developers, in response to the need to inform the translation process of the EQ-5D. It demonstrates that, whilst there is much shared intention of the meaning of questions, even EuroQol Group members have slightly different interpretations of the questions. The second section indicates some of the reactions and thoughts that respondents had to the EQ-5D in the source language version - UK English. The third part reports examples of meanings amongst people who complete the EQ-5D in other languages[1]. It highlights some of the differences between interpretations amongst respondents and between respondents and the original developers. The discussion reflects upon the implications of the varying interpretations for the EQ-5D for the future layout of the instrument, as well as future research by the EuroQol Group and other developers of HRQoL instruments.

10.2 STUDYING INTENDED MEANING OF THE EQ-5D AMONGST EUROQOL GROUP MEMBERS

Aim and methods of the study

The investigation of the intended meaning of the EQ-5D by EuroQol Group members was undertaken for 3 reasons: the EQ-5D was going to be translated into other languages; the Group preferred a meaning-based rather than literal translation; and preferred to establish intended meaning themselves rather than relying on future translators. Given this, Larson suggests beginning with an analysis of the semantic structure of the source text (the EQ-5D), part of which involves an identification of the key words or phrases for which meaning is crucial and needs to be transferred.

---

1. In this chapter we report findings only from completed studies using an official translation. For details of issues arising during the process of translation, readers are referred to Chapter 12 of this book.

The principal advantage of this process is that "most of the implicit information is made explicit and the secondary and figurative senses eliminated" (Larson, 1984).

A self-completed questionnaire was sent to members of the EuroQol Group who had been involved during the initial stages of development (Fox-Rushby, 1997). Key terms were selected for investigation, and included: those that had proved difficult to translate (such as 'self-care', 'extreme'); terms used to categorise people's health state (both in titles and descriptors e.g. 'mobility', 'walking about'); and the centrality of an idea to understanding valuation (such as 'best/worst imaginable health state'[2]). Each person was asked to write about what they thought the EuroQol Group meant to convey by a set of words or phrases as well as whether there were any specific items meant to be included or excluded. Responses for each term were considered in relation to: the most common idea presented; stated inclusions or exclusions; the range of alternative words proposed; the existence of contrasting ideas; the level of specificity of answers; and missing responses, or responses using the same words as the original text.

Response rate and quality of data

Of the 23 questionnaires sent out, 20 were returned. Of these, 3 returned only the first page and 1 form was spoilt. The response rate for each question was high, with the exceptions of 'best/worst imaginable health state' (5 missing responses[3]), 'pain' (14 missing responses) and the last long phrase concerning health after 1 year (8 missing responses). Few alternative phrases/words were elicited for 'the state dead', 'walking about' and 'best/worst imaginable health state'. Some terms such as 'anxiety/anxious', and 'pain' elicited more detailed responses and long lists of alternative words.

2. The list of key terms/phrases inquired about included: 'walking about', 'confined to bed', 'usual activities', 'pain', 'discomfort', 'anxiety/anxious', 'depressed', 'mobility', 'unconscious', 'the state dead', 'some problems', 'moderate', 'extreme', 'health/your own health state', 'today', 'best/worst imaginable', 'a person like you', 'personal view', 'when thinking about each health state imagine that it will last for one year. What happens after that is not known and is not taken into account'.
3. Defined as completely missing, or the respondent wrote he/she was unable to think of an alternative description of the word/phrase.

Main Findings

The results highlighted 6 principal findings. First, they showed that a range of implicit and intended meanings behind the words/phrases selected did exist. For example:

(i) Anxiety/anxious is not intended to refer only to a clinically defined state.
(ii) Mobility is intended to refer to walking as well as other movement.
(iii) Walking about is not intended to mean strenuous activities or country walks.
(iv) The state dead is not intended to refer to the actual process of dying.

Second, there were particular words/phrases for which there was close agreement about meaning. For example, the majority of responses elicited for 'today' included 'this day', 'this particular calendar day', and 'current' 24 hours. One of the main surprises, given the problems in translation (see Chapter 12), included the intended meanings of 'self-care' - there was much more agreement than expected. The most common idea presented was that self-care was about washing and dressing (17 responses mentioned this, and 6 exclusively). Some specific activities noted for exclusion were social and role activities, and 1 person questioned whether continence and transfer should be included in this category. The important underlying idea of this dimension points towards independence in basic daily care activities and, whilst the level of specificity was fairly general, 3 people gave quite detailed examples (some of which are not included in the examples in the questions), such as 'hand or foot care', 'brushing teeth', and 'can wipe own bottom'.

Third, the responses also highlighted some inconsistencies in the name given to a dimension and the content of questions covered in the dimension. This was clearest for the dimension mobility, for which the main ideas presented encompassed the ability to move from one place to another and included walking, moving in a wheelchair, and driving/transport. The levels of the mobility dimension however, focus on walking. The most common responses involved 'walking about on two feet' and being able to walk without constraints (e.g. having to stop, using a wheelchair, and 'difficulties'). However, walking about for 1 person included 'any steps taken even with crutches, walking frames or support'. There were some definite exclusions given, such as 'strenuous activities', 'country walks', and 'sport' and 1 answer also excluded arm movements. Some people asked where people moving around in wheelchairs should be located on the EQ-5D, with suggestions that they would be excluded from walking without any/some difficulty (although debate during the 1996 EuroQol conference questioned whether this was appropriate).

Fourth, the results showed that EuroQol members found some ideas particularly difficult to describe. For example, 1 person said they had to make use of a dictionary to define unconscious and 14 people could only use the word 'pain' to describe 'pain'. Indeed a few people wrote about how much more difficult the exercise was than they expected. Occasionally, members raised questions about, for example, how regular 'usual activities' are meant to be (whether daily or not).

Fifth, the results showed that there were a number of contradictory views held within the Group concerning the intended meaning of parts of the EQ-5D. For example, the analysis of 'discomfort' highlighted a wide range of replies, which seemed to fall into two main categories: those that stated it was intense pain and those which included non-pain physical sensations. Group members also differed in their views about whether discomfort only concerned physical and/or psychological disturbances, whether discomfort was something which could be disregarded or not, and whether physical comfort was about how you felt about physical discomfort. Some of the ideas covered whether people were able to adapt to discomfort or not and that discomfort was not considered as intense or acute as pain. On the whole, responses tended to be very general but when people did give examples, the most frequently cited were itching, followed by pain, aches, nausea and tiredness. Others mentioned were dizziness, bloatedness, pins and needles, and ringing in the ears.

As much of the work of the EuroQol Group has focussed on quantifying levels of health and the values attached to health states, there was particular interest in the terms used to indicate degree of (dis)ability. Alternatives given for 'some problems' and 'moderate' were varied. 'Some problems' tended to be described in terms of frequency of problems rather than intensity (e.g. 'not daily', 'chronic number 1-3', 'small number', 'more than one problem', 'every now and then', and 'from one to many'), whereas others explained it in terms of how people would react ('problems which may need medical intervention', 'independent problems which do not compromise subject's ability to self-care'; 'they would be noticeable to the individual'; 'unable to perform task/activity as would wish'; 'problems do not overcrowd normal life, bearable'). The word 'moderate' elicited similar diversity in views, and it was interesting to see the diversity concerning the location of the word on the scale (e.g. 'towards lower end of pain scale', 'middling to bad', 'central tendency', 'somewhat above average'). With respect to 'extreme', 'very severe' was the most commonly used rewording, although other words used were 'very much', 'very very strong', 'a lot', and 'very high degree of'. Other indications were given to exemplify, and included 'almost intolerable', 'life almost not worth living', '100% of the problem'.

Finally, it is interesting to gain an insight into how the EuroQol Group members conceive of the notions 'best/worst imaginable health state' as these are the limit points on the EQ VAS and the EQ-5D VAS. Other words used for 'best' were: 'optimal/ideal', 'very good', 'best level', 'well', and 'most'. In describing the 'best', some applied definitions of health such as 'absence of dysfunction', 'capacity to perform', or 'fully occupied living'. Contrasting beliefs highlighted were whether or not the health state imagined was influenced by the EQ-5D itself, whether the respondent may or may not have experienced their best imaginable state, or whether it existed or not. Phrases used for 'worst' were: 'very bad'; 'alive but that's all'; 'unable to function independently in all areas of life'; 'as bad as it is possible to be'; 'presence of all dysfunction in human system compatible with life'; 'and serious limiting consequences'. One response gave notably vivid examples for worst imaginable health state: 'meningococcus septic shock, big bullae, losing your skin, extreme pain, knowing you will die in 4-5 hours'.

Response to findings

These findings were discussed at the EuroQol Group's 1996 plenary conference in Oslo and used to gain consensus on intended meanings to help in the translation process and for assessing the semantic equivalence of source and target questionnaires. The main product of this process was the development of an outline defining the concepts of the EQ-5D considered to be key by the EuroQol Group (see Appendix 7). As the EQ-5D was developed for self-completion, this document should *not* be given to respondents. The document is primarily intended for researchers and translators of the EQ-5D to help in the choice of the most appropriate words in another language, but it was recognised that it may also contribute to an explanatory background for EQ-5D application studies. It should also be noted that the document is liable to change as the EuroQol Group learns from experience.

10.3 INTERPRETATIONS OF THE EQ-5D AMONGST PEOPLE WHO HAVE COMPLETED THE QUESTIONNAIRE IN UK ENGLISH WITHIN THE UNITED KINGDOM

The recommended steps to be taken in the development of any new questionnaire, or scale, are now well documented in the literature (Juniper *et al*, 1996). One important stage is a piece of qualitative research where items are tested on a sample of respondents who are encouraged to tell the interviewer what that question or item *meant* to them and what they were considering before replying. This process is sometimes known as 'cognitive debriefing', and it is now an obligatory part of the EuroQol translation protocol (see Chapter 11). By contrast, it is of interest that relatively little formal cognitive debriefing was undertaken in the early development of the EQ-5D. This perhaps partly explains why, as described above, the survey of EuroQol Group members showed a number of inconsistencies in the intended content of the questions covered in the EQ-5D dimensions.

Although very little research was designed with the explicit goal of exploring the meaning of the UK English EQ-5D in the UK, some qualitative data have been collected and reported by EuroQol Group members (see Table 10.1). These data have usually been elicited incidentally, when questions and comments arose during the administration of a study using the EQ-5D. In this section, we summarise a selection of key findings from these studies, grouped by dimension of the EQ-5D and exemplified by respondents. The findings do not represent a comprehensive survey but are interesting both in themselves and as a backdrop to the work on translations and cross-cultural comparison of EQ-5D data.

Table 10.1. UK-based studies, by EuroQol Group members, collecting qualitative data alongside the EQ-5D

Sample characteristics	References
A microstudy of 40 patients, 23 of whom completed the EQ-5D descriptive system, EQ VAS and the EQ-5D valuation task.	Selai and Rosser, 1995a
43 members of the general population who completed the EQ-5D valuation task using VAS and TTO and were willing to be re-interviewed	Robinson *et al*, 1997
A total of 270 epilepsy patients: 125 patients starting new anti-epileptic drugs; 145 patients being considered for definitive surgical treatment for epilepsy. All completed the EQ-5D descriptive system & EQ VAS.	Selai, 1997 Selai *et al*, 1999 Selai *et al*, 2000b
A study of 35 patients with dementia and their carers completing the EQ-5D descriptive system & EQ VAS.	Selai *et al*, 2000a
Ongoing studies of various students completing the EQ-5D descriptive system, EQ VAS and EQ-5D valuation task.	Selai, 2000c

Mobility

The level 'some' covers a broad range of health-related phenomena. In a study of patients with neurological conditions, patients with Parkinson's disease suggested that 'some' problems in walking about covers the whole range from slight tremor to walking with a stick to a patient who is wheel-chair bound (Selai, 1995b). A number of patients with epilepsy hesitated in answering this question because they said they did not have a physical problem with walking but they liked or needed someone to accompany them (Selai, 1997). Other health-related problems considered in this dimension were problems with balance, dizziness, unpredictability of seizures, tiredness, and epilepsy-related migraines.

Self-Care

Some patients hesitated when answering this question because they could (physically) wash themselves but were not allowed to take a bath alone (Selai, 1997). Other problems considered were urinary incontinence (a frequent problem with some types of seizures) and being wired up in hospital (monitoring of seizures and other behaviour known as 'telemetry').

Usual Activities

There are a number of problems with this dimension as many patients and carers are unsure about what is meant by usual activities. It has been especially difficult in situations:

(i) Where slow deterioration in health is occurring (e.g. dementia) so that it is no longer clear what 'usual' means. In a recent study, patients with dementia and their carers said that the patient had often had to give up work because of dementia, sometimes weeks or even months before the interview (Selai, 1998a). So is work a 'usual' activity?

(ii) In cases of chronic illness where the patient has adapted. For example, if epilepsy has caused unemployment for many years (or if the patient has never worked) then is their health condition causing a problem with 'usual activities'? One might argue that the answer is "yes" if the patient is being compared to other adults of a similar age (Selai, 1995b).

Patients interviewed in hospital whilst being monitored with a view to undergoing definitive surgical treatment for intractable epilepsy were thinking of a range of things when answering questions in this dimension (Selai, 1997). These included sports, housework and other daily activities, feelings of apathy, the fact of just having had a seizure, memory problems, feeling slowed down, not being able to bend over, having an epileptic aura (a warning that a seizure is imminent), finding the right word and the impact of this on conversation, blurred vision, and the need to be accompanied when going out.

Pain/Discomfort

On the whole, this dimension has been straightforward. Occasional comments from patients have concerned whether 'tension' or 'boredom' should be included here. Epilepsy patients interviewed in hospital (Selai, 1997) mentioned that they were thinking of a range of things including pain in the back after a seizure, 'feeling funny' as a result of taking new medication, pain related to falls, mouth bitten to pieces, arm out of socket, pins and needles, and feelings of tension. Many patients also mentioned headaches and migraine. Other comments concerned co-morbid conditions e.g. wisdom teeth, stomach-ache, rheumatism, stomach pain and sickness, menstrual pain and 'feeling heavy'.

Anxiety/Depression

Some problems appear to arise because this dimension combines 2 items. Some patients with epilepsy wanted to make it clear that they were anxious but not depressed (possibly due to the stigma of depression) (Selai, 1995b; OHanlon and Buxton, 1993). One epilepsy patient had difficulty deciding because he/she was "mentally better but physically the same" whilst a patient with Parkinson's disease was "mentally better but physically worse"(Selai, 1995b).

Of the epilepsy patients interviewed in hospital, 12 out of 57 mentioned being anxious or depressed about hospitalisation, being anxious about the future, and the risks and outcome of major surgery. Some comments suggested the patients were undergoing an existential re-appraisal with the patients thinking about what had happened over the last few years and thoughts about their family and loved ones (e.g. "if brain surgery goes wrong what will happen to my kids?"). Comments indicated that patients were also thinking about other things e.g. the menopause, lack of confidence at work, memory problems and their traumatic divorce (complicated by a battle for custody of their children).

Understanding the meaning of level 2

A small study was conducted to look at how people understand the meaning of level 2 (the middle level) in each dimension (Selai, 1998b). In this task, the respondents (n=100) were asked to scale the middle level of each of the EQ-5D dimensions against the endpoints (the wording used in that particular dimension). Although we might hypothesise that the middle level would always fall halfway between 0-100 i.e. at 50, this was not the case. In this study, the mean score of level 2 was always higher than 50 (range 51.50 to 79.75) and there were significant differences between the mean scores per dimensions. It was hypothesised that there might be different 'thresholds' with a respondent only indicating a problem on the EQ-5D if it is quite considerable. The results suggest that the EQ-5D does not have *interval* scale measurement. As discussed in the paper, the findings clearly have implications for the valuation and modelling techniques.

Rating own health between 'best'/'worst imaginable health state'

Patients are not always clear what is meant by the concept 'health'. They often have a concept of general 'fitness' and this is seen as quite separate from their health or disease condition (Selai, 1996). Patients with epilepsy, for example, see their health, which many describe as 'good', as distinct from their seizures which might be infrequent (Selai, 1995b). Patients with rheumatoid arthritis (OHanlon & Buxton, 1993) gave similar comments.

Patients and carers can have difficulty giving 1 score on the EQ VAS because it is difficult to condense everything, including health, family and social life into a single number (Selai, 1995b). In a study of the HRQoL of patients with dementia, respondents (patients and their carers) found difficulties completing the EQ VAS. In particular, they wanted to give separate scores for 'mental' and 'physical' well-being (Selai, 1998a; Sela *et al*, 2000a). Patients with epilepsy also said it was difficult to give a score taking into account "the occasional effect of an epileptic fit" (Selai, 1995b).

The anchor points on the EQ VAS (best/worst imaginable health state) raise particular problems. One epilepsy patient asked of the scale "is this compared to *me* on another day or the average man on the street?" Another patient said "I'll put myself half-way down the scale because I am normal" (Selai, 1995b). A further patient asked of the label 'best imaginable health state', "what does this mean; is this like a top athlete?" In a study of patients before and after surgical treatment for epilepsy, 42% of patients said that they thought that 'health' did not include their epilepsy. These patients said that if the EQ VAS score was to include their epilepsy, they would have given a score up to 70 points lower on the EQ VAS.

In the same study of epilepsy patients, another patient said: "Shall I put 100% because I feel fine? Well, I'd better put 80%" (Selai, 1995b). Other patients in this study said they had many problems but decided to adjust the score and rate the EQ VAS as 70, writing "because millions of people are worse off than me". In each of these cases, the original score would appear to have been adjusted taking into account some additional information. A related issue is that of coping mechanisms, particularly in cases of chronic illness. In a study of in-patients in a London teaching hospital, where most patients were seriously (some terminally) ill, it is of interest that many rated their health state as 'fairly good' on the EQ-5D descriptive system (Selai and Rosser, 1995a).

EQ-5D VAS Valuation task

Robinson *et al*, 1997 questioned respondents about their thinking when valuing EQ-5D health states using the EQ-5D VAS and TTO. Part of their analysis showed that 29 out of 43 respondents rated health states differently in relation to the state dead depending on whether the EQ-5D VAS or TTO valuation method was used. They concluded that, of the 29 respondents, many did not appear to keep the intended time scale[4] in mind when making their valuations using the EQ-5D VAS, whereas all 29 had mentioned the time scale consistently using TTO. They also found respondents treated 'immediate death' differently on the TTO and EQ-5D VAS; some (n=14) automatically put death at the bottom of the scale because "it had to be" or because it is the "final event" in people's lives. They also showed that 12 out of 43 respondents interpreted the EQ-5D VAS as percentage scores of fitness and 7 out of 43 respondents mentioned the effect of a health state on their family when making their valuations.

10.4 INTERPRETATIONS OF THE EQ-5D AMONGST PEOPLE WHO HAVE COMPLETED THE QUESTIONNAIRE IN OTHER LANGUAGES:

To date there have been 2 studies that have investigated aspects of respondents' views following completion of the EQ-5D in other languages[5]. Busschbach *et al* presented their observations on 105 students from the Netherlands filling in the EQ-5D (Busschbach *et al*, 1993). More recently, Pedersen *et al* investigated whether 144 people in Denmark perceived certain EQ-5D dimensions in the same way. They also looked at the ordinal scale properties of selected EQ-5D dimensions (Pedersen *et al*, 2000). With the exception of a question focussing on anxiety and depression, the studies were completely different and hence are reported separately.

Busschbach *et al* commented on a range of aspects including the instructions to respondents, labelling of scales, and approaches respondents used in making their valuations[6]. Most notably, they highlighted a number of mistakes made by respondents, for example:

"One of the most striking mistakes was the interpretation of the label 'best imaginable health state' which is located above the calibrated line and the interpretation of the instruction 'Remember we want you to indicate how good or bad each of these states would be for a person like you'. Sixteen students thought that the aim was to indicate how well one could imagine being in that health state themselves. Since most students have never been in a bad state, they found it difficult to imagine the bad health states" (Busschbach *et al*, 1993)."

---

4. In this study, the time scale was 10 years for all health states.
5. This excludes the results of findings from translation exercises that are presented in more detail in Chapter 12 and in the results of research on the EQ-5D outside Europe (Chapter 13).
6. When this questionnaire was administered, death was valued as a health state within the valuation exercise. We do not report the qualitative results here because the current EQ-5D VAS valuation task values death relative to health states by drawing a line across the scale or implicitly through the TTO technique.

While all students did eventually complete the exercise correctly (through self-correction (n=7) or interviewer correction (n=9)), there was particular concern about what happens in practice with a self-completed questionnaire and a less well educated audience. A second difference between the expectations of researchers and actions of students was exemplified in their use of the instruction 'When thinking about each health state imagine that it will last for one year. What happens after that is not known and should not be taken into account.' Of the total number of students, 34.5% remembered the instruction about the time being 'for 1 year'. Of the remaining students, 28% thought of 'a chronic state', 25% 'a period longer than 1 year, without clear boundaries', 8% thought of no time period at all, and 8% thought either in terms of months, weeks or days. Busschbach *et al* also observed the kind of strategy students used when completing the valuation task. They found that 54% valued states in the left column and then the right column, 14% valued one state from the left and then right (like reading a book), 9% ranked states first prior to placing them on the scale, 9% chose the best and the worst first, and for 13% the strategy wasn't clear (Busschbach *et al*, 1993).

Pedersen *et al*, (2000) first asked respondents about their personal interpretation of the following words/phrases: walking about, confined to bed, self-care, pain, discomfort, moderate pain, extreme pain, anxiety, moderate anxiety, extreme anxiety, depression, moderately depressed, and extremely depressed. Second, they asked respondents to give examples of moderate and extreme pain, anxiety and depression. Within the mobility dimension, they found that 52% and 64% of respondents interpreted 'walking about' and 'confined to bed' as intended[7]. Only 23% of respondents specifically mentioned walking about 'inside and outside', and around 10% of respondents talked very generally about what it meant to them to be able to walk about or be confined to bed. 73% of respondents interpreted self-care as expected and none interpreted it to include social or role activities.

'Pain' and 'discomfort' were asked about separately and elicited both similar and different ideas. Pain was defined by 32% as being more than 'hurt' or 'ache', with a further 9% saying it would require a painkiller. Respondents drew out issues of duration (for example saying a 'stab' of pain would not count as pain) and intensity, and noted it was a relative concept that required an 'anchor-point' from which to judge it. 15% considered it as something unpleasant and 7% saw it in both somatic and mental terms (Pedersen *et al*, 2000). The examples given to describe discomfort included nausea/vomiting (21%), pain/ache/hangover (24%), and general feelings of being unwell (more than 25%).

The findings regarding differentiations between 'moderate' and 'extreme' are interesting. For both pain and discomfort, 'extreme' was described more often in

7. Judged by comparing responses to the outline in Appendix 7.

terms of being of longer duration and intensity compared with 'moderate', but in 10% of cases this position was reversed. Of the sample, 60% were able to give examples of both 'moderate' and 'extreme pain', but 22% did not give an example of 'moderate' pain and 36% did not exemplify 'extreme pain'.

Finally, it is interesting to turn to the example of the anxiety/depression dimension as the 1 area studied by both research groups in the Netherlands and Denmark. Busschbach *et al* asked the students if they saw this psychological dimension as dependent or independent of the physical dimensions. They found that 49% viewed it as independent, 35% as dependent and that 17% didn't know (Busschbach *et al*, 1993). The findings of Pedersen *et al* would appear to argue more strongly for anxiety/depression being independent of physical concepts. For example, anxiety was described in terms of being apprehensive, anxious about others, worried, nervous, depressed and uncertain/restless. Depression was more frequently described in terms of being sorry/unhappy about something, feeling 'down', negative or 'low', unable to concentrate or think, feeling isolated or cut off and being in a bad mood. Of the respondents, 11% mentioned something related to a psychiatric condition or needing medical help. In terms of the differentiation between moderate and extreme, 'extreme' was more likely to be regarded as having a higher intensity, being of longer duration, having a psychiatric diagnosis and needing medical treatment. However, 10% did not hold this ordinal view and 22% were unable to give examples for both moderate and extreme levels (Pedersen *et al*, 2000).

10.5 DISCUSSION

This collection of research findings from qualitative investigations in a range of studies gives some indication of the variety of intentions and interpretations of the EQ-5D by the developers and respondents. With respect to the intentions of the developers the findings suggest that there may be more agreement on the purpose and implicit exclusions of the dimension 'self-care' than for 'discomfort'. Whilst many of the intended implicit meanings may not be a surprise to members of the EuroQol Group, they are not ideas which are readily accessible by researchers outside the Group. The exposure of implicit understandings can facilitate understanding of what the EQ-5D is trying to measure and as different types of information are held explicitly or implicitly in different languages, a semantic re-write may improve translation decisions made in other languages.

It is also interesting to note the direct questions raised by EuroQol Group members about what activities were included under 'mobility' and the differences in opinion concerning the meaning of 'some' and 'moderate' in level 2 of each dimension. In one sense this is surprising, as the Group has worked together on the instrument since 1987, is familiar with the same literature, and shares characteristics such as a similar level of education. However, there are several other reasons such variation would be expected: the view of a group is likely to change over time; asking individuals to think of the group view is likely to produce variety; group members will hold different views individually which reflect personal experiences of life, and an instrument developed by a group will represent a compromise of opinions; some people said they had been influenced by the interpretation of people completing the EQ-5D whilst others may have been influenced by more regular use of alternative language versions; and, studies of meaning will always uncover the ambiguities of language.

Showing the similarities and differences of intended meaning amongst EuroQol Group members was useful in drawing up Appendix 7, which clarified several aspects of implicit exclusions in the minds of the developers that would not normally be available to translators. At the same time it provides a basis from which semantic equivalence can at least be judged partially during the translation process. It was also useful in highlighting differences in the views of developers - and that any process of translation reliant on different or specific people within the group may result in very different or specific interpretations of questions and hence future translations. It is also interesting to reflect on which concepts were considered 'key' by the developers and how sufficient this view is likely to be, given the increasing world-wide translation of the EQ-5D. For example, Fox-Rushby *et al* reviewed and discussed a different range of concepts inherent to 4 health state valuation techniques[8] (including conceptions of the future, perceptions of time, life and death, and the nature of individual choice) in addition to the model of health represented (Fox-Rushby *et al*, 2000). Perhaps in the future the EuroQol Group needs to consider an even broader set of implicit meanings behind the survey questionnaire.

Whilst it is important that researchers are clear about what they want to measure, it is equally important that the interpretations of respondents who complete questionnaires are understood. Whilst Appendix 7 may be helpful in clarifying the intended meaning of parts of the EQ-5D, it says nothing about how the instrument is likely to be interpreted in practice. With the noticeable exception of Pedersen *et al* (2000), to date, very few researchers have set out with the specific aim of collecting qualitative data to ascertain how respondents understand the meaning of questions asked in the EQ-5D[9]. Indeed, it is unusual to see such information reported for generic HRQoL instruments. Qualitative data have most often been reported as incidental data and we have noticed that some qualitative data presented at EuroQol Plenary Meetings were not included in subsequently published papers. Those that have been published tend to represent the research interests of individual members of

8. Including the TTO, SG, EQ-5D VAS and PTO.
9. Much of the data from non-English language versions arises from the translation process and whilst this is interesting there are 2 problems. First the information does not always refer to the final official version produced. Second the data is collected from very few people (as the requirements from the EuroQol Group have changed over time).

the EuroQol Group and hence there is an unusual mix of populations that leaves many disease areas, interventions and countries untouched by this area of work. The findings (which show a range of interpretations given to aspects of the EQ-5D in English, Dutch and Danish) are therefore better discussed in terms of testing future hypotheses.

Our findings show that some interpretations of the EQ-5D by respondents appear to accord with the Group's intentions and some do not. For example, in asking about ability to walk without problems or wash/dress oneself, respondents have hesitated and questioned the intended meaning. In both cases this hesitation appeared to be partially related to their or another's expectations of a future adverse event, thus showing that respondents do not always think only of the time period 'today'. That respondents think of other time periods when valuing the health states was well demonstrated by Busschbach *et al*, 1993 and Robinson *et al*, 1997. However, whether this finding holds for all populations is unknown and remains untested. If there were systematic differences, it could conceivably account for variation in the valuation of health states.

The evidence to date also points to wide ranges in interpreting the meaning of levels within each dimension. It suggests that different people with the same degree of (im)mobility may classify themselves differently and value the same condition differently. Perhaps of most concern is the findings of Pedersen *et al* (2000) that between 25-35% of people were unable to exemplify different levels of severity in pain/discomfort and anxiety/depression and that 10% of people did not appear to believe in the ordinality of levels within dimensions. Given the work on inconsistencies (Ohinmaa and Sintonen, 1999) it would appear to be very important that qualitative and quantitative data collection is collected together in the future. This would facilitate the assessment of whether the same people are the cause of inconsistencies, and to find out why.

It is interesting to note some similarities in the concerns of the EuroQol Group members and respondents. For example, there do seem to be commonly perceived difficulties with the expression 'usual activities'. Whilst the EuroQol Group members wondered how frequent 'usual' meant, the patient groups were particularly concerned about whether 'usual' meant before or since their illness. This links partially to how people adapt to chronic illness over time. The more people adapt or accept their illness, the more likely they are to view their state of being as usual, and the less likely they are to record being unable to do their normal activities. The most extreme example of this might be where a person defines his/her usual activity as being ill. Such a person could define themselves logically as having no problems with usual activities. The extent to which this exists for the EQ-5D is unknown, but again it would be an empirically testable hypothesis. We would suggest at least investigating whether interpretations are likely to vary systematically by disease group and age. If this is proven, and it is not what the EuroQol Group intends, it would provide a clear case for changing 1 of the EQ-5D dimensions and/or levels.

The difficulties raised by patients completing the question on anxiety/depression highlight the possibility of people wanting to give socially desirable answers - a common problem with survey instruments (Streiner and Norman, 1995). This raises broader questions of the extent to which there are gaps between what the respondent thinks in reality and what is recorded on a survey. It is also well-documented in the psychology literature that there is often a 'gap' between understanding an item, choosing how to respond, and the answer that actually gets recorded by the respondent (Donovan *et al*, 1993). It is important to assess whether the EQ-5D is likely to suffer from these differences in any systematic way. Is there likely to be a systematic difference in the way that social groups consider what is a socially acceptable answer? If so, this might be an explanatory factor that is currently excluded from existing measurement and models of valuations. It may, for example, lead to an over- or under-explanation of between-country differences in the measurement and valuation of health states.

Our main recommendations for further research include first, broadening the range of methods used to investigate meaning. For example, adopting the full range of methods under the CASM (cognitive assessment of survey methods) approach (see, for example, Jobe and Mingay, 1989; Stone *et al* 2000). Second, we recommend broadening the base of investigations to include a wider range of countries and disease groups. Third, we recommend that quantitative and qualitative methods are used alongside each other to investigate the relationship between interpretations of words and scales and valuations of health, in relation to socio-economic, demographic and geographic variables. Finally, we consider it important that this research is undertaken in a way to maximise the comparability of findings, and that this requires planning from the outset.

11
Producing other language versions of the EQ-5D

Michael Herdman, Julia Fox-Rushby, Rosalind Rabin, Xavier Badia and Caroline Selai

11.1 INTRODUCTION

The measurement and valuation of HRQoL is increasingly important as a measure of the impact of disease and the outcomes of treatment from the patient's point of view. A plethora of questionnaires have been developed to measure HRQoL, and these questionnaires are frequently translated for use in languages other than the original. Questionnaires are adapted for various reasons, sometimes to be able to compare or aggregate results obtained in different countries, and sometimes to provide a measure in a given cultural setting where none existed before. When data are to be compared or aggregated across countries it is especially important to ensure that equivalence between translated versions is assessed (Herdman *et al*, 1998). This requires close attention to the way in which health status and HRQoL measures are developed and adapted for use in different countries. Ideally, before beginning to adapt a questionnaire the extent to which a questionnaire's content appropriately reflects local concepts of health and quality of life should also be determined.

Various recommendations and guidelines have been produced within the HRQoL field that aim to ensure some degree of equivalence is assessed between different language versions of the same measure (Guillemin *et al*, 1993; Keller *et al*, 1998; Gandek and Ware *et al*, 1995; Bullinger *et al*, 1998). Many of these guidelines emphasise the need for a relatively elaborate process of forward and back translation complemented by panel discussion and patient testing. An alternative, perhaps more sophisticated (and certainly more labour intensive), approach to the development of HRQoL measures for use in international settings is that exemplified by the development of the World Health Organisation Quality Of Life questionnaire, or WHOQOL (Sartorius and Kuyken, 1994; WHO, 1994; WHOQOL Group, 1998). In this case, the instrument was developed simultaneously in various national settings, which permitted an exploration of the extent to which elements or facets of HRQoL were common to the various countries involved in its development. Although such an approach offers intriguing possibilities in terms of justifying the cross-cultural content validity of the measure, it is an approach which at present is probably beyond the means of many, and the most common approach to the cross-cultural measurement of HRQoL remains that of adapting existing instruments.

The international development of the EQ-5D (Brooks *et al*, 1996) has to some extent combined these 2 approaches. The early versions of the instrument were originally

R. Brooks et al. (eds.),
The Measurement and Valuation of Health Status Using EQ-5D: A European Perspective, 183–189.

developed by researchers from 5 European countries, in a process which allowed researchers from all of those countries to contribute to the instrument's content and design. However, as demand for the instrument grew in countries where no language version of the instrument existed, it became necessary to develop and implement translation procedures which would ensure a certain degree of rigour when translating the instrument for use outside the original group of languages.

The purpose of the present chapter is to review the way in which international versions of the EQ-5D have been produced to date; to present and review the latest version of the translation Standard Operating Procedures (SOPS), which have been produced as part of the recent EQ-net project; and to describe the current status of EQ-5D in terms of existing language versions.

11.2 TRANSLATING THE EQ-5D: A BRIEF HISTORY

The EQ-5D was initially developed as a joint effort by researchers from Finland, the Netherlands, Norway, Sweden and the UK (EuroQol Group, 1990), the aim being to produce an instrument which included a 'common core' of content related to self-perceived health status which would "capture the key descriptive elements in which everybody was likely to be interested, not to create an exhaustive system for descriptors which would serve all purposes". This was done initially through meetings and by asking the original group members to "circulate instruments they were likely to be using up to 1990, as a way of indicating interest in particular aspects of health" (Fox-Rushby *et al*, 1996). The original version of the instrument measured health in 6 dimensions with 2 or 3 levels of severity in each dimension. This version was later reduced to 5 dimensions and the number of levels of severity was standardised to 3 in each dimension.

As the working language of the EuroQol Group is English, the original version of the EuroQol instrument (EQ-6D) was designed in English but "tempered by discussion in Swedish, Norwegian, Dutch and Finnish" (Fox-Rushby *et al*, 1996) alongside discussions of whether the researchers felt that concepts, described using English words, would be perceived differently and could be translated into their languages. Following the development of the English version in this way, researchers translated (often with assistance from professional translators) the EQ-6D questionnaire into their own languages.

In 1992, researchers from Spain became involved in the Group, and the instrument was translated and validated in Spanish and Catalan. The Spanish version was produced using what was, by then, becoming the standard methodology in the HRQoL field, i.e. the process of forward and back translation, followed by testing of the translated versions on a panel of members from the target population. In this respondent testing stage in the Spanish version, participants were asked for the first time to provide ratings of clarity, use of colloquial language, and the appropriateness of the questionnaire content. These aspects were all rated on a scale from 1 to 10 (Badia *et al*, 1995a).

At about this time, the Group became aware of the need to standardise the methodology and procedures used to produce translated versions of the instrument. The procedures used to produce the Spanish and Catalan versions of the EQ-5D served as a model for draft translation guidelines developed by Group members between 1994 and 1995. The essential features of these initial draft guidelines, which have remained in place over the years, are:

(i) The production of 2 (non-literal) forward translations by 2 translators working independently.
(ii) Forward translators should be native speakers of the target language but fluent in English, and at least 1 of the forward translators should be a professional translator.
(iii) Production of a first consensus version is based on combining the 2 forward translations in a meeting between translators and the research team.
(iv) Production of 2 back translations from the first consensus version.
(v) Back translations produced by 2 professional translators working independently, although in this case the translators should be native English speakers who are fluent in the target language.
(vi) Testing of the final version of the questionnaire in a small number of potential respondents to determine clarity, acceptability and relevance.

In 1995, a similar methodology was used to produce French and German versions from the English version. Since that time, versions of the EQ-5D have been produced which are suitable for use in 63 different countries (see Table 11.1). Forty-one language versions have received official status[1] whilst 22 are expected to receive official status in 2002.

The Group's growing awareness of the importance of translation issues also led to efforts to determine the extent to which the earliest language versions of the instrument (Dutch, Finnish, Norwegian and Swedish), produced before the development of translation procedures, are semantically equivalent to the standard English version (see Chapter 12). In 1998 at the Group's annual Plenary Meeting in Hannover, minor changes were agreed for the UK English version and accordingly in the other ver-

---

1. Official status is assigned to translations which have been approved by the EuroQol Translation Committee based on a review of all of the documentation produced during a given translation process. In order to be assigned official status the local translating team should have closely followed the guidelines included in Appendices 8, 9 and 10, and the EuroQol Group review team should be agreed that the content of the translated version is as similar as possible to that of the UK English version. Copies of the translation reports are available from the EuroQol Business Management on request.

sions available at that time. This illustrates the evolutionary nature of the development of the EQ-5D itself and the development of language versions, with updates being performed to keep abreast of changes introduced within the instrument over time.

Table 11.1 EQ-5D Language versions: June 2002

EQ-5D official language versions		*EQ-5D "best available" language versions (awaiting official status)*
Afrikaans Bulgarian Catalan Croatian Czech Danish Dutch (for Belgium & the Netherlands) English (for Australia, Canada, New Zealand, South Africa, UK (includes Ireland), USA) Finnish French (for Belgium, Canada, France, Switzerland) German (for Austria, Germany, Switzerland) Greek	Hungarian Italian Japanese Norwegian Polish Portuguese Rusian Spanish (for Argentina, Colombia, Costa Rica, Guatemala, Mexico, Peru, Spain, USA, Venezuela) Swedish Turkish	Armenian Basque Chinese (for China, Hong Kong, Singapore, Taiwan) English (for Singapore) Estonian Hebrew Icelandic Korean Latvian Lithuanian Portuguese (for Brazil) Romanian Russian (for Israel) Shona (for Zimbabwe) Slovakian Slovenian Spanish (for Chile & Uruguay) Xhosa (for South Africa)

The initial draft translation guidelines have evolved gradually into a set of SOPS for translation (Appendices 8, 9 and 10), the production of which was one of the milestones in the EQ-net project. These SOPS are now provided to all researchers interested in producing new language versions, and are designed to ensure a standardised approach to translation and better quality translations.

The latest version of the translation SOPS has incorporated some innovations. In particular, feedback from an increasing number of translation processes indicated that it would be helpful to provide explanations of a number of key words and phrases used in the instrument. A first step towards gaining some insight into the interpretations EuroQol Group members intended for key words and phrases was to circulate a questionnaire asking members for their own interpretations. The results of this exercise have been described in (more) detail in Chapter 10. A number of the interpretations provided by that exercise are now included as part of the translation package sent to researchers interested in producing new versions of the EQ-5D (see Chapter 10 and Appendix 7).

In order to provide some control over the quality of translations produced, and to standardise the process used, regular contact between local researchers translating the EQ-5D and members of the EuroQol Group is sought. Group members involved in the translation process review each stage of the process, provide help and suggestions to the local translation team, ensure that the reports produced contain all relevant information, and generally ensure that the translation guidelines are followed as closely as possible. Once any changes have been discussed with at least one member of the Group, and any differences have been harmonised and incorporated into the local version, that version is tested in 8 respondents from the target country (Appendix 9). Local research teams are informed that not following the guidelines will mean that the version will not be assigned 'official status'. This means effectively that the Group will not be able to vouch for the quality of the translation process and hence any data obtained with that version. To help in the translation process, local research teams are provided with a copy of an earlier report which met the Group's criteria for the process required in translation.

When it is necessary to produce variants of existing language versions, for example, variants of the Castillian Spanish version for use in Mexico or Argentina, or variants of the French and German versions for use in Switzerland, a different set of guidelines have been used (Appendix 10). In such cases, the closest and most appropriate language version is used as a starting point for the adaptation (for example Castillian Spanish for Argentina) and is reviewed by the local research team and at least 1 linguist in the target country, to determine whether any changes are needed. Once any such changes have been discussed with at least 1 member of the Group, and any differences have been harmonised and incorporated into the local version, that version is tested in 5 respondents from the target country.

11.3 QUALITY CONTROL

To ensure the thoroughness of the translation process, the reports produced during the translation process are reviewed by at least 2 members of a translation review team, who make a recommendation as to whether the version should be granted official status. The final decision rests with the Translation Committee, who might ask for certain points to be clarified before deciding that a given language version will be the Group's official version. Versions which are produced without the cognisance of Group members are not likely to be awarded official status. A version completed in cooperation with the Group and following the Group's translation guidelines may however be used as 'the best available version', while awaiting official ratification by the Translation Committee.

From early in the process of developing international versions of the EQ-5D, the Group has required documented information regarding the process followed, the details of the people involved, and the nature of any problems arising during the translation process, together with information on the way the problems were resolved. This not only provides a record of the translation process, but also a means of determining whether translation difficulties may play a part in any discrepancies arising in the measurement or valuation of health using translated versions. This aspect of the translation process is dealt with in more detail in Chapter 12. Currently a further rating sheet is being developed to record the degree of semantic equivalence achieved between the UK version and the new language version according to the perceptions of the local translation team.

The type of translation process set out here aims, at best, to achieve semantic equivalence between versions, and specifically with the original UK English version (Herdman *et al*, 1998). Whether or not the translated version will be equally reliable, valid and sensitive to change, whether the levels will measure equivalent levels of function or dysfunction, and whether or not respondents will respond similarly to the levels, can only be tested more fully when the translated version is used in relatively large samples. Moreover, there is obviously no guarantee that the translated version will adequately reflect local concepts of health and/or QoL (Guyatt, 1993), though this is an issue which should be dealt with before deciding whether it is appropriate to translate an existing HRQoL questionnaire, and if so whether the EQ-5D is appropriate for use in a given cultural setting. At the same time, it can be argued that all generic HRQoL instruments fall somewhat short of adequately reflecting health and/or QoL, because of the need to reduce a complex concept to a relatively small number of written items.

These issues are becoming more prominent as the EQ-5D (and other HRQoL instruments), is translated into other languages and where researchers seek to access respondents' understanding and views about the questions. For example the translation of the EQ-5D into Shona (one of the official languages of Zimbabwe, see Chapter 13), showed that although the EQ-5D was deemed to be suitable for translation and use in Shona, it soon became apparent that some of the concepts described by the EQ-5D "do not sit comfortably in the Shona worldview" (Jelsma *et al*, 2000a). For example, expressions such as 'I am confined to bed' prove problematic because statements of this type require an agent "who .... has confined the person to bed" and at the same time "not everyone sleeps in a bed". The combination of these 2 factors meant it was impossible to use a direct translation of the original level and the local researchers had to use an expression meaning "I cannot even walk at all". Finally, on another level the emphasis in Shona culture on humility meant that describing oneself as having no problems at all in dimensions such as 'self-care' or claiming to be in the 'best imaginable health state' would be viewed as being extremely arrogant, and these expressions had necessarily to be softened for inclusion in the Shona version of the EQ-5D (Jelsma *et al*, 2000a).

11.4 CONCLUSIONS

The development of new language versions of the EQ-5D reflects the development of the area of cross-cultural adaptation and development in the HRQoL field in general. The EuroQol Group has used a combination of methods, including the development of an initial version of the instrument which relied on simultaneous input of content from researchers in several European countries. From the early stages in the development of the instrument, the Group has provided translation SOPS which are based on internationally recommended guidelines, and which have permitted a considerable amount of control to be retained as regards the quality of the translation process. Though the guidelines aim towards producing translated versions that are semantically equivalent to the original version, local researchers should also be aware of the need to test the new version's measurement properties of reliability, validity and sensitivity to change. They should also be aware that the content and assumptions of the instrument (that, for example, respondents will be capable of responding to a visual analogue scale) may not be equally relevant in all languages and that the examination of an instrument's cross-cultural validity is a complex and on-going process. In the case of the EQ-5D the analysis of similarities and differences between values obtained for EQ-5D health states in different cultural settings may be used (alongside careful qualitative research) not only to determine whether there are differences in values between respondents in different countries, but also as a further check on the extent to which meaning has been transmitted successfully between languages (Johnson *et al*, 2000a; Badia *et al*, 2001).

12
Exploring the results of translating the EQ-5D into 11 European languages

Rosalind Rabin, Michael Herdman,
Julia Fox-Rushby and Xavier Badia

12.1 INTRODUCTION

One of the 3 principal aims of the EQ-net project was to increase the number of European translations of the EQ-5D. An early requirement of anyone undertaking translations was the production of a series of reports at different stages for review by at least 2 members of the EuroQol Group Translation Committee (see Appendices 8-10). This was considered an important part of ensuring consideration of semantic equivalence between source and target versions of the EQ-5D and has provided an unusual opportunity to examine the results of the translation process[1]. Such information is rarely written up in the international field of health outcomes assessment so it is hoped that the information provided here will be helpful to other researchers working in the HRQoL field.

The aims of this study were modest, given the available resources, and focussed primarily on highlighting problems encountered during the translation process with a view to examining how satisfactorily they were resolved and to consider any potential effect on valuations. For example, how comparable are back translations and the original forward translations? If a word is back translated as 'very' instead of 'extreme' or as 'daily' instead of 'usual', does it make a difference? Can these kinds of differences affect what is measured and valued and if so, how should similarities and differences in measurements and valuations of HRQoL between countries be interpreted? These issues are important, as researchers need to be confident of the comparability of the content of health questionnaires used in different countries if results are to be compared. This chapter moves cautiously towards examining these questions using the limited evidence available. The first section describes which language versions were selected and how they were reviewed. The results section focusses on how the main differences between the UK English and target language versions were resolved and whether any between-country differences in values might be attributed to decisions taken in the translation process, while the discussion evaluates such evidence, as well as suggesting future research that might be carried out by the EuroQol Group and other developers of HRQoL instruments.

---

1. Bowden and Fox-Rushby (2001) have shown that, of the translation/adaptation guidelines for 7 generic HRQoL measures, the EuroQol group has the largest reporting requirement for the translation process.

R. Brooks et al. (eds.),
The Measurement and Valuation of Health Status Using EQ-5D: A European Perspective, 191–205.

12.2 METHODS

This review was undertaken in 2 sections. The first considered the results of the translation of the source language version (UK English) into 11 European languages (Croatian, Czech, Danish, Dutch, Finnish, French, German, Italian, Polish, Portuguese and Spanish). The second section considered the language versions for which there was a set of values for health states using the EQ-5D VAS and TTO (Dutch, German, Finnish, Spanish) to see whether any differences could be related to findings of the translation process.

Selections of the language versions and sources of evidence used

The versions were selected because, first, they were all official translations approved by the EuroQol Group and second because they were European (bearing in mind the European focus of the EQ-net project). The selection of the French, Italian and Portuguese versions was based largely on evidence of increasing EQ-5D use in these countries, while the Croatian, Czech and Polish versions were chosen because it was thought important to include versions from Eastern Europe. An additional reason for selecting the Finnish, Dutch, Spanish, German and Danish versions was because valuations had already been elicited for these versions (or were in progress as in the Danish case).

The Dutch and Finnish versions were translated in 1987-8. The translations were based on a simultaneous group process and are reported in Chapter 11. Briefly, discussions were "held in English but 'tempered' by interludes of discussion in ... Dutch and Finnish" (Fox-Rushby and Badia, 1996). No back translations or formal reports exist for these versions which, as Fox-Rushby and Badia pointed out, "reflects the thinking of the HRQoL field at that time" so we have relied for this investigation on reviews from the various researchers who were key participants in the process. The Spanish version was translated according to more standardised guidelines and is described briefly in Badia *et al* (1995a). The remaining versions, Croatian, Czech, Danish, French, German, Italian, Polish and Portuguese, were translated after 1990, and followed the standardised guidelines produced by the Group (which were revised over time). While the Group has tried to ensure that experienced translators were involved in these later versions, it cannot be guaranteed. Some problems with the German translation, for example, were detected by German members of the Group and subsequently amended.

Review methods

The first section of the review concentrated on the EQ-5D descriptive system, the EQ VAS and the associated instruction text together with the socio-demographic questions (SDQ). The second section of the review also included the EQ-5D VAS valuation task and the associated instruction text for countries where valuation work had been (or is) taking place.

To facilitate the review of each official translation, a standard data extraction questionnaire was developed. This recorded brief details of the procedure followed for each translation, i.e. forward, back, lay review and whether there was contact with the Group during the process. The reviewers were also asked to describe the difficulties encountered during the translation in relation to the consistently problematic words and phrases from each section of the questionnaire (based on earlier work by Fox-Rushby, 1997), as well as how they were resolved. Finally, a judgement was made about which, if any, aspects of the translation process might affect the comparability of health and socio-demographic data. A group of reviewers were asked to share the task of providing a qualitative subjective review for each language based on the reports and back translation material provided. Review members consisted of the authors plus 1 other EuroQol Group member involved in EQ-5D translation issues. The Finnish and Danish translations were reviewed by 2 EuroQol Group members who had been closely involved in the translation of these versions.

12.3 RESULTS

Main differences between the language versions and how they were resolved

EQ-5D descriptive system

The instruction text for the EQ-5D descriptive system generally causes few problems. For most versions too, few problems are recorded relating to 'mobility' although in German two words are used 'Beweglichkeit/Mobilität', as the former is considered more understandable by ordinary people. In the Italian version 'mobilità' is substituted by 'capacità di movimento', as the former is more normally associated with social mobility. 'Walking about' is substituted by 'walking' in Spanish, Dutch, Finnish, Italian and Portuguese and 'walking around' in German. For many languages the expression 'walking about' simply does not exist. In the French version the expression is translated as 'se déplacer à pied' to capture the idea of a space restriction (i.e. not necessarily walking a long distance) and to allude to everyday movement. The alternative 'marcher' appears to refer more to going for a stroll or walking as recreation. In Finnish there are 2 words for walking, i.e. 'kävely' which means the act of walking (as in a walking competition) and 'käveleminen' a broader expression that does not just include walking competitively. The latter was chosen. 'Confined to bed' proves more problematic in capturing the English implication of being in bed either on a short or long-term basis. In other languages 'confined to bed' is translated in Dutch as 'ik ben bedlegerig' and 'sono costretto/a a letto' in Italian. Both expressions imply 'being bedridden'. Some translators circumvented the problem by using 'I have to stay in bed' (Polish, French and Spanish). An early Spanish version used 'estoy siempre en la cama' which apparently has a slight connotation of staying in bed because of laziness, but this was changed in later versions to 'tengo que estar en la cama' (I have to be in bed), which can refer to short or long periods. Similarly the Portuguese translation 'Tenho de estar na cama' can also refer to short or longer periods.

The expression 'self-care' has caused difficulties, although there are problems inherent in the English source which specifies 'self-care' in level 1 but then goes on to give the examples of 'washing and dressing' in levels 2 and 3. In at least one instance, the Dutch version, level 1, 'I have no problems with self-care', had to be substituted for grammatical reasons with 'I have no problems washing and dressing myself', which is arguably more consistent. Self-care has been translated as 'taking care of myself' (in Finnish) and 'personal care' (in Danish). Both expressions (as well as the more literal Dutch translation) have a broader meaning than in English but would not include, for example, 'coping with finances'. In the 1994 German version 'self-care' is translated as 'personal bodily hygiene' ('körperpflege Hygiene') but this was considered too restrictive and changed for the 1997 German valuation study to 'für sich selbst sorgen'. This is quite a broad concept and could include for example shopping and cooking. In the Italian version, too, 'cura della persona' is quite broad and could also imply cooking food, while in French, self-care has been translated as 'autonomie de la personne' which is related to independence. Otherwise there are no reported problems with washing and dressing in the European languages although the Spanish word used for washing 'lavarme' could imply washing the face and hands only.

'Usual activities' is often back translated as 'daily or everyday activities', while the examples listed under the dimension may not be carried out on a daily basis, for example in the Dutch version 'dagelijkse activiteiten' and in the 1994 German valuation study 'ubliche Tätigkeiten'. However for the German 1997 valuation study this is replaced with a phrase closer to the English source 'allgemeine Tätigkeiten'. This is also used in the level descriptors and implies 'normal or customary activities'.

'Pain' is generally not difficult to translate, but translating 'discomfort' is often problematic. The Dutch word chosen, 'klachten', back translates as 'complaints' and in Finnish the word 'vaiva' is back translated as 'unpleasant physical symptoms'. Both 'kipu' (pain) and 'vaiva' (discomfort) are used in the plural in the Finnish version and in Danish also for pain, but not for discomfort. In German the title refers to 'körperliche Beschwerden' to emphasise that it refers to 'physical discomfort', while in the Czech version 'discomfort' ('obtíe') was back translated as 'difficulties'. The translators were asked if this included feelings of physical discomfort such as 'itching', 'nausea', 'dizziness'. While this was confirmed, Group members reviewing the Czech version did not agree that examples could be included in only 1 particular language version. In translating 'I have no/moderate/extreme pain or discomfort', the corresponding verb 'to have' is retained but not without controversy. For example, in the French version 'ressentir' meaning '(to) experience' was preferred but 'to have' was retained so the questions might sound rather unnatural in French. In Italian, Croatian and Polish however, 'to feel' was chosen (and retained) as the corresponding verb so the translation is therefore less forced.

The fifth dimension of the EQ-5D descriptive system 'anxiety/depression' is translated as 'stemming' meaning 'mood' in the Dutch version and in the levels, anxiety is translated as 'fear'. In English, 'depression' can imply clinical depression but also covers feeling 'cheerless', 'gloomy', 'dejected', 'down', 'sad', 'miserable', and 'unhappy'. For many languages the options are often either a word that means a pathological state or a word denoting feeling 'low', 'blue', 'down' etc. The Dutch, for example, opted for 'somber' meaning 'sad', 'low' or 'gloomy' instead of 'depressie' meaning something more clinical. Nowadays 'depressief' is more widely used in Dutch health questionnaires other than EQ-5D. For the German 1994 study the word 'Niedergeschlagenheit', which has a less clinical connotation, was used for the dimension and in the level descriptors, but the 1997 German study substituted 'deprimiert' in the level descriptors which denotes a more clinical depression, illustrating the more evolutionary nature of the EQ-5D German version.

Selai (1998b), has explored the difficulties of ascertaining the English meaning of the use of 'some' and 'moderate' in level 2 of the EQ-5D dimensions. In Italian 'some' is translated as 'qualche' meaning 'partial presence of', while in the French version the decision was made to use 'des' instead of 'quelque' because while the latter apparently refers to a level of problems midway between the 2 extremes, it does not cover the full range, whilst 'des' is a vaguer term which is more similar to the original 'some'. In the Polish version, 'some' is back translated as 'certain' as this was the closest word the translators could find. 'Certain' was also initially back translated as 'some' in the Czech version, but a more appropriate word 'urèité', closer to the meaning of some, was eventually agreed. The translation of 'moderate' is back translated in Finnish as 'kohtalainen' which means 'to some extent', and in Danish 1 back translation used 'some'. In Spanish, while 'moderado' is back translated as 'moderate', it is not a common word to describe health problems in Spain, although in various clinical studies respondents appear not to have reacted adversely to its use and have no problems understanding the meaning. In French 'modérée(s)' is used, although it was found to be artificial when talking about 'pain/discomfort' and 'anxiety/depression', but not when talking about 'discomfort'. This might then make the translation a little forced. The same seems to apply to the Italian translation 'moderati' (although not when used with 'anxiety/depression') but there were no adverse comments by the Italian lay panel. In Czech, one back translator used 'mild' for 'moderate' for level 2 of 'pain/discomfort' and 'anxiety/depression'. In fact, finding an appropriate word for 'moderate' in Czech caused the most problems in all the languages reviewed. The appropriate word according to the Czech translators was 'mírný', but only for a scale using mild/moderate/severe as the response options. This word was therefore not considered because the surrounding words and context were different, i.e. no/moderate/extreme. Finally, 'støednì' was chosen as it represents 'in the middle', i.e. between 'no' and 'extreme'.

There have always been difficulties in translating 'extreme' as it is not widely used in some languages to quantify health dimensions like 'pain/discomfort' and 'anxiety/ depression'. It is variously translated as 'very serious' in Dutch ('zeer ernstige') for both dimensions and 'very strong' in Finnish ('ankaria') with regard to 'pain/discomfort'. In Danish 'ekstreme' is borrowed from the English and in some contexts can mean 'way out'. One person in the Danish lay panel thought 'ekstreme' was an academic word but others thought it would be well understood by ordinary Danes. The word is retained in the Danish translation. 'Extreme' is translated as 'I have a great deal of pain' in the Spanish version. Spanish translators were reluctant to use the direct translation, as it is not used at all in the context of 'pain/discomfort' or 'anxiety/depression', at least in lay populations. Similarly in the French translation. Although the French lay panel objected strongly to the use of 'extreme', stating that people never used this word to describe 'pain/discomfort' or 'anxiety/depression' in France (they recommended using the word 'very') 'extreme' however is retained. There was also resistance to using 'extreme' in the Italian version too although, as with the French version, it is retained. The Polish translators preferred a word meaning 'considerable' but another word more closely resembling 'extreme' was finally chosen. These translations therefore are to a certain extent forced.

EQ VAS

One of the main criticisms of the English instruction text for the EQ VAS is that it is repetitive. This has caused problems in certain languages where it is not viewed as merely stressing something (as in English) but as a serous language error. Interestingly the Italian translators reported that repetition was practically a hanging offence in Italy. Both the Finnish and German translations use a simplified text that is less repetitive and sounds more natural in these languages. In Finnish for example, the translation has simplified the instructions, splitting the long sentence into 2 in paragraph 1 and removing 'how good or bad' and 'in your opinion' in the second paragraph.

EQ-5D VAS valuation task

There are no problems reported in translating the anchor points 'best imaginable health' and 'worst imaginable health' in any of the languages reviewed. There also appeared to be no problems generally with the instruction text relating to the valuation task, except for the state 'dead' in France as death seems to be a delicate subject, and a neutral way of including it in the valuation task was sought (which would not refer to 'how good or bad' death was). Respondents prefer the simple form of 'la mort' rather than a slightly longer version 'le fait d'être mort'. In Danish 'being dead' and 'death' have the same translation.

EQ SDQ

A notable number of language differences occur in the standard socio-demographic questions (SDQ) regarding employment and education, implying that for between-country valuation research, these 2 variables will be non-comparable on the basis of the current translations. In Dutch under 'main activity', 'seeking work' is split into 'unable to', 'out of a job' and 'voluntary' because in the Netherlands it would be considered inappropriate to exclude voluntary work as so many people are involved in the voluntary sector. In Finnish 'in employment or self employment' simply refers to 'työssä' (working). More generally however, difficulties are routinely experienced with question 7: 'did your education continue after the minimum school leaving age?' and question 8: 'do you have a degree or equivalent professional qualification?' In the German 1994 version, Dutch, and Spanish versions, the questions are combined and there is no reference to 'minimum level of education'. In the Dutch version respondents are asked to choose a level of education from a number of options (e.g. 'lower', 'middle', 'higher', 'university') - 8 levels in total. The Spanish version asks respondents to choose from 5 levels. In Finland the questions are not appropriate so question 7 asks about basic education with 3 levels and question 8 asks about professional education with 5 levels. In many countries, there is no minimum school leaving age while in others, e.g. Denmark, people would not necessarily know what it is. It was agreed to refer to 'folkeskolen' which is compulsory education to ninth class (age 15-16 years). Moreover there is no direct translation of 'a degree or equivalent professional qualification'. This was translated as 'education from a higher institution'.

Are the decisions made during the translation process likely to affect valuations and comparability of health and socio-demographic data and/or can different valuations be attributed to differences in translation?

For all the languages, the reviewers considered that there were translation differences that might affect valuations and/or comparability of between-country results. For example: the French, Italian and Polish versions retained 'extreme' although it was considered unnatural in the context of 'pain/discomfort' and 'anxiety/depression'; the Polish version retained 'certain' problems instead of 'some'; the substitution of 'feeling' pain (although more natural in these languages) instead of 'having' pain in Croatian, Italian and Polish versions; and, the use of 'having' pain in the French version when 'feeling' was preferred.

However, 4 main concerns (relating to the Dutch, Italian, Polish, Spanish and Finnish versions) were raised:

(i) In the Dutch, Italian and Polish versions, the wording chosen for third level 'mobility', 'confined to bed', implies being bedridden. This could result in the Dutch, Italian and Polish values being lower for health states incorporating level 3 for 'mobility'.

(ii) In the Dutch version, 'usual activities' is back translated as 'daily activities'. This could result in the Dutch values being lower for health states incorporating levels 2 or 3 for 'usual activities'.

(iii) In the Spanish, Dutch and Finnish versions, 'very' is used instead of 'extreme(ly)' for level 3 for 'anxiety/depression' and 'pain/discomfort'. This might result in Spanish, Dutch and Finnish values being higher in these countries for health states incorporating level 3 for 'anxiety/depression' and 'pain/discomfort'.

(iv) In the Dutch version 'anxiety' is translated as 'fear' and 'depression' as 'gloomy'. While 'fear' could be viewed as being worse than 'anxiety', 'gloomy' would probably be regarded as not being as bad as 'depression' so it is difficult to know how the Dutch values for health states incorporating levels 2 or 3 of 'anxiety/depression' could be affected.

As no valuation data currently exists for Italy and Poland, we were not able to explore our concerns relating to these countries further. Although German and (more recently) Danish EQ-5D valuation data is available we did not explore these data as the review had not revealed any major concerns regarding the Danish or German (1997) translations.

We were, however, able to undertake a preliminary exploration of the Dutch version regarding (i) and (ii) and of the Finnish and Spanish versions regarding (iii) as data were available from the EQ-net project (see Chapters 6-9).

We used data that were, as far as possible, similar in terms of methodology. Table 12.1 shows the differences between Finnish, Dutch and UK (Frome) postal valuations for a set of EQ-5D health states using the EQ-5D VAS technique. Finnish values were higher than the UK values for health states that include level 3 for 'pain/discomfort' and 'anxiety/depression' although only 2 states (22233 and 33333A) were significant.

Table 12.2 shows the differences between 2 Spanish interview-based valuation studies (Cat_Hos and Navarra) and postal valuations elicited in the UK (Frome) study for a set of EQ-5D health states using the EQ-5D VAS. Spanish values were lower for health states incorporating level 3 'pain/discomfort' and 'anxiety/depression' (except for 21232) than the mean values for the UK (Frome) for these health states. Another

Spanish study (Cat_Cor) was compared with the UK MVH study. Both elicited interview-based valuations for a standard set of EQ-5D health states using TTO. Table 12.3 shows small, non-significant variations except for 'unconscious' and 'dead' where the Spanish values are significantly lower.

When comparing the socio-demographic data between-countries, the individual reviews concluded that the demographic questions relating to 'main activity' and 'education' were unlikely to be comparable with the source version, and particularly so for the Finnish, Dutch, Danish, Spanish and 1994 German versions. Chapter 6 on the construction of the EQ-net VAS database describes how the education variables for the different countries had to be recoded to low, medium and high levels of education so that the studies could be made more comparable.

Table 12.1. Differences between Finnish, Dutch and UK (Frome) postal valuations for a set of EQ-5D health states using the EQ-5D VAS

					95% CI		
Finland v UK Frome	State	Mean Finland	Mean UK (Frome)	Mean Diff.[a]	Lower	Upper	Sig.
	21232	38.7	35.2	-3.5	-8.0	0.9	0.118
	22233	29.1	24.0	-5.1	-9.3	-0.8	0.019
	22323	25.4	23.4	-2.0	-6.2	2.1	0.336
	33333A	9.5	4.9	-4.6	-7.97	-1.18	0.008
	33333B	9.4	6.9	-2.5	-5.76	0.728	0.128

					95% CI		
Netherlands v UK Frome	State	Mean NL	Mean UK (Frome)	Mean Diff.[a]	Lower	Upper	Sig.
	11211	80.2	73.5	-6.7	-10.2	-3.2	0.000
	32211	41.7	33.9	-7.8	-12.3	-3.3	0.001
	33321	21.9	16.3	-5.5	-9.2	-1.9	0.003

a. Mean differences calculated using Independent-Samples t-tests

Table 12.2. Differences between Spanish (Cat_Hos and Navarra) interview-based valuations and UK (Frome) postal valuations for a set of EQ-5D health states using the EQ-5D VAS

State	Mean Spain (Cat_Hos & Navarra)	Mean UK (Frome)	Mean Diff.[a]	95% CI		Sig.
				Lower	Upper	
11111B	97.3	94.5	-2.8	-4.2	-1.4	0.000
11111A	96.9	95.7	-1.1	-2.6	0.3	0.129
11121	72.7	70.1	-2.6	-5.8	0.7	0.118
11112	71.4	72.5	1.1	-2.2	4.4	0.517
21111	70.2	73.0	2.7	-0.1	5.5	0.060
11211	67.9	73.5	5.5	2.4	8.6	0.001
12111	52.8	62.0	9.3	6.2	12.3	0.000
11122	52.0	56.3	4.3	1.4	7.2	0.004
21232	35.5	35.2	-0.3	-3.0	2.4	0.831
22233	21.9	24.0	2.2	-0.2	4.6	0.078
32211	19.7	33.9	14.2	10.4	17.9	0.000
33321	11.1	16.3	5.2	2.8	7.6	0.000
DeadA	6.9	13.9	7.1	4.3	9.8	0.000
DeadB	6.2	14.2	8.0	5.5	10.6	0.000
33333B	4.1	6.9	2.8	1.0	4.5	0.002
Uncon	3.4	13.1	9.7	7.6	11.9	0.000
33333A	3.4	4.9	1.6	0.0	3.1	0.043

a. Mean differences calculated using Independent-Samples t-tests

Table 12.3. Differences between Spanish (Cat_Cor) and UK (MVH) interview-based valuations for a set of EQ-5D health states using TTO

State	Mean Spanish (Cat_Cor)	Mean UK (MVH)	Mean Diff.[a]	95% CI Lower	95% CI Upper	Sig.
11111A	98.5	98.7	0.3	-0.3	0.8	0.331
11112	81.4	82.3	0.9	-1.8	3.7	0.510
21111	81.3	81.5	0.2	-2.5	2.9	0.876
11121	81.2	82.9	1.7	-0.8	4.1	0.191
11211	79.6	82.2	2.6	-0.1	5.2	0.062
12111	78.8	80.7	1.9	-0.9	4.7	0.188
11122	72.1	70.7	-1.4	-5.0	2.2	0.436
21232	42.1	38.9	-3.2	-7.4	1.1	0.144
32211	33.4	36.2	2.8	-2.0	7.6	0.253
22323	29.6	30.1	0.5	-3.8	4.7	0.834
22233	26.7	25.6	-1.0	-5.0	2.9	0.605
33321	18.6	22.0	3.4	-0.3	7.1	0.073
DeadA	11.9	9.8	-2.0	-4.3	0.2	0.074
Uncon	3.6	9.7	6.1	4.2	7.9	0.000
33333A	2.7	5.5	2.8	1.7	3.9	0.000

a. Mean differences calculated using Independent-Samples t-tests

12.4 DISCUSSION AND FUTURE DIRECTIONS

The aim of this investigation was to investigate the pitfalls and hurdles encountered during the translation of the EQ-5D into a number of different European languages. The presence of differences between the UK English source version of EQ-5D and 11 different European language versions was highlighted, primarily by comparing the source with back translations, reports and reviews. The UK English version was used as the reference version because it is considered to be the source version for the translation process. A simultaneous comparison of all existing versions was felt to be beyond the scope of the review. The investigation did, however, provide an opportunity to explore whether or not any of the differences that we were able to flag were likely to be reflected in differing between-country valuations. Likewise, the differences in valuations highlighted in Chapters 6-9 provided an opportunity for us to explore whether these could be the result of differences in the way words or phrases were translated.

Our analyses showed Finnish postal EQ-5D VAS values to be higher than UK postal EQ-5D values for health states that include level 3 for 'pain/discomfort' and 'anxiety/

depression' which might be expected in view of the substitution of 'very' instead of 'extreme' for 'pain/discomfort' and 'anxiety/depression' in the Finnish version. However, Dutch postal EQ-5D VAS values for states 32211 and 33321 were higher than UK postal EQ-5D VAS values which is contrary to what we might expect if level 3 'mobility' in the Dutch version does indeed imply 'being bedridden'. We might also expect Dutch values to be lower if levels 2 and 3 for 'usual activities' for these states (as well as 11211) are translated in Dutch as 'daily' activities. The Dutch values were in fact significantly higher for these 3 states. It is of course very difficult, if not impossible, to differentiate between these effects so we should be cautious in interpreting these results. Actual values given will depend on a combination of factors, including people's reaction to the aspect of health being valued (for example, whether they think 'pain/discomfort' and/or anxiety/depression' is worse than being immobile or being unable to perform their daily activities), the way in which the levels are worded, and the response effects due to the valuation method.

Comparison of Spanish interview-based EQ-5D VAS values and UK postal EQ-5D VAS data showed Spanish values to be lower for health states incorporating level 3 'pain/discomfort' and 'anxiety/depression' (except for 21232) than the mean values for the UK (Frome) for these health states. This is contrary to what we might expect as 'very' instead of 'extreme' for 'pain/discomfort' and 'anxiety/depression' has been substituted in the Spanish version. But again, caution is required when attempting to differentiate between these effects. It is possible, for example, as Badia *et al,* (2001) have suggested, that UK respondents ascribe greater importance to dimensions of 'pain/discomfort' and 'anxiety/depression' than Spanish respondents who think that the dimensions of 'mobility' and 'self-care' are more important. It could also be argued that if the word 'extreme' had been used in the Spanish version, the differences between Spain and other countries might have been even greater. Furthermore, there were differences in methodology between the studies which might also account for the different values. Both the Spanish studies were interview-based, unlike the UK Frome study which was a postal survey.

No substantial differences in methodology, however, were observed between another Spanish study (Cat_Cor) and the UK (MVH) study. Both elicited interview-based valuations for a set of EQ-5D health states using TTO. The data revealed small, non-significant variations except for 'unconscious' and 'dead' where the Spanish values are significantly lower. It seems therefore that no concrete conclusions can be drawn from these analyses and more qualitative research is required.

Data from the EQ-net project provided us with an opportunity to explore whether valuation differences might be attributed to differences in translation. The main conclusion from Sintonen *et al* (in Chapter 7) is "that there appears to be a considerable degree of agreement between (EQ-5D VAS) health state valuations in studies from several European countries, with the exception of Spain". Health states incorporating 'confined to bed' in one of the Spanish studies (Cat_Hos), report markedly lower values although the other Spanish studies did not report similar results. More between-country differences using TTO are reported in chapter 9, however, where German valuations were found to differ from Spanish and UK valuations. German respondents gave fewer negative health states and generally valued them higher than Spanish and UK respondents. One of the conclusions reached in the chapter is that translation differences were not responsible and that the differences were more likely to be associated with socio-demographic factors in the German sample. This conclusion was reached mainly because the differences did not show up when German respondents used the EQ-5D VAS methodology, but this might not necessarily be a correct assumption. It may be that TTO happens to be more sensitive to these sorts of differences, or other method artefacts, such as response spreading on the EQ-5D VAS, mask differences that might be due to translations. It is also possible that the differences could be attributed to disparities in German culture that were highlighted by the particular nature of the TTO methodology. More qualitative work is needed in this area to find out how and why people give the valuations that they do.

Some evidence for the role of translation differences impacting on valuation data does however arise when comparing the German valuation studies of 1994 (Graf v.d. Schulenberg *et al*, 1996) and 1997 (Claes *et al*, 1998). The 1994 German version used 'daily activities' for the heading and levels of 'usual activities' but this was replaced by 'customary activities' in the 1997 version to more accurately reflect the UK English source version. This resulted in slightly higher values being assigned to this dimension in the later study. For 'depression', the German 1994 study used 'Niedergeschlagenheit' for the heading and levels and while retaining this expression in the heading for the 1997 valuation study, the levels were replaced with 'deprimiert'. This resulted in lower values being assigned to the 'anxiety/depression' dimension in the 1997 study as 'deprimiert' in German means a much poorer health state than 'Niedergeschlagen' (Claes *et al*, 1998). This lends some support to the view that different wording may have been responsible but more work is needed to determine a more definite link.

The study reported here has been complicated for 2 reasons. First, as Fox Rushby *et al* report in Chapter 10, there is some uncertainty over the shared intention of the meanings of questions for some words/phrases in the English source version among EuroQol Group members. This however appears to be a common problem that has to be addressed when translating HRQoL questionnaires. Words such as 'self-care', 'discomfort' 'extreme', 'some' and 'moderate' can be difficult to translate precisely into other languages as sometimes there simply will not be a direct equivalent in English (and because the English word is not used as a precise term itself). Second, the forward and back translation approach has been criticised as being insensitive to differences in meaning between source and target language versions. For example, Amuyunzu *et al* (1995) showed that forward and back translations into Kikamba were apparently absolutely comparable but investigation of the use of words in context showed differences in meaning. Sartorius and Kuyken (1994) have suggested that one step to understanding whether words and phrases are the same in different languages is to examine the extent to which "semantic space is shared, and what items in the source instrument address this semantic space". It appears from the material we reviewed that these issues have been at least partly addressed in the identification of alternative words. However, we have not yet attempted or recommended a back and forward dictionary-based analysis of synonyms, for example. Even so, this is still only one step as dictionary based searches do not always reflect common understandings and extensive dictionaries do not exist to facilitate this approach for all languages.

There has been little published research comparing the valuations of health states between countries and even fewer clear explanations of the reasons for between-country differences. The EuroQol Group, in its first corporate paper, reported that valuations for a selection of EQ-5D health states across the Netherlands, Sweden, Norway and the UK were "broadly similar" (EuroQol Group, 1990). In a comparison of UK and Spanish general population values for EQ-5D health states using time trade-off (TTO), valuations were considered to be generally similar although Spanish respondents placed more importance on functional dimensions (Badia *et al*, 2001). In a comparison between countries, using the US English version, (almost identical to the UK English version), Johnson *et al* compared Finnish and US VAS-based valuations of EQ-5D and found that the US respondents tended to give higher values for some mild and moderate states and lower values for some severe states (Johnson *et al*, 2000a). In an earlier version of this paper, Murti *et al* (1998) suggested that a value set developed in one country could not be used in the other. Such findings mirror the findings of Ustun *et al* (1999), who asked groups of 15 'experts' in 14 countries to rank the valuation of disease states and concluded that there was sufficient evidence to shed doubt on the assumption of universality of the disability rankings.

The cause of any differences and the lack of differences in valuations have never been attributed to differences in translation between countries. Indeed, Johnson *et al* (2000a) go as far as stating that the reasons were methodological and "that there is no significant conceptual difference between the translations" (Johnson *et al,* 2000a). Similarly, Badia *et al* (2001) reject the view that differences in translation might have affected UK and Spanish valuations but concluded that there was a strong possibility of 'genuine cultural variations' between valuations for health states elicited in Spain and the UK.

Indeed, when we explored the data from the EQ-net project, the issues considered likely to affect valuations were in general not confirmed. Although Finnish values were higher (as anticipated) for the selected states, it is not possible to conclude that this was attributable to translation differences. Likewise while 'confined to bed' was valued lower in 1 Barcelona valuation study in the EQ-net data, no qualitative information is available from the translation reports as to why this might be case and the finding was not repeated in the other Spanish studies, suggesting that translation was unlikely to be the reason for the differences. However, none of these studies was designed from the outset to test for the impact of translation differences on valuations so current conclusions could be premature. There is a paucity of qualitative data regarding the translation procedures from those countries with existing valuation data sets and little qualitative research accessing the interpretations of the EQ-5D in the target languages. In 1 country, however, this is likely to change in the future. Pedersen *et al's* (2000) exploration of Danish wording experiments based on EQ-5D (and outlined in Chapter 10) have the potential to be related to health state valuations. This could prove to be a fruitful line for incorporating qualitative experiments into future valuation work.

Finally it should be remembered that translation differences are only one of a number of possible explanations as to why valuations might differ between countries, including differences in the use of scales, sampling, study design, respondent characteristics, understanding of the valuation method and the way health is conceptualised and defined across cultures. While this investigation should be viewed as a preliminary qualitative exploration, it has proved useful in providing a starting point while highlighting the necessity for further work. The EuroQol Group has also made progress by providing explicit translation guidelines and insisting on Group involvement in the process, but we still need to go further to explore and achieve good quality translations that are semantically equivalent. Assessing the impact of differences in the translation of questionnaires has to be supported with empirical research. The Group could investigate equivalence models offered by researchers such as Herdman *et al* (1998) or consider certain aspects of the approaches adopted by the WHOQOL Group (1994) or the IQOLA project (Ware *et al*, 1995, Gandek *et al*, 1998, Keller *et al*, 1998). The acceptability and conceptual equivalence of the existing translations could be further evaluated and improved using qualitative methods (e.g. use of cognitive assessment methods with a wider range of people, and ethnographic approaches that examine the relevance of concepts implicit to the EQ-5D in other cultures), and quantitative methods (e.g. exercises to examine the feasibility and relevance of different measurement techniques, comparison of the use of scales in different countries). These would all improve the understanding of the semantic equivalence between 2 questionnaires. However, we recognise that this will not be sufficient for reliable international comparisons as additional aspects of conceptual, item, operational, measurement and functional equivalence need to be investigated. For example, further research (and development of EuroQol Group guidelines) could be directed at methods for investigating each of these. This would be a challenging task but the work is important if the EuroQol Group is to be confident of the comparability of the content of EQ-5D language versions used in different countries.

13
EQ-5D in selected countries around the world

Richard Brooks, Stephen Joel Coons, Paul De Cock, Nancy Devlin, Willy De Weerdt, Paul Hansen, Naoki Ikegami, Jennifer Jelsma, Jeffrey Johnson and Carlo Marra

13.1 INTRODUCTION

This chapter focuses on the use of the EQ-5D in a variety of different countries across the world. The EQ-5D was specifically developed in the European context, and most of the detailed valuation work has been undertaken in Europe, as is made clear in this book. The instrument has, however, been used in a wide range of countries. EuroQol Group plenary meetings, held once per year, have witnessed a substantial increase in papers from countries outside Europe, and contributors to this chapter have themselves presented papers at these meetings. Since these contributions come from a variety of different countries, from different parts of the world, and from very different cultural backgrounds, it is of considerable interest to the Group and worthy of wider exposure, how the EQ-5D 'performs' in these wider contexts. The 4 sections are from Japan, New Zealand, North America, and Zimbabwe.

This chapter focuses largely on the valuation tasks, and, as will be evident, this is inter-related with the 'translation' issues treated in detail in the EQ-net project. The Japanese section contains specific examples of how words and phrases in the English EQ-5D were translated into Japanese, and shows the cognitive/conceptual problems that can arise. The author also speculates that health dimension values may be affected, specifically in the mobility dimension.

The section on Zimbabwe discusses translation and conceptual issues with regard to 1 of the major language groups, namely Shona. The authors conclude that, despite Shona people having a different view on aspects of health status from that portrayed in the EQ-5D, it would still be possible for people to respond to the questionnaire. This is borne out in the empirical results.

The New Zealand section contains some interesting discussion of health valuations across the 3 major ethnic elements of New Zealand society, namely Maori, European/ Paheka and Pacific Islands people. Despite the possibility of different conceptualisations of health, these do not appear to be borne out by the valuations, so the authors feel it is appropriate to generate social preferences from the electoral roll.

R. Brooks et al. (eds.),
The Measurement and Valuation of Health Status Using EQ-5D: A European Perspective, 207–227.

There is less direct reference to cross-cultural issues in the North American section, although the authors do refer to potential problems in cultural adaptation in a US-Finnish data comparison (Johnson *et al*, 2000a) and also point to a population-base feasibility study in Montreal, Canada involving a French-Canadian translation of EQ-5D (Mayo *et al*, 1997).

All 4 sections include detail on valuation exercises in their respective parts of the world, both VAS and TTO valuations. In all sections there is comparison with previous European results, in particular the UK MVH study. There were important differences in valuations, for example in Japan and Zimbabwe, which are reported in the relevant sections.

13.2 JAPAN

Japan's health care environment

Although there is universal health insurance coverage, financing is fragmented among over 5000 social insurance plans while delivery is mainly in the private sector. Despite the fee-for-service basis of reimbursement, cost containment has been achieved by relying on the national uniform fee schedule that determines the price of all procedures and materials. All payers and providers must use this fee schedule; thus it has become a powerful instrument that strongly influences both the extent and the quality of technology in Japan. When a new technology is developed, its price is determined by comparing its efficacy with the nearest existing technology, with little consideration given to its actual costs. Although this should provide an ideal opportunity to utilise the results of a health economics analysis, very few analyses have actually been undertaken, let alone had any impact on policy (Ikegami and Hisashige, 1994; Ikegami and Campbell, 1999). One of the barriers has been the lack of standardised generic instruments to evaluate HRQoL. It is in this context that we focussed on the use of the EQ-5D.

The translation process

A EuroQol translation team undertook this task, official approval being given by the EuroQol Group in late 1997. The Japanese version of the EQ-5D was subsequently placed in the public domain, following the principles laid down by the Group.

In the translation process, the following words posed particular difficulties.

'Mobility'. The literal translation of this word into Japanese would be "ability to move" (*kadousei*) which would not be a familiar term to the general public. Thus, the phrase "range of movement" (*idou no teido*) was used instead. In Japanese, *idou* (movement) is usually used to describe that of the whole body, and not parts such as an arm or a leg.

'Confined to bed'. In this case, although there was a corresponding colloquial word in Japanese (*netakiri*), this has more negative connotations than the original English. Many Japanese would say that they would like to avoid this state because of the high prevalence of strokes and because of the perceived poor quality of formal services for those with this condition. However, because of our inability to find alternative words, we used this word. This may have led to low values for health states that included this level in the mobility dimension.

'Self-Care'. Since there was no corresponding word in Japanese, we had to use the expression of "*mino mawari no kanri*" which would be retranslated into English as "management of things around oneself".

'Wash oneself'. The English word includes washing the body. However, in Japanese, the corresponding word would limit the washing to the face (*senmen*). Nevertheless, this word was used after considering the greater difficulty involved in taking a bath in a Japanese style bath.

Appropriate adaptations were also performed for 'usual activities' and the use of the term 'box'.

The above factors had to be taken into consideration when interpreting the data using the Japanese version. This meant that any differences in self-reported health among respondents with similar characteristics could be the result of the translation, and not necessarily substantive. Hence, in order to deal with this situation, we proceeded to develop a Japanese value set.

Japanese EuroQol valuation project team

This team had the following 2 objectives: the first was to obtain data on the valuation of health status from the Japanese general population, and the second was to develop a Japanese value set where all possible EQ-5D descriptors are listed together with their corresponding uni-dimensional HRQoL. The same subjects were used for both objectives, with interviews being conducted over August and September of 1998. Each interview comprised:

(i) The full EQ-5D valuation questionnaire.
(ii) Ranking of 19 hypothetical health states expressed in 5 dimensions.
(iii) TTO evaluations of 17 of these 19 hypothetical health states.

The general population study

The subjects were those aged 20 and over living in 3 prefectures, i.e. Saitama, Hiroshima and Hokkaido (Ikeda *et al,* 1999). No upper age limit was stipulated. A 2-stage random sampling was undertaken by first selecting the smallest geographical unit within each municipality, and then selecting individuals within each unit so that the total would reflect the demographic structure of the general population. In total, 972 were selected of which 505 (52%) responded. In the 2 areas where the response rates were low, additional subjects were recruited by randomly selecting those living in the same geographical unit with the same age and sex characteristics as that of the non-respondents. With the addition of these respondents the number sampled totalled 621.

The responses on the EQ-5D descriptive system were skewed, with a median response of 'no problem' for all dimensions. A 'moderate problem' on at least 1 dimension was reported by 25.0% of respondents, whereas only 2.1% of respondents reported any 'extreme problem'. Problems were most often recorded in the pain/discomfort dimension (20.0%). Rates of reported problems generally increased with age, with those who had experienced serious illness, had lower education, were retired, or doing housework. There were no differences due to sex, except for women aged 70 and above who reported higher rates than men of the same age group, and for women of all ages in the pain/discomfort dimension. Our results generally reflected those from the previous UK study (Kind *et al*, 1998). However, the proportions of respondents having problems in mobility and usual activities were lower in Japan.

Development of the value set

The methodology was similar to that adopted by the MVH project in using a 10-year TTO and in the design of 'props' (Dolan, 1997). Where the 2 studies differed was in the number of health states: whereas it was 42 in the original, the minimum set of 17 was used in Japan. (Macran and Kind, 2000). With this reduced number of health states valued, a value set of comparable robustness with the MVH study has been estimated. This value set has been made available to the public (Tsuchiya *et al*, 2002).

Conclusion

A number of other studies using EQ-5D have been undertaken (Nawata *et al*, 2000; Sakamaki *et al*, 2000), and other projects under way include the simultaneous administration of EQ-5D and SF-36 in cancer and Parkinson's disease patients. With the growing interest in economic evaluations, we envisage a wider dissemination of the EQ-5D in Japan.

13.3 NEW ZEALAND

Background

New Zealand (NZ) is notable, internationally, for its attempts to implement explicit, economics-based priority setting in the health sector. In 1998, the Health Funding Authority (HFA), the purchaser of publicly-funded health services, proposed a 'principles-based' prioritisation framework incorporating cost-utility analysis (CUA) (HFA, 1998). Pharmac, the government's pharmaceuticals purchaser, also employs CUA (Pharmac, 1999).

Governmental reviews of these agencies' proposals highlighted a number of practical concerns with CUA (Ashton *et al*, 2000; Devlin *et al*, 1999). These included criticism of the proposed adoption of the QLHQ (Hadorn and Uebersax 1995), to which both agencies responded by shifting to routine use of the EQ-5D. Another issue was the lack of basic research on the health state preferences of New Zealanders - local CUAs have had to rely on other countries' health state valuations, principally the UK's EQ-5D value set (Dolan *et al*, 1997). Hence, an over-arching objective of the NZ programme of research has been the creation of a NZ EQ-5D valuation set.

Population study

To this end, health state valuations were sought in 1999 from 3000 adult New Zealanders (randomly selected from the electoral roll) using a visual analogue scale (VAS) via 3 versions of a self-completed postal survey. 1360 questionnaires were completed and returned (a 50% response rate of those who received them). However a third of them could not be used for estimating a value set, mostly because states 11111 or dead (both necessary for 're-scaling' the valuations) had not been scored or the values for the other heath states surveyed were 'missing'.

Of the 919 responses that were useable, 80% had at least 1 logical inconsistency, almost a third had more than 3 inconsistencies, and 10% had more than 10 (Devlin *et al*, 2000a). A logically inconsistent valuation is one that violates the logical orderings implicit in the EQ-5D classification system, namely a state with a less severe rating on a particular dimension than another state, given its other ratings are no more severe ought, logically, to be scored higher by the respondent making the comparison (e.g. 11121>11122). Here, as in Dolan and Kind (1996b), violation of such an ordering is counted as 1 logical inconsistency and the valuations for *both* states are classified as logically inconsistent. This definition is in marked contrast to Ohinmaa and Sintonen (1999) where "a state was considered inconsistent if it had a higher preference value than at least one higher ranked (logically better) state." A higher ranked (logically better) state that had a lower preference value than another state was not considered inconsistent.

As there appeared to be *systematic* inconsistency in the groups with 2 or more inconsistencies, we opted for 2 data sets from which *two* valuation sets would be estimated: the full sample (n=919) and, as an alternative, a sub-sample of respondents with at most 1 inconsistency (n=396).

Ethnic valuations

But first, given that the value sets are intended to reflect the health state preferences of the NZ *general* public (as tax-payers and potential patients), we sought to discover the relevant group characteristics determining the representativeness (in this sense) of our samples. Of particular relevance was the possibility of differences between Maori (12% of the population) and non-Maori health state valuations, arising from alleged different cultural perspectives on health (Durie, 1998). It is also conceivable that Pacific Islands people, NZ's other predominant ethnic minority (about 5%), perceive and value health differently than Maori and Pakeha/Europeans.

The usual approach to investigating valuation differences between population subgroups is to model each health state individually; however, this can create problems for generalisability if some background characteristics emerge as significant explanators for some states but not others. Instead, therefore, for the full and sub-samples respectively, we combined them all in a single data set by calculating for each valuation its difference in percentage terms from the relevant sample mean for that particular health state (Buckingham *et al*, 2001). We found that none of a range of the usual socio-demographic variables (including ethnicity), nor respondents' self-assessed EQ-5D profiles and VAS scores of their own health, nor their experience of illness (in themselves, their family and others) were important explanators of differences in New Zealanders' health state valuations.

In related work, drawing upon the same data, we examined the extent to which these socio-demographic variables could explain variations in respondents' EQ-5D self-classified health states and EQ VAS scores of their own health (Devlin *et al*, 2000b). Most of the background characteristics were related to self-reported health in expected ways. For example, respondents were more likely to report problems on each of the 5 dimensions and to have a lower global score if they smoked, if they were unemployed, a house-worker or retiree, and if their education did not continue past the minimum school leaving-age. Problems on all dimensions were more common the older the respondent and the global score was lower for over-70 year olds than for younger people. However, notably, neither the global score nor the incidence of problems on any of the dimensions was related to respondents' ethnicity (Maori versus non-Maori versus 'other').

This lack of difference in self-reported health between Maori and non-Maori is of concern given the relatively poor health status of Maori in NZ (National Health Committee, 1998). A possible explanation for this finding, and also the apparent lack of difference between Maori and non-Maori valuations of hypothetical states, is the adequacy or otherwise of the EQ-5D in reflecting cultural differences in the conceptualisation of health. However, in response to the question "Do you feel that the way of describing 'health' used in this questionnaire covers all the aspects of your health that are important to you?", nearly three-quarters of respondents answered "yes", and there were no differences between Maori and non-Maori. Furthermore, in answers to the follow-up question "If you ticked 'no', please tell us what *other* aspects of health are important to you?", the concept of spiritual health, for example, was raised as frequently by non-Maori as Maori (Devlin *et al*, 2000b).

Another possible explanation for these findings regarding ethnicity is sampling and response bias arising from the use of the electoral roll and reliance on English language survey instruments. This raises the concern that the Maori in our electoral roll sample may not be representative of the Maori community generally. Hence a pilot study was undertaken in which subjects were identified through Maori networks and approached in a culturally appropriate manner (Perkins *et al*, 2001). Although based on a small sample (n=66), this work suggests little difference between the health state valuations of this sample of Maori, and those of both Maori and non-Maori from the electoral roll data. While there undoubtedly remains further work to be undertaken in relation to the perception and valuation of health by New Zealand's principal ethnic groups, our findings to date suggest that the valuation data derived from the electoral roll survey may appropriately be used as a basis for deriving a value set for New Zealand.

VAS value sets

Accordingly, we proceeded to estimate the values for the full (n=919) and sub-samples (n=396) respectively, experimenting via a 'random effects' model with 9 specifications involving different combinations of dummy and interaction variables (Devlin *et al*, 2000a). On the basis of the logical consistency of the resulting value sets we settled on the 2 most parsimonious equations. Both restrict the effect on the estimated health state values of moving from level 1 (no problems) to 2 (some problems) to being the same as going from 2 to 3 (extreme problems), while the sub-sample equation is augmented by a dummy variable that is activated if any of the dimensions are at level 3. Due to this variable, 243 (85%) of the full sample values are higher than their sub-sample counterparts.

As noted above, the UK value set has mostly been used in NZ CUAs to date; hence we were interested in gauging the sensitivity of CUA results to the valuation set applied. We conducted 6 actual CUAs using 3 value sets: the 2 NZ value sets discussed above and the UK 'A26' value set from the UK MVH Group - chosen since it is also derived from a VAS survey of the general adult population (MVH Group,

1995). Like the NZ full sample value set, the UK values are consistently higher than the NZ sub-sample value set. The question therefore, which can only be resolved empirically, was what effect these substantial and systematic differences between the 3 value sets would have on the respective estimates of QALYs gained - the relevant denominator in CUA.

A data set was accessed comprising over 1000 patients from the Cornwall and Isles of Scilly Health Authority (UK), on which CUAs of 6 types of elective surgery had been conducted (Buckingham, 1999). Spearman's correlation coefficients of the rankings of the QALYs gained for all patients were 0.94 between the NZ value sets and 0.99 and 0.92 for the sub- and full sample value sets respectively against the UK value set (Buckingham *et al*, 2001). These strong correlations were supported by comparisons of rankings of individual patients within each of the 6 procedures. In terms of mean cost per QALY gained, the UK and NZ sub-sample value sets rank the 6 procedures identically, as did the NZ full sample value set except that the placings for 2 procedures (incontinence and prostatectomy) were reversed. Finally, despite the NZ sub-sample valuations being consistently lower than the other 2, the estimates of QALYs gained from them were neither consistently smaller nor greater across the 6 types of surgery.

Future directions for NZ research

Just as health sector developments - the proposed routine use of CUA in priority setting - provided the initial catalyst to this research programme, the future direction of NZ EQ-5D research is likely to be shaped by the changing political landscape. A general election late in 1999 resulted in a new Labour-led coalition government, which rejected the quasi-market model, replacing the single, national purchaser (HFA) with 21 mainly locally elected Boards. It is uncertain whether the new Boards will have the capacity to build on previous efforts at explicit prioritisation (Devlin *et al*, 2000c) and on what basis resource allocation decisions will be made. A growing (and worrying) tendency to reject economic analysis in favour of 'needs assessment' will influence the impetus for further basic research on health state valuation.

Pharmac, however, remains intact, and continues to use the EQ-5D as its preferred instrument. A recent workshop involving academics and government officials concluded that the main challenge facing analysts undertaking CUA is the lack of effectiveness evidence reported in terms of the EQ-5D (or any preference-based generic outcome measure). In the absence of evidence of this sort, CUA often proceeds on the basis of highly arbitrary and subjective exercises to 'map' outcomes from disease-specific to preference-based systems. The immediate goal therefore lies in encouraging studies of effectiveness - and routine clinical service quality audits - to include the EQ-5D as one means of gauging patient outcomes.

13.4 NORTH AMERICA

Introduction

Due to the popularity of the EQ-5D in European countries, North American researchers and policy makers are increasingly interested in utilising the instrument for studies in a variety of settings and conditions. The EQ-5D has been included in guideline recommendations in both Canada and the United States for the indirect measurement of preferences suitable for calculating QALYs. In many cases, the brevity and simplicity of the instrument have made it an attractive choice when investigators desire or require a preference-based index measure of HRQoL.

13.5 UNITED STATES

Introduction

In 1996, Johnson and Coons embarked on an investigation to establish a set of US-based population weights for the standard set of health states for the EQ-5D instrument, to determine weights for the entire 243 health states defined by the measure, and to compare results from the SF-12 to those provided by the EQ-5D (Johnson *et al*, 1998a; Johnson and Coons, 1998b). Thus, the authors set out to determine the reliability, construct validity (self-reported EQ-5D validations compared to pre-specified hypotheses), convergent validity and discriminant validity of the EQ-5D in this population (through comparisons with measurements from the SF-12).

Of the 3500 questionnaires mailed out for the valuation exercise, only 905 (25.8%) were returned in a usable condition. Half of the sample had also received a combined EQ-5D/SF-12 questionnaire; the usable response rate for this group was lower (427 out of 1800 or 23.7%). The mean age of the respondents was 52.4 years and tended to be male (66%), Caucasian (90%), married or in a partnership (71%), and employed (60%). Respondents were most commonly in the low to middle income groups (62%) and had some college education (73%). The sample reported having the following chronic medical conditions: arthritis (24%), hypertension (24%), heart disease (13%), diabetes (8%), asthma (8%), COPD (4%), and cancer (3%). Over half of the respondents (58%) indicated some level of feeling depressed.

EQ-5D health status

The distribution of the responses to the EQ-5D was skewed with the median response being 'no problem' on all dimensions. Seven health states (11111 [50%], 11121 [14%], 11112 [8%], 11122 [8%], 11221[4%], 21121 [3%], 21221[2%]) accounted for almost 90% of all the respondents. Interestingly, 219 of the 243 possible states did not occur in this survey. The instrument displayed a substantial ceiling effect with over 85% being at the ceiling for the functional dimensions; however, for the pain dimension, 59% responded at the ceiling. When only the VAS scores for the self-valuation of individuals' health states were considered, the ceiling effect was less pronounced (median VAS 85 out of 100).

Validity

With respect to the construct validity of the instrument, the hypothesized relationships between the proportions of those patients reporting any problem were significant for age and socioeconomic variables (education, income, employment, and relationship status) and were consistent with the observed responses, as had been the case in most European general population health surveys. Respondents with a chronic condition were more likely to report a problem on all of the dimensions. These relationships were also true for the mean VAS scores between the above groups. In addition, when the most common specific medical conditions were considered, significantly more patients with the condition reported problems in at least 3 dimensions (range 3-5) than those without the illness.

Reliability

In terms of the reliability assessments for the study, there were no differences in health state valuations for the 2 versions of the questionnaires (i.e. with or without the embedded SF-12). However, there were differences in the responses from the 6 variants of the valuation question; specifically, in the proportion of respondents not valuing 'dead'. The authors explored reasons for these differences but were unable to identify a satisfactory explanation beyond stating that they may have been due to chance because of the large number of statistical tests performed (i.e. the rationale being that with more tests performed at an alpha level of 0.05, there is an increase in the probability of some of them being significant due to chance alone).

EQ-5D health valuations

45 health states were valued by respondents. All of the 45 health states had a minimum valuation of 0 and all but 3 had a maximum valuation of 100. 22% of the respondents did not value all 14 standard health states and 5% did not value any health state. The number of health states valued by an individual was negatively correlated with chronic conditions and positively correlated with his or her VAS score. In addition, the number of health states where a valuation was not supplied was significantly larger for individuals with lower education ($p < 0.001$) or lower levels of income ($p < 0.001$). 25% did not provide a valuation for the state of 'dead'. For those that provided a valuation for the other 14 health states, 15% did not provide a value for dead. Respondents who did not value dead were significantly older (59.6 years vs. 50.3 years, $p = 0.001$) and had significantly lower levels of income and education

(both p = 0.001). These findings indicate that respondents had difficulty and may have introduced bias in the valuation exercise.

The valuations of the 8 health states (those on page 5 of the EQ-5D instrument) also revealed significant relationships. Respondents who were older, less educated, or from a lower income group tended to give a higher value to health states with at least 1 moderate or severe problem. In addition, these individuals assigned a lower health valuation to the best state of health (11111) than others. Logical consistency in the EQ-5D involves comparing pairs of health valuations in which one should be least as good as its comparator (e.g. 22222 and 22232). If comparisons are undertaken and this hypothesis is not supported, the logical consistency of the valuations must be questioned. The investigators found that the logical inconsistency in this study was 18.6%, much higher than those achieved by European investigators.

The investigators employed an ordinary least squares (OLS) regression approach, using the valuations from the 8 health states, to attempt to interpolate scores not directly valued, again following the approach in the UK MVH study. However, this regression model was found to violate several assumptions (normality and homoscedasticity) despite the fact that the regression coefficients (dimensions and scores) were all significant. Despite these difficulties, the model was reasonable at predicting, from the standard states, the 43 health states for which valuations were obtained. The absolute value of the difference between the observed and the predicted scores exceeded 10 (out of 100) for only 2 of the 43 states.

Comparison of the EQ-5D with the SF-12

The convergent and discriminant validity of the EQ-5D was tested in this sample by examining the relationship between the EQ-5D and the physical and mental composite summary scores of the SF-12 (i.e. PCS-12 and MCS-12, respectively). The relationships between comparable dimensions from each instrument (i.e. anxiety/depression from the EQ-5D to the MCS-12, and the mobility, self-care, usual activities and pain/discomfort EQ-5D dimensions to the PCS-12) were postulated to be stronger than less comparable dimensions. In addition the VAS was postulated to correlate with both the MCS-12 and the PCS-12 scores. Further, the purported greater discriminative ability of the SF-12 at identifying respondents with less severe, but significant, health problems was investigated. The authors found that respondents indicating a problem on the EQ-5D had significantly lower SF-12 component scores. As postulated, this relationship was the strongest for the anxiety/depression dimension (EQ-5D) to the MCS-12 (SF-12), and the functional dimensions (EQ-5D) to the PCS-12 (SF-12).

Those reporting 'no problem' on the EQ-5D (i.e. a health state of 11111) were divided into 2 groups according to the median SF-12 component scores (the upper group was considered to have 'better health' whereas the lower group was considered to have 'worse health'). Significant differences were found between these 2 groups in age, relationship status, employment, chronic medical conditions, and mean VAS score with the better health group being consistently superior to the worse health state. This finding suggests that the SF-12 had better discriminating properties than the EQ-5D in the US population.

Comparisons in valuations between US and European populations

Recently the VAS valuations for EQ-5D health states obtained in the US were compared to the VAS valuations obtained from postal surveys in Finland (Johnson *et al*, 2000a). This study was unique in that it was the first published study to compare EQ-5D health state valuations between samples from different countries. When combined, the US and Finnish surveys covered a total of 43 EQ-5D health states with 32 being common between the 2 samples.

The authors utilized a weighted least squares regression approach to test whether VAS valuations for the 32 health states common to both surveys differed by country. The model allowed for the weighting of differences in the distributions in socio-demographic factors between the 2 countries through a standardised age-gender distribution. In addition, the regression analysis allowed for the differences in specific VAS valuations through the interaction terms between country and specific dimension weightings.

The Finnish sample appeared to be of similar mean age but differed in employment status. It was not possible to compare ethnicity, income, or marital status between the 2 samples, as this data was not collected in the Finnish survey. Mean valuations of EQ-5D health states were significantly different in 18 out of the 32 common health states, with the US sample supplying more extreme values (higher values for mild health states and lower values for severe health states).

The authors acknowledged several limitations with their study such as: potential problems with the EQ-5D in cultural adaptation that make comparability across countries difficult, the fact that the 2 surveys were conducted in different time periods (the US survey in 1996 and the Finnish survey in 1992), and the low response rates in the US survey (25%) which limit generalisability. In addition, the authors addressed further problems with logical inconsistency in health state valuations, the presence of multicollinearity and heteroscedasticity in the regression models, and the fact that the regression model only applied weights to known differences in distributions (i.e. age and gender) between the 2 samples, whereas many parameters were not collected in the Finnish survey. Despite these limitations, the authors concluded that the EQ-5D VAS valuations for common health states were different between US and Finnish populations; however, these differences were unlikely to be of sufficient magnitude to affect EQ-5D scores in international studies.

13.6 CANADA

The EQ-5D has also been applied in population surveys in Canada. Johnson and Pickard essentially replicated the previous US survey methodology in the general adult population in Alberta, one of the Canadian provinces (Johnson *et al*, 2000b). Of the 4200 randomly selected subjects who were mailed surveys, 1518 (36%) were returned in a usable fashion. The respondents' mean age was 53.5 years and they tended to be male (67%), Caucasian (85%), married or in a partnership (71%), and employed full-time (59%). In addition, they were most likely to come from lower or middle income categories (59%) and have some at least some college or technical school education (61%).

As with the study conducted in the US, the median response for all dimensions was 'no problem' (health status 11111). In fact, 47% of the respondents replied in this manner. Of the 243 possible EQ-5D health states, respondents reported 52 unique health states. However, 11 of these 52 accounted for more than 90% of all responses. As with the study in the US, hypothesized relationships were confirmed between the proportions of those patients reporting any problem that were significant for age and socioeconomic variables (education, income, employment, and relationship status). Respondents with a chronic condition were more likely to report a problem on all of the dimensions. Thus, the construct validity of the measurement of health status in Canada appeared to be supported.

The comparison of the comparable dimensions between the SF-12 and the EQ-5D yielded similar results to the US study. For example, the authors found that respondents indicating a problem on the EQ-5D had significantly lower SF-12 composite scores for all dimensions. As postulated, this relationship was the strongest for the anxiety/depression dimension (EQ-5D) to the MCS-12 (SF-12), and the functional dimensions (EQ-5D) to the PCS-12 (SF-12). The EQ VAS scores were positively correlated with the SF-12 summary scores for the PCS-12 ($r = 0.68$, $p < 0.01$), but less strongly with the MCS-12 ($r = 0.38$, $p < 0.038$).

To assess the ceiling effect of the EQ-5D, those reporting no problems on the EQ-5D dimensions (state 11111) were divided into 2 groups depending on whether they had reported any chronic conditions. The mean SF-12 scores were compared between these groups and it was found that those reporting no medical conditions had significantly higher PCS-12 scores than those reporting at least 1 condition. In addition, in those respondents who had stated 'depression' as a chronic illness on the descriptive portion of the survey but stated no problems on the EQ-5D, their mean MCS-12 standard was significantly lower than those who did not report this condition. Thus, again it would appear that the EQ-5D has an important ceiling affect and the SF-12 has better discriminating properties when applied in a generally healthy sample of the population.

One other population-based study of the EQ-5D has been conducted in Canada, involving both English- and French-speaking respondents from the Montreal, Quebec metropolitan area (Mayo *et al*, 1997). The purpose of this study was to assess the feasibility and measurement properties of the EQ-5D in a survey of English- and French-speaking Canadians. Postal surveys were mailed to 2000 subjects, half of whom were identified as French-speaking and received a French-Canadian translation of the EQ-5D. The overall response rate was 30.5%, with no difference by known first language.

As with other population surveys, the most prevalent health state was 11111 (44.2%), with moderate pain/discomfort and moderate anxiety/depression the next most common states, with 18.9 and 7.7%, respectively, and 11.1% combined (i.e. 11122). These 4 health states accounted for 83% of respondents. Mean EQ VAS rating for the full sample was 82.4 (SD 13.1). Respondent characteristics, such as age, gender, education, employment status, and self-rating of health were assessed for their relationship with the EQ VAS rating. Age over 65 years, presence of chronic health problems, and poor general health ratings were associated with lower VAS scores. The authors concluded that this initial information on the use of the EQ-5D in a French-speaking Canadian population would be helpful in future applications of the measure in Canada.

Some limitations of EQ-5D use in North America

These population health studies reflect some important limitations in using the EQ-5D to determine population-health status in North America. The studies had high non-response rates, thus limiting the interpretability of the findings. In addition, due to the selection of addresses from the telephone directory, the 2 larger survey samples were biased in selecting out predominantly white males, again limiting the extrapolation to other North American populations. For the US health state valuation component, the non-response rate for specific health states (including dead) lead to biased estimates of the values. As most people responded with the best possible health state (11111), this indicates that there was a high ceiling effect of the EQ-5D. This finding is further supported by the comparisons with the SF-12 where it is evident that the EQ-5D lacks the discriminant properties to detect less serious but important deficits in health status. Thus, the SF-12 measure is likely to be better than the EQ-5D at capturing some nuances of health status. However, the limitations with the SF-12 (and SF-36, for that matter) are that it does not supply an index measure of health status, nor are the scores preference-weighted. Thus, it may be preferable to use the 2 measures together in order to avoid the limitations of using either instrument alone.

Summary

In the past 5 years the EQ-5D has gained prominence in North America, based on a number of population health studies and applications in specific clinical areas, as well as involvement of investigators in multi-national clinical trials. Clinical applications include subarachnoid hemorrhage (Haley *et al*, 1997), HIV/AIDS (Wu *et al*, 1997b; Delate and Coons, 2001), stroke (Poissant *et al*, 2000), rheumatic disorders (Wolfe and Hawley, 1997), and cystic fibrosis (Johnson *et al*, 2000c).

The EQ-5D has been included in guideline recommendations in both Canada (Canadian Coordinating Office, 1997) and the US (Gold *et al*, 1996) as an indirect preference measure for the purpose of calculating QALYs in cost-utility analyses. Initial concern that a 'European-based' measure of health status would not be appropriate for measuring health status and HRQoL in North America seems to have been overcome. The simplicity and brevity of the descriptive system appear to be its strongest attributes in choosing to use the EQ-5D as a measure of health status in most applications. In general, most of the applications of the EQ-5D have provided broad support for its measurement properties.

When the purpose of using the EQ-5D multi-attribute descriptive system has been to generate an overall index of HRQoL and/or QALYs, analysts have most often applied the TTO-based scoring algorithm derived from the general population from the UK (Dolan, 1997) However, there is currently no comparable preference-based weighting system for North America.

The degree to which North American and European preferences for health states differ is not clear. Initial comparisons indicate that some differences in VAS valuations exist, but these differences may not be important in terms of impacting on health policy or resource allocation decisions. Further research is required to determine if there is a need for country-specific preference weighting systems for the multi-attribute classification system of the EQ-5D.

Future work

To redress the need for preference values noted above a new research project has been established. The primary objective of the study is to establish population-based preference values for the EQ-5D's 243 health states for use in the US. This proposal is in direct response to the recommendation by the US Public Health Service's Panel on Cost-Effectiveness in Health and Medicine to establish US-based weighting systems for preference-based health status measures, including the EQ-5D.

The specific aims are to:

(i) Determine preference values for 45 of the EQ-5D's health states through time trade-off (TTO) exercises conducted in a representative sample of the general US population.
(ii) Based on the data collected for the 45 health states, impute values for the full set of 243 health states represented in the EQ-5D.
(iii) Compare the US population-based EQ-5D health state values among the major racial/ethnic groups sampled (i.e. Hispanic, non-Hispanic Black, and 'other') and with values generated in a population survey in the UK.
(iv) Establish US population norms, by age groupings, gender, and major racial/ ethnic groups for self-reported health status as measured by the EQ-5D.

This project will be a cross-sectional study involving a face-to-face interview design on a nationally representative US sample. A total of 4007 face-to-face interviews will be conducted throughout the US. Each interview will consist of 3 stages:

(i) Rank-ordering 15 health states.
(ii) Rating the 15 health states on a VAS.
(iii) Making a series of choices (i.e. TTOs) based on hypothetical situations for each of the health states. During these stages, the self-reported health status of the subjects will be elicited via the EQ-5D and the Health Utilities Index. An ordinary least squares (OLS) regression model will be constructed to interpolate scores for the health states not directly valued in the EQ-5D TTO exercise.

13.7 ZIMBABWE

Introduction

Zimbabwe is a country of approximately 12 million people. There are 2 main language groups, Shona and Ndebele. Shona speakers comprise the majority language group but English is the official language. In 1980, Zimbabwe gained independence from the UK and since that time, there has been free compulsory primary education (7 years of schooling) and the adult literacy rate is high, 91% (compared to 84% in South Africa) (Tandon, 1999). Significant gains in health care were also achieved. Unfortunately the worsening economic climate and the catastrophic impact of HIV/ Aids have eroded these advances.

In 1995, the Zimbabwe National Burden of Disease and cost-effectiveness study was initiated to assist government to define national control priorities. As the study progressed, it became apparent that the global burden of disease quality of life measure, the disability adjusted life year (DALY) did not reflect local health preferences. As the EuroQoL Group had had extensive experience with valuations of health states, the EQ-5D was chosen as the measure with which to assess the preferences of Zimbabweans. The EQ-5D was therefore introduced to Zimbabwe through a multi-disciplinary research committee, with the specific purpose of establishing values that could be used in conjunction with epidemiological studies and with cost-effectiveness analysis.

Translation

The EQ-5D was translated into Shona under the guidance of the EuroQol Group. This entailed forward and backward translation and testing the results on a lay panel of 18 participants.

It was clear from the outset that the concepts described by the EQ-5D do not sit comfortably in the Shona worldview. For example, the English concepts of health sound inappropriate when translated because some health states are seen to have a spiritual rather than a physical origin. Mararike (1999) states that within Shona culture, illnesses may be normal (i.e. an illness with an impersonal cause) or abnormal (an illness with interpersonal causes). Abnormal diseases can only be treated by traditional healers because modern medicine cannot address the ultimate cause of the illness, namely witches or the various types of spirits. Attitudes towards these health states are therefore understood and interpreted differently in Shona culture and experience.

Several problems were encountered with the process of translation. The innate modesty of the language makes definitive statements unacceptable in Shona idiom. The words used to translate "I have no problems with self-care" are " don't need anyone to help me" which come across as arrogant. Similarly people would hesitate to say that their health state approximates the "best imaginable health state" or "worst imaginable health state" and these words were replaced with "very good health" and "very bad health".

It was concluded that Shona respondents would be likely to identify the EQ-5D as a forcign instrument but would be able to recognise the concepts and respond appropriately, while maintaining the awareness that the questions do not relate directly to "their world" (Jelsma *et al*, 2000a.)

Reliability, validity and sensitivity

Several related studies were then undertaken to determine the reliability, validity and sensitivity of the instrument (Jelsma *et al*, 2002b). On the basis of these studies, it was concluded that the Shona EQ-5D was a reliable and valid instrument that could be used with confidence in an urban Zimbabwe population. The English version was reliable in those with a minimum of 7 years of education. However, the VAS should be used with caution in those with less than primary school education as not all respondents would be able to understand the concept.

Home-based survey – health status

In March 2000, 2488 residents of randomly selected stands in Glenview, a high-density suburb of Harare were interviewed in their homes. The entrance criteria included completion of primary school education and a minimum age of 15. The oldest person in each household who met the criteria was interviewed. The demographic details of the respondents were compared with published profiles of the area (Central Statistical Office, 1994, 1998) and results indicated that the sample was representative of the general adult population in terms of gender, marital status, residence and age. A total of 2182 respondents had completed some or all of the EQ-5D self-report information of which 104 (4.4%) reported a disability and 290 (12.2%) had had a serious illness in the prior 3 months.

In both this sample and the UK MVH sample nearly one third of the respondents reported either some or severe problems in the dimensions of pain/discomfort (Kind *et al*, 1998). However, the number reporting some or severe anxiety/depression (30.5%) was higher than in the UK sample (21%). As the study was undertaken at an uncertain time in the political and economic history of Zimbabwe (just prior to a general election), it was not surprising that there was a high degree of anxiety amongst the respondents. Both samples reported very few problems in the area of self-care, or extreme problems with mobility or usual activities. The mean score on the VAS in the Zimbabwe sample (79.8, SD 17) was comparable to that of the British sample of 82.5 (SD 17). At first it may seem surprising that, even in the light of the HIV/AIDS pandemic, the health descriptors were so similar between the UK and Zimbabwe populations. However the Zimbabwe sample was much younger and it is possible that the morbidity reported was related more to infectious disease, whereas the morbidity in the UK sample was due more to ageing.

Home-based survey – valuations of health states

The TTO method of valuation of health states was used to determine Zimbabwean preferences for health states. The respondents in the home-based survey were asked to value different sets of 7 randomly selected health states based on English descriptors of combinations of the 5 EQ-5D domains (Dolan, 1997). All respondents also valued the 33333 state.

Following recommendations from other valuation studies (Ohinmaa and Sintonen, 1999), inconsistent data were excluded. Dummy independent variables were created and the variables representing the levels of moderate and extreme on each dimension were entered in forward stepwise linear regression analysis. The dependent variable was the TTO score divided by 10. Residual analysis was done through descriptive statistics. Comparison with the MVH data was based on the published data set (Dolan, 1997).

After exclusion of incomplete and inconsistent replies, the responses of 2182 subjects and 16488 values of 38 health states were analysed. The 33333 state was the only state that was valued as being worse than death (mean value = -0.27). Figure 13.1 depicts the observed MVH scores compared to the Zimbabwe scores for the 38 health states.

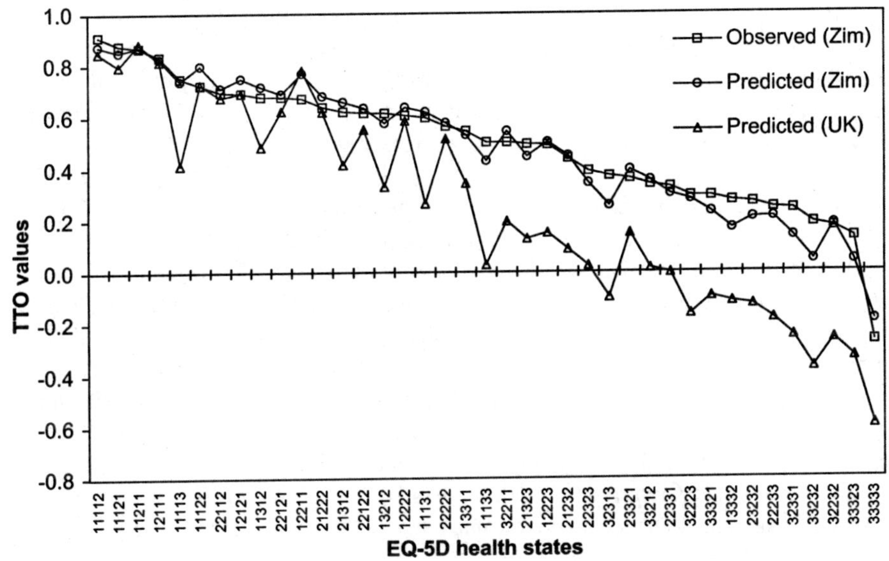

Figure 13.1. Plot of predicted and observed TTO scores (divided by 10). The UK predicted scores from the MVH are included for comparison

Whereas there was initial convergence in scores between the Zimbabwe and MVH sample, values diverged as the health states become more severe and dimensions at an extreme level were included. Pearson's correlation between the values for the 38 different states was $r = 0.945$ ($p < 0.01$). Linear regression indicated that the dummy variables representing moderate and extreme levels on each dimension accounted for 55.0% of the variance ($R^2 = 0.550$, standard error of estimate = 0.3001).

A credible model was developed and the R^2 of 0.55 compared favourably with the MVH model ($R^2 = 0.46$) which is regarded as being very high given the type of (cross-sectional) data analysed (Dolan, 1997). The mean absolute difference between actual and predicted value and residuals for each health state was 0.040 (cf.

MVH = 0.039). The rank correlation between the MVH and Zimbabwe sample coefficients for the different domains was rho = 0.879 (p = 0.001).

The most striking finding of the study is the similarity in preferences between the UK and Zimbabwe samples. The correlations between the values of the health states and the coefficients generated were very high. Although valuation studies based on the EQ-5D had reported similarities of valuations, with low sensitivity for socio-demographic variables across European countries (Krabbe *et al,* 1996), the results of this study were unexpected. A previous study on the rank ordering of the 22 index health states used by the global burden of disease study had found no correlation between the international and locally determined Zimbabwean ranking (Jelsma *et al*, 2000b). It would appear that a deconstructed approach to valuation, in which impairments or activity limitations (WHO, 1999) are valued (e.g. pain or mobility) rather than specific health states (e.g. rheumatoid arthritis), is more likely to tap into commonly understood constructs and yield universal preferences.

However, there were important differences between the samples. Respondents in the UK study valued 16 health states as being worse than dead, whereas in the Zimbabwe sample only the 33333 state was awarded a negative value. This obvious reluctance to value states as worse than dead might reflect the general state of health of the population. Primarily due to the HIV/AIDS pandemic the expected number of years to be lived in what might be termed the equivalent of 'full health' (DALE) is now estimated to be 32.9 (cf. UK 71.7) (WHO, 2000). For many of the respondents death is a reality, rather than an abstraction, and consequently more to be avoided. This conclusion is supported by a Spanish study of preferences of 103 severely ill patients who rated no states as worse than dead. The authors concluded that within the EQ-5D descriptive system, there are no health states worse than dead for seriously ill patients (Badia *et al,* 1996).

Another notable difference between the Zimbabwe and UK studies is that, although highly correlated, the ranking of the coefficients of the different levels of the 5 dimensions differs. For Zimbabweans, the inability to wash and dress oneself is a major contributor to poor quality of life and self-care level 3 was ranked second. In contrast, self-care level 3 was only ranked fourth in the MVH study. It is regarded as insulting to ask whether people are able to wash or dress themselves, if in any way it is implied that they have not done so (Jelsma *et al*, 2000a). Being confined to bed and severe depression are regarded as being more serious by the UK sample.

It is therefore recommended that the parameter estimates developed in this study be used to both describe HRQoL and as an outcome measure of health interventions in the Zimbabwe urban population.

Conclusion

The EQ-5D appears to be a robust measure of HRQoL that demonstrates reliability and validity in a cultural context very different to that in which it was developed. The similarities between the Zimbabwe findings in both the community survey and the valuation study are striking and it is possible that QALY weights based on EQ-5D descriptors might be developed which are valid globally. However, as there are important differences in the absolute values of more severe states and the relative importance attached to the different domains, locally generated values should be used to investigate local quality of life issues.

13.8 CONCLUDING REMARKS

This chapter provides insights into the use of the EQ-5D in different parts of the world. The emphasis, as in much of the book, is on valuation exercises in the different countries. It is evident from the authors' own conclusions that EQ-5D is likely to have a considerable part to play in HRQoL measurement and valuation in their respective parts of the world. Furthermore, given that the instrument is one of the few generic measures currently available that can be used for valuation in economic appraisal, it is likely to play a prominent role in studies aimed at giving advice to policymakers. We should not, however, ignore the difficulties in using the EQ-5D in different contexts around the world, nor indeed the perceived limitations of the instrument in its present form. This chapter's contributors have raised and discussed a number of these matters.

The EuroQol Group welcomes the interest shown in the EQ-5D around the world. Further development of the instrument will depend in part on the continued willingness of analysts in a variety of countries to collaborate with us in our efforts.

14
Summary and future EQ-5D work

Richard Brooks and Frank de Charro

It will be evident from the contents of this book, which reports on the work accomplished by the EuroQol Group in the context of Biomed II funding - the EQ-net project - that the measurement and valuation of health-related quality of life is a comprehensive undertaking, even for a measurement instrument, the EQ-5D, which is probably the simplest and shortest of the generic instruments currently available. This final chapter summarises the EQ-net project, highlighting some of the key points and issues in what proved a complex set of inter-locking tasks. The opportunity is also taken to reflect upon the current status of the Group's work with EQ-5D and how this might proceed.

Biomed II funding provided the Group an opportunity to proceed with our research and development programme in a systematic fashion by focussing our work within a number of key categories: application, valuation, translation and communication.

In the first part of the book the emphasis is on the application of EQ-5D where we present guidelines on the analysis and reporting of EQ-5D outcomes (Chapter 2), advice on alternative modes of administration (Chapter 3), and guidelines for value sets to be used in economic and non-economic studies (Chapter 4). We also point in Chapter 5 to evidence on the test-retest performance of our instrument.

14.1 APPLICATION

Chapters 2 and 3 are devoted to various practical aspects of EQ-5D: the implications of using EQ-5D with various research designs, data collection, statistical techniques required for data analysis, some suggestions for reporting EQ-5D data, and modes of administration alternative to the standard pencil and paper self-report – face-to-face interview, telephone interview, and self-completion in the presence of an interviewer. Chapter 3 also considers computer-assisted data collection, proxy report for respondents who may be physically incapacitated or severely cognitively impaired and a brief commentary on recall periods. The work undertaken for this chapter clearly demonstrates the Group's awareness of important issues concerning how to administer HRQoL measures and how these issues can be handled in the context of EQ-5D.

Chapter 4 provides an essential link to the valuation material by focussing on key concepts and constructs in valuation. The relationship between values and prefer-

R. Brooks et al. (eds.),
The Measurement and Valuation of Health Status Using EQ-5D: A European Perspective, 229–244.

ences is discussed at the outset, followed by a consideration of EQ-5D presentational formats, in which the chance is taken to discuss measurement properties, including ordinality and cardinality. A key point made is that since a range of value sets for EQ-5D index is now available, there is no longer reason to believe that researcher-based value assumptions, by contrast with values generated, e.g. from survey data, have any particular legitimacy. The use of EQ-5D in measuring HRQol is then taken up, followed by an outline of sources of values, with particular emphasis on the VAS approach, given the detailed investigations that have been undertaken using this approach from the Group's early days. The application of EQ-5D in economic studies is treated in some detail, with a table providing a summary of the choice factors in selecting EQ-5D weights for such studies. The application of EQ-5D in non-economic studies is discussed, followed by a tailpiece listing the variety of population value sets constructed using EQ-5D; with some suggestions concerning how researchers may proceed in the absence of a set of weights representing a particular general population's preferences.

Measurement instruments need to be reliable. Chapter 5 reports on the exploration of one aspect of reliability, namely the test-retest reliability or the reproducibility of scores, for the EQ-5D descriptive system and the EQ VAS. Work undertaken with 2 samples, one the 1993 UK MVH survey and the other a group of rheumatoid arthritis patients in Edinburgh, Scotland, is detailed. It is concluded that EQ-5D demonstrates acceptable test-retest reliability (or reproducibility) when administered to both a general population and a clinical sample over a 3-month period. The arthritis data also demonstrated that the EQ VAS was responsive to self-reported clinical change, thus giving some evidence to counter the view that generic health outcome measures are not responsive. The chapter concludes by noting that the reported reliability of a measure is always context specific, and hence reliability coefficients should always be interpreted with caution outside the context of the specific populations for which they were calculated.

14.2 VALUATION

The next part of the book focuses on the considerable volume of work undertaken by the Group on valuation. EQ-5D was explicitly developed with the aim of providing HRQoL valuations, with particular emphasis on the search for a common value set that might be constructed and applied across countries. This process started in a small number of countries. The EQ-net project allowed the Group to build up databases for the VAS and TTO valuation approaches, using material from a variety of studies from a number of countries. These studies were not completely standardised, so a lot of effort had to be put into pooling the data in appropriate ways. Chapter 6 reports on this endeavour. Once this was accomplished, detailed analysis of the data could be undertaken. Chapter 7 provides an analysis and comparison of the VAS scores generated. From a research point of view considerable fascination surrounded the attempt to construct a common EQ-5D value set based on VAS values. For the original members of the Group a common value set had been a key aim from the outset. Chapter 8 reports this in detail. Equally fascinating have been the experiments in obtaining EQ-5D TTO valuations, especially for those seeking the choice-based valuations deemed to be required for the measurement of QALYs, thus opening up the possibility for the use of EQ-5D in, e.g. economic evaluation of health projects. Chapter 4 set the scene for such evaluation and Chapter 9 details the EQ-net work in this area.

Chapter 6 commences by listing the 'standard' set of 18 EQ-5D health states on which much of the valuation work has been undertaken. These comprise the 13 states employed from the outset of the Group's empirical work (usually referred to as the 'common core'), 'dead' valued twice, 'unconscious', and 11111 and 33333 (core states) both valued twice.

Owing to the wide variety of responses in different studies (both response rates themselves, and how respondents handled the tasks posed by EQ-5D) the Group established a set of exclusion criteria to enable consistent comparison across EQ-5D studies. These are listed. It should be stated that this set of criteria has been adopted as a 'working rule' by the group; on-going research may well lead to modification. The individual studies providing the material for the VAS and TTO databases are described. Annotations of background variables follow, classified into respondent characteristics and sample features. The characteristics are: age, sex, experience of illness, working status, level of education, ease of filling in the questionnaire, own health scores on the EQ-5D descriptive system, and EQ VAS scores. Sample features are: time of data collection, sample method, RIT-variable (ranked interview-based ten-year duration study protocol), and interviewer participation. This is a considerable list, and leads to the provision of very detailed tables involving these background variables and their impact on valuations, with further detail on the adjustment of the data for exclusions and inconsistencies.

The major points to emerge from this work were:

(i) Analysis of respondent characteristics showed some differences between the study populations, which were partly influenced by the differences in sample features, e.g. differences in the methods of collecting valuations.

(ii) The number of exclusions and inconsistencies differed significantly between the studies, these differences being connected to differences in the VAS valuation methods used. The quality of data was much better in the interview-based TTO data sets.

As a consequence, the analysis of the evaluation data conducted in subsequent chapters utilizes different kinds of weighting techniques. This evidence has also informed the ongoing deliberations within the Group concerning modes of administration, referred to in Chapters 2 and 3.

The purpose of Chapter 7 is to pool the data from the European VAS-based studies conducted since 1991, and to compare the valuations across studies and countries in a rigorous way by accounting for measurable differences in methods used, study features, and respondent characteristics. Explored are:

(i) The extent to which the variation in the valuations of different health states, when considered separately, can be explained by the background variables employed.
(ii) To what extent median VAS valuations differ between the studies.

In order to investigate the similarities in the VAS valuations from the studies, singular value decomposition (SVD) was carried out on the median VAS scores.

A number of features emerged from this work as follows:

(i) Since a striking difference between the studies was in sample sizes, in order to prevent the larger studies from dominating the data, the analyses were carried out with weighted data (the reciprocal of the number of respondents per study after exclusions).
(ii) The studies differed in study features and respondent characteristics. These differences had an effect on valuations, although the proportion of variance they explained was very low.
(iii) From the variables considered, the RIT variable appeared to have had the clearest and most consistent effect on valuations, resulting in generally higher valuations than the standard approach.
(iv) Age and education also seemed to have some effect: higher age tended to be associated with higher valuations, but for education there was no systematic pattern.
(v) After controlling for these factors, the origin of the study did not have a consistent effect on valuations with the exception of 2 studies from Spain. The reason for this exception is unclear.
(vi) The SVD analyses show how similar are the median valuations of the studies for the standard states.

The conclusion is drawn that there appears to be a considerable degree of agreement between health state valuations in studies from several European countries, with the exception of Spain. The valuations from 3 RIT-based studies from 3 countries were even more similar. There is also some evidence comparing Finnish and US valuations which shows just small and inconsistent differences in valuations.

The evidence so far thus appears to suggest that the Western industrialised countries at least may share a similar value climate. Hence in this cultural area it appears unnecessary to replicate expensive and detailed valuation studies in each country in order to arrive at valid preference-based HRQoL instruments.

This conclusion leads naturally to the question whether a European value set based on VAS scores can be constructed from the database, and this is considered in Chapter 8, which is a lengthy chapter reflecting the complexity of the task. Essentially the task was to see if the joint data sets of the VAS scores in the database could be described by 1 model. Since the database provides data on a range of health states (not just the 'standard' set) this wider information can be used to model in such a way that it is possible to assign a unique HRQoL value to each possible health state as defined by EQ-5D (243 in all).

The analyses were performed on a total of 114220 scores from the pooled data of the 11 studies included in the database. To avoid skewness on the raw VAS scores, the data was transformed by a logistic transformation. In order to provide a scale from 'full health' = 100 and 'dead' = 0, the data was also rescaled. Multi-level regression modelling was then undertaken. Results are first presented with respect to the influence of the number of inconsistencies. Then the effect of exclusions on the number of valuations is reported. Next, background variables are brought into the picture, with results shown from an OLS regression on both the raw and transformed VAS scores. These results are compared with the outcomes from a 'CANALS' model from the SAS programme. Detailed CANALS results are presented. Multilevel regression analysis is applied at 3 levels, allowing for both fixed and random effects. The model improves considerably if random effects are incorporated. This analysis also incorporates dummies for the RIT variable, for N2 (any score including EQ-5D dimension level 2), for N3 (score includes level 3), and for the interactions RIT and N2, and RIT and N3. The results in terms of rescaling are also shown. Annex 8.3 provides the estimated and rescaled estimated scores for all 243 EQ-5D states, as intended at the outset of the exercise.

Key aspects of the analysis and its results include the following:

(i) Exclusions had the effect that the data on which the regressions were performed were from respondents who were younger, healthier, and more educated.

(ii) The regression on the transformed values resulted in a much lower R^2 compared to the regression on the non-transformed data. After applying a non-linear regression analysis, it turned out that the best transformation was linear over the major range of the scale, with exceptions at the ends of the scale. The improvement in the model (in terms of the R^2) was, however, small. Hence it was decided to maintain the use of the linear regression model.

(iii) In order to take individual and study differences other than the RIT-model into account, the multi-level (random effects) model revealed that 28.3% of the total error variance was due to individual differences and 1.6% was due to study differences. However, this had only a small effect on the parameter estimates in the model.

(iv) A major aim of the analysis was the impact of modelling on the basis of EQ-5D characteristics, compared with modelling on the basis of difference in study methodology used (i.e. the ranking effect'). The 3 'RIT studies' were interviewer-based TTO studies in which a VAS valuation task took place after the health states were ranked by the respondents, by contrast with the standard postal approach. The major effect of the difference in methodology concerned the level of scoring, rather than the scores on the separate EQ-5D dimensions. In particular the very mild and, to a lesser extent, the less serious health states, were rated higher. So for evaluation studies comparing different forms of treatment, the absolute value of scoring is less important than its relative weight.

(v) Chapter 6 indicates that there is a considerable influence of study design on the valuations. To account for this influence, a dummy variable was included in the model that described the influence of the RIT studies. For future valuation studies, it should be kept in mind that VAS valuations differ between RIT and non-RIT studies and that the RIT-methodology produces more consistent outcomes. Future VAS valuation studies therefore should be designed to incorporate the ranking task.

(vi) From a theoretical point of view, rescaling (e.g. full health =100 and dead =0) is necessary for a data set to be used in economic evaluation studies. Rescaling can take place on the individual valuations, using the individual scores for full health and dead, or it can take place at the end of the analysis on the estimated VAS values. A problem with the rescaling procedure on the individual valuations is that this procedure sometimes results in rescaled values greater than 1 and less than minus 1. The rescaled scores of less than minus 1 can be extremely negative, causing standard deviations to double in the mild health states and to increase by more than a factor 2 in the more severe states. All the rescaled health states had a high negative skewness. To counter these effects, the negative values were truncated at minus1, which is an arbitrary cut-off point. A rescaling procedure was carried out on the estimated values where the estimated value for 11111 was the upper anchor and a measure of central tendency for dead was the lower anchor. When rescaled with the mean value for dead (10.0) the estimates, especially at the lower end of the spectrum of health states, are clearly lower.

(vii) Given the high value for the R^2 in the regression analyses, the overall conclusion is that there is strong evidence that it is possible to describe the joint VAS data set, gathered by the EuroQol Group, by one common model which could, e.g. be used for cost-effectiveness analyses in socio-economic evaluation studies. The results from the multilevel regression do not contradict the expected characteristics of the value set derived by the EQ-5D. All the coefficients have the right signs, while the values all differ from zero, with values that are plausible. For all the dimensions of the EQ-5D, a 3 on the descriptive system has a stronger negative effect on the estimated VAS values than a 2.

(viii) The results of this exercise on the basis of pooled data from 11 European studies (some with differences in study design e.g. ranking or selection of hypothetical health states) should be compared with valuation data from future work with a uniform European, or even world-wide, approach. The results suggest that valuation studies need not be confined to national borders. There is scope for widening the context of research on VAS-based instruments such as EQ-5D and finding solutions that can be generalised, at least for Western European industrialised countries.

Chapter 9 turns to EQ-5D valuations derived using the TTO approach, and codified in the TTO database, which contains valuations from studies undertaken in the UK, Germany, and Spain. Comparison of these values gives the opportunity to test differences in TTO values between these countries. As with the VAS analyses, exclusion criteria have been applied. Four multi-level regression models are used in order to handle nested data (health states nested within respondent, respondents nested within nations). Background variables are incorporated into the analysis.

Key points to emerge included the following:

(i) There were differences in EQ-5D valuations: the Spanish values resembled the British, but the German values were higher. The differences, small but larger than the differences found in the VAS values, cannot be explained by differences in the distribution of background variables.

(ii) The results suggest that health is valued systematically differently in different countries, when measured using TTO. Part of the variance could be attributed to the way education interacted with age differently in each country. The differences seemed to be driven by differences in the proportion and magnitude of the negative valuations of health states.

(iii) The small differences found may have been the result of subtle differences in the administration of the TTO task, perhaps, e.g. in relation to the handling of negative values in the interviewer-based scoring task.

(iv) The differences may not represent differences in health valuation, but differences in the translation of the health states.

(v) The different results in VAS and TTO comparisons may mean that the VAS technique is less influenced by cultural differences, or perhaps VAS is easier to replicate, resulting in less variation between studies.

Practical implications are:

(i) Since there may be national differences in TTO values, choice of a particular TTO value set, say for economic evaluations, has to anticipate these national differences.
(ii) Within international trials, it might be appropriate to use 1 TTO-based value set. Given its design and construction and the large sample employed, the UK MVH value set has been the most often used in this context.
(iii) Even where 1 value set was used in an international trial, it is recommended that the best local valuation set be used for (local) reimbursement decisions.

It will be evident that the TTO evidence is somewhat more limited then the VAS material. More studies can be expected to be reported, e.g. a large-scale Danish study has been undertaken, but in general the Group is keen that further work be undertaken using choice-based methods such as the TTO.

14.3 TRANSLATION

The translation category was viewed broadly to encompass issues concerning the nature and meaning of health and HRQoL in the context of EQ-5D, its construction, design, and wording. As EQ-5D spread to languages other than the original ones in which it was developed (with English as the 'reference' language), the process of translation began to point to difficulties in language usage, and even more fundamentally, to differences in the conceptualisation of entities, such as EQ-5D dimensions and items, across countries and languages. This experience, amongst other considerations, led the Group to consider more closely the meanings of concepts and the related wording used in EQ-5D, not least in the reference English language. Chapters 10-12 report in detail on the EQ-net work in this area.

Chapter 10 concerns interpretation of EQ-5D concepts. It considers 3 main areas of research: the range of shared and different meanings among EuroQol Group members, interpretations of EQ-5D amongst people who have completed the questionnaire in UK English within the UK, and interpretations amongst people who have completed the EQ-5D in other languages.

There are evident variations in interpretation of EQ-5D concepts by Group members. At first sight this may seem surprising given that work on the instrument has proceeded since 1987. Part of the reason is that members were required to try to be explicit about concepts and terms which often contain implicit meanings. Other reasons could be: the view of a group is likely to change over time, asking individuals to think of the group view is likely to produce variety, group members will hold different views individually which reflect personal experiences of life, and an instrument developed by a group will represent a compromise of opinions. Appendix 7 provides a taxonomy of interpretations of EQ-5D terms which resulted from the research reported in this chapter.

Evidence from respondents indicates:

(i) Some interpretations of the EQ-5D appear to accord with the Group's intentions, and some do not.
(ii) Wide ranges in interpreting the meaning of levels within each dimension.
(iii) Some similarities in the concerns of Group members and respondents, e.g. with the expression 'usual activities'.
(iv) Difficulties for patients in completing the anxiety/depression question, raising broader questions of the extent to which there are gaps between what the respondent thinks in reality and what is recorded in a survey.

The main recommendations for further research include:

(i) Broadening the range of methods used to investigate meaning.
(ii) Broadening the base of investigations to include a wider range of countries and disease groups.
(iii) Using quantitative and qualitative measures alongside each other to investigate the relationship between interpretations of words and scales and valuations of health, in relation to socio-economic, demographic, and geographic variables.

Chapter 11 reviews work undertaken on producing other language versions of the EQ-5D. A brief history of translating the instrument is presented, followed by a discussion of current translation standard operating procedures and the 'quality control' of the translation process. Two appendices give detailed guidelines.

In concluding, the chapter notes:

(i) Development of new language versions of the EQ-5D reflects developments in the area of cross-cultural adaptation and in the HRQoL field in general.
(ii) Local researchers should be aware of the need to test a new version's measurement properties of reliability, validity, and sensitivity to change.
(iii) Analysis of similarities and differences between values obtained for EQ-5D health states in different cultural settings may be used, alongside careful qualitative research, to determine whether there are differences in values between different respondents in different countries, and as a further check on the extent to which meaning has been transmitted successfully between languages.

Chapter 12 contains a detailed account of an exploration of the results of translating the EQ-5D into 11 European languages: Croatian, Czech, Danish, Dutch, Finnish, French, German, Italian, Polish, Portuguese, and Spanish. Information on the translation process in the HRQoL field is rarely written up in the international field of health outcomes assessment, so the material presented in this chapter is offered as an insight into the translation process, in particular the difficulties encountered and how they were resolved, and how health state valuations might be affected. First, there is a fascinating description of the translation of the EQ-5D dimensions into languages other than English, replete with interesting examples. Then a number of studies of the potential impacts of decisions made during the translation process on valuations are presented. These impacts are discussed at some length.

A number of pointers to future work emerge from this preliminary, and essentially qualitative, exploration:

(i) The need to explore and achieve good quality translations that are semantically equivalent.
(ii) Assessing the impact of differences in the translation of questionnaires has to be supported with empirical research.
(iii) The acceptability and conceptual equivalence of existing translations could be further evaluated using both qualitative and quantitative methods.
(iv) For reliable international comparisons additional aspects of conceptual, item, operational, measurement and functional equivalence need to be investigated. This would be a challenging set of tasks, but the work is important if the Group is to be confident of the comparability of the content of EQ-5D language versions used in different countries.

14.4 NON-EUROPEAN STUDIES

Usage of the EQ-5D instrument has now spread far and wide from its original European base, and indeed EQ-5D has been used in many more European countries. Some of the issues raised by these developments are considered in the latter part of the book, as just noted in respect of the translation material. Chapter 13 contains 4 contributions from across the world – Africa, Asia, Oceania and North America. The choice of these contributions was largely motivated by researchers from these '4 corners of the world' becoming active members of the Group and joining us in our common endeavours. It is no surprise that language/semantic issues again feature in this chapter.

This chapter focuses largely on the valuation tasks and these are inter-related with the 'translation' issues treated in detail in the EQ-net project. All 4 sections include detail on valuation exercises in their respective parts of the world, both VAS and TTO valuations. In all sections there is comparison with previous European results, in particular the MVH study from the UK. There were important differences in valuations, for example in Japan and Zimbabwe, which are reported in the relevant sections.

The Japanese section contains specific examples of how words and phrases in the English EQ-5D were translated into Japanese, and shows the cognitive and conceptual problems that arose. It is speculated that health dimension values may be affected, specifically mobility.

The section on Zimbabwe discusses translation and conceptual issues with regard to 1 of the major language groups, namely Shona. It is concluded that, despite Shona people having a different view on aspects of health status from that portrayed in the EQ-5D, it would still be possible for people to respond to the questionnaire. This is borne out in the empirical results.

The New Zealand section discusses health valuations across the three major ethnic elements of New Zealand society, namely Maori, European/Paheka and Pacific Islands people. Despite the possibility of different conceptualisations of health, these do not appear to be borne out by the valuations, so it is appropriate to generate a value set by selecting samples from the electoral roll.

There is less direct consideration of cross-cultural issues in the North American section, although there is reference to potential problems in cultural adaptation in a US-Finnish data comparison (Johnson *et al*, 2000a). This North American section reviews work undertaken using EQ-5D in Canada and the United States. It is indicated that the degree to which North American and European preferences for health states differ is not clear. Initial comparisons indicate that some differences in VAS valuations exist, but these differences may not be important in terms of impacting on health policy or resource allocation decisions.

To redress the need for preference values noted in the North American review a new research project has been established. The primary objective of the study is to establish population-based preference values for the EQ-5D's 243 health states for use in the US. The project is a cross-sectional study involving a face-to-face interview design on a nationally representative US sample (4007 interviews. Each interview will consist of 3 stages: 1) rank-ordering 15 health states, 2) rating the 15 health states on a VAS, and 3) making a series of TTO choices based on hypothetical situations for each of the health states. An ordinary least squares (OLS) regression model will be constructed to interpolate scores for the health states not directly valued in the EQ-5D TTO exercise.

It is evident from the authors' own conclusions in Chapter 13 that EQ-5D is likely to have a considerable part to play in HRQoL measurement and valuation in their respective parts of the world. Furthermore, given that the instrument is one of the few generic measures currently available that can be used for valuation in economic appraisal, it is likely to play a prominent role in studies aimed at giving advice to policymakers. We should not, however, ignore the difficulties in using the EQ-5D in different contexts around the world, nor indeed the perceived limitations of the instrument in its present form, matters that are raised and discussed in this chapter. The EuroQol Group welcomes the interest shown in the EQ-5D around the world. Further development of the instrument will depend in part on the continued willingness of analysts in a variety of countries to collaborate with the Group in our efforts.

14.5 COMMUNICATION

The EuroQol Group initially comprised a group of researchers in different countries whose aim was to combine their methodological research efforts in the area of HRQoL. This intellectual partnership has proved to be very rewarding. The founding members of the Group, who were already involved in the application of HRQoL questionnaires in their respective countries, were aware of the vastness of the field. They realized the difficulties of making meaningful progress and generating sufficient resources to take on the substantial work required. Furthermore, research was often limited to a small number of academic institutions in various European countries. Members who were involved in the methodological research field lacked a forum for interdisciplinary research and interaction with other research units who were involved in application studies. All Group members were therefore eager to take on the methodological challenges involved and pursue a common agenda.

As the Group approaches its 15th anniversary, the pleasure of the intellectual debate within the Group continues as the primary stimulus for researchers to retain their membership and for others to join the Group. The unique feature of the Group's yearly meetings is that there is always time for lengthy debate on topical HRQoL issues both within the scientific meeting and outside in a more informal context. There are also opportunities for interaction between different researchers within the Group from different countries and disciplines that has lead to enduring and productive collaborative efforts, often resulting in joint articles. Achieving communication internally between EuroQol Group members has therefore been one of the Group's important successes.

Over the years since the inception of the Group, valuation studies have been carried out in various European countries. The resulting valuation sets were often applied solely for the purposes of national policy, and institutions where Group members were working were frequently commissioned to undertake this work. Over time, however, there was a common awareness that the body of knowledge produced by Group members should be made available to users and HRQoL researchers generally. As a result, the Group created a small management office, located in Rotterdam, the Netherlands, that provides services for distribution, co-ordination, quality control and

support for maintaining a focal point for communication. At the end of 1999, the EuroQol Business Management mailed a newsletter and survey of usage to more than 1000 researchers worldwide on the Group's mailing list. Further newsletters will be distributed electronically. A web address has been registered: www.euroqol.org
The site (which is continually updated) includes current information about Group membership, meetings, useful references, and an electronic version of the EQ-5D registration form that can be completed and returned directly to the EuroQol Business Management via the Internet. A large database of studies has been established as a result of this facility, thus enabling the EuroQol Business Management to provide information on the use of EQ-5D in various clinical areas, on the condition that the user has indicated a willingness that his or her research can be made available to other researchers.

A number of meetings and workshops have been arranged with users from the academic world and users with commercial interests, often within the context of international conferences. These provide useful information about the usage of EQ-5D and offer a forum to exchange experiences. More detailed and/or specialist information or support for users is provided by a number of Group members. These consultancy contracts are a matter to be decided upon by individual Group members and the institutions requesting support.

14.6 EQ-5D: THE FUTURE

The development of EQ-5D has been supported by the European Union as part of the Biomed programme (project number PL 963118). The grant has provided support in the form of a network resource that has enabled the Group to make progress in a number of key areas described in this book. Research focussing on integration and systematic analysis of values sets derived in European countries probably stands out as the most ambitious and noteworthy aspects of this programme. To date, as discussed in chapters 6-9, the data suggest that values elicited using the VAS method appear to reflect common values over Europe while those collected with TTO show fewer similarities. More research is needed in this area and members of the EuroQol Group will continue to contribute to the important methodological work that is required.

Membership and language versions

Over the last 10 years the EuroQol Group has developed from a group of mainly European researchers to a world-wide group of researchers. Ten years ago Group membership was derived from a total of 6 European countries. Currently there are Group members from 17 different countries, 5 from outside Europe (Canada, Japan, New Zealand, South Africa and the US). Current individual membership has increased to 60 as at the beginning of 2003. The dynamics underlying this increase in world coverage are also reflected in the EQ-5D language versions now available. In 1993 the EQ-5D was available in just 6 languages. EQ-5D has now been translated or adapted into 63 language versions and new versions currently in progress include versions for Indonesia, Malaysia, Bangladesh, Thailand, South Africa (Sotho) and the Philippines. The 'Euro' part of the Group's title now only refers to the region of origin of the instrument and is no longer an indication of a constraint on input from Europe. This is exactly as it should be.

Valuation projects

Since the Biomed project, valuation data has become available from Canada, Denmark, Japan, New Zealand and Zimbabwe. A large valuation study is currently taking place in the US. Field interviews were completed in October 2002 and data are now being analysed. It is anticipated that a US value set will become available by the end of 2003, early 2004.With such a rich array of data sets, the Group will be undertaking comparative work to provide insights into possible cultural, local, national, or regional differences and suggest ways of handling these differences. This information will of course be made widely available to HRQoL investigators.

Further development of EQ-5D

The Group's success is partly due to its commitment to produce a reliable questionnaire, capable of describing and valuing health which is also simple and brief so it can easily be added where required to a battery of other questionnaires. The willingness of the Group to adhere to this mission has been important for the success of the EQ-5D. The future research agenda of the Group will reflect the commitment to the support of the current version of the EQ-5D. In the middle to longer term the group will investigate whether there is potential to enlarge the scope of the core mission of the Group. One item on the research agenda is the exploration of whether a large gain in sensitivity can be achieved by increasing the number of response levels in the current version. In order to address this issue a number of research projects will be undertaken in 2003 and 2004 in different countries. If these projects prove that the idea is feasible, a version of the EQ-5D will be available that will potentially be more sensitive, yet will still be consistent with the value sets currently in use.

Development in the area of modes of administration continues. A large exercise is underway to translate the text of the proxy version of EQ-5D into more than 20 different languages. Work is also currently underway to produce electronic versions of EQ-5D that can be used on websites and also to provide computerized versions for collecting patient data. Software for the analysis and presentation of results is also being tested. In addition, a task force of EuroQol members will meet in 2003 to investigate electronic methods for collecting valuation data.

Work is ongoing in the UK to produce a child-friendly version of the EQ-5D. The current adult version has been revised and a study undertaken to demonstrate the feasibility of administration of the new version to children. The project also aims to establish normative data on HRQoL for children of school-age using the modified measure.

EQ-5D inclusion in population health surveys

There has been an exponential increase in the world-wide demand for concise information on HRQoL, inter alia, within countries, regions and age groups. A number of projects in different countries have made it clear that EQ-5D has an important role to play in population health surveys. These surveys can generate population norms which are of value in themselves. The prevalence of problems on the 5 dimensions is also potentially of interest to health policy makers. So too is the average EQ-5D index that results in applying one of the available value sets generated from the EuroQol Group to information on the EQ-5D descriptive system collected in such surveys. These population values can also be used as reference values or norms for groups of patients who suffer from specific diseases.

Other Group activities

The Group continues to hold successful scientific meeting meetings where, increasingly, non-EuroQol Group members are invited to participate and present their research using EQ-5D. For the first time in 2002, the Group initiated a programme of internally commissioned research. The results were presented at the 2002 EuroQol Group meeting in York, UK. Topics included:

(i) Looking at alternative ways to elicit valuations for health states via postal surveys.
(ii) Investigating the determinants of self-reported quality of life among the residents of Woodstock, Cape Town, South Africa.
(iii) Investigating the parametric relationship between EQ-5D values elicited using TTO and VAS.
(iv) Determining whether EQ-5D can shed any light on international differences in self-reported health problems by age, sex and educational level.
(v) Further guidance on the collection of EQ-5D data via proxies.
(vi) Comparison of valuation methods used to generate the EQ-5D and the SF-6D value sets in the UK.

These topics represent just a part of the ongoing work of the Group, but should give an indication of the variety of issues members are addressing. The programme is continuing throughout 2003 and results will be presented at the EuroQol Scientific Meeting scheduled for Bled in Slovenia in September 2003.

The success of the EuroQol Group evidently relies ultimately on the continued cooperation between Group members and their willingness to make the results of their efforts generally available to users. This commitment remains steadfast as we proceed into the 21st century.

In presenting the fruits of our efforts in this book we in the EuroQol Group hope we have portrayed how we have met, and continue to meet, the exciting challenges posed in the complex tasks of measuring and valuing health-related quality of life.

References for all chapters

Agt H M E van, Essink-Bot M L, Krabbe P F M, Bonsel G J. Test-retest reliability of health state valuations collected with the EuroQol questionnaire. Social Science & Medicine 1994;39:1537-1544.

Altman D G. Medical Statistics for Medical Research. London: Chapman and Hall, 1991.

Amuyunzu M, Allen T, Mwenesi H, Johnson K, Egesah O, Parker M, Fox-Rushby J. The resonance of language: health terms in Kenya. Quality of Life Research 1995;4(5):388.

Ashton T, Devlin N, Cumming J. Priority setting in New Zealand; translating principles into practice. Journal of Health Services Research and Policy 2000;5(3):170-175.

Badia X, Fernández E, Segura A. Influence of sociodemographic and health status variables on valuation of health states in a Spanish population. European Journal of Public Health 1995a;5:87-93.

Badia X, Alonso J. Re-scaling the Spanish version of the Sickness Impact Profile. An opportunity for the assessment of cross-cultural equivalence. Journal of Clinical Epidemiology 1995b;48:949-957.

Badia X, Diaz-Prieto A, Rue M, Patrick D L. Measuring health state preferences among critically ill patients. Intensive Care Medicine 1996;22:1379-1384.

Badia X, Roset M, Monserat S, Herdman M. The Spanish VAS tariff based on valuation of EQ-5D health states from the general population. In: Rabin R E, Busschbach J J V, Charro F Th de, Essink-Bot M L, Bonsel G J, editors. EuroQol Plenary Meeting, Rotterdam 1997, 2-3 October. Discussion papers. Centre for Health Policy & Law, Erasmus University, Rotterdam, the Netherlands, 1998:93-114.

Badia X, Roset M, Herdman M, Kind P. A comparison of UK and Spanish general population time trade-off values for EQ-5D health states. Medical Decision Making 2001;21:7-16.

Björk S, Norinder A. The weighting exercise for the Swedish version of the EuroQol. Health Economics 1999;8:117-126.

R. Brooks et al. (eds.),
The Measurement and Valuation of Health Status Using EQ-5D: A European Perspective, 245–258.

Bleichrodt H, Johannesson M. Standard gamble, time trade-off and rating scale: Experimental results on the ranking properties of QALYs. Journal of Health Economics 1997;16:155-175.

Bonsel G J, Essink-Bot M L, Hout B A van, Stouthard M E A. EuroQol 1991 - The Rotterdam survey- introduction. In: Björk S, editor. Discussion paper no 1. EuroQol Conference Proceedings, Lund, October 1991. IHE working paper 1992:2. Institute of Health Economics, Lund, Sweden, 1992:11-15.

Bowden A, Fox-Rushby J A. The adaptation and use of generic health-related quality of life measures in Africa, Asia, Eastern Europe, the Middle East and South America: A critical review of the literature, Final report presented to Global Health Outcomes. GlaxoSmithKline, 2001.

Brooks R, et al. EuroQol: The current state of play. Health Policy 1996;37:53-72.

Buckingham K. For debate: Is the EuroQol health profile and associated tariff sensitive to change in perceived quality of life? [unpublished paper] Wellington: Health Services Research Centre, 1999.

Buckingham K, Devlin N, Hansen P. Does it matter whose valuations are used to estimate health state tariffs, and which tariffs are used for CUA? In: Cabasés J M, Gaminde I, editors. 17th Plenary Meeting of the EuroQol Group, Pamplona, 28-29 September 2000. Discussion Papers. Universidad Pública de Navarra, Spain, 2001: 137-151.

Bullinger M, Alonso J, Apolone G, Leplege A, Sullivan M, Wood-Dauphinee S, Gandek B, Wagner A, Aaronson N, Bech P, Fukuhara S, Kaasa S, Ware J E. Translating health status questionnaires and evaluating their quality: the IQOLA Project approach. International Quality of Life Assessment. Journal of Clinical Epidemiology 1998; 51:913-923.

Busschbach J J V, Hessing D J, Charro F Th de. Observations on one hundred students filling in the EuroQol Questionnaire. In: Sintonen H, editor. EuroQol Conference Proceedings, Helsinki, October 1992. Discussion Paper No 2. Kuopio University Publications E. Social Sciences 8, Kuopio, Finland, 1993:55-62.

Busschbach J J V, McDonnell J, Hout B A van. Testing different parametric relations between the EuroQol health description and health valuation in students. In: Nord E, editor. EuroQol Plenary Meeting, Oslo 17-18 October 1996. Conference Proceedings. Working paper No 2/97. National Institute of Public Health, Oslo, Norway, 1997.

Busschbach J J V, McDonnell J, Essink-Bot M L, Hout B A van. Estimating parametric relationships between health description and health valuation with an application to the EuroQol EQ-5D. Journal of Health Economics 1999;18(5):551-571.

Canadian Co-ordinating Office for Health Technology Assessment. Guidelines for the economic evaluation of pharmaceuticals: Canada. 2nd ed. Ottawa: Canadian Co-ordinating Office for Health Technology Assessment (CCOHTA), 1997.

Central Statistical Office. Census 1992: Provincial Profile Harare. Harare: Central Statistical Office of Zimbabwe, 1994.

Central Statistical Office. Intercensal Demographic Survey Report. Harare: Central Statistical Office of Zimbabwe, 1998.

Claes C, Greiner W, Uber A, Schulenburg J-M Graf v.d. The new German version of the EuroQol quality of life questionnaire. In: Rabin R E, Busschbach J J V, Charro F Th de, Essink-Bot M L, Bonsel G J, editors. EuroQol Plenary Meeting, Rotterdam 1997, 2-3 October. Discussion papers. Centre for Health Policy & Law, Erasmus University, Rotterdam, the Netherlands, 1998:1-24.

Claes C, Greiner W, Uber A, Schulenburg J-M Graf v.d. An interview-based comparison of the TTO and VAS values given to EuroQol states of health by the general German population. In: Greiner W, Schulenburg J-M Graf v.d, Piercy J, editors. EuroQol Plenary Meeting, 1-2 October 1998. Discussion papers. Centre for Health Economics and Health Systems Research, University of Hannover, Germany. Uni-Verlag Witte, 1999:13-38.

Coast J, Peters T J, Richards S H, Gunnell D J. Use of the EuroQol among elderly acute care patients. Quality of Life Research 1998;7:1-10.

Cohen J. A coefficient of agreement for nominal scales. Educational and Psychological Measurement 1960;20:37-46.

Cohen J. Weighted kappa: nominal agreement with provision for scaled disagreement or partial credit. Psychological Bulletin 1968;70:213-220.

Cook T D, Campbell D T. Quasi-experimentation: Design & analysis issues for field settings. Boston (MA): Houghton Mifflin, 1979.

Coucill W, Bryan S, Bentham P, Buckley A, Laight A. EQ-5D as a measure of health related quality of life in patients with cognitive impairment: an investigation of inter-rater reliability. In: Badia X, Herdman M, Roset M, editors. 16th Plenary Meeting of the EuroQol Group. Sitges, 6-9, November 1999. Discussion Papers. Institut de Salut Pública de Catalunya, Spain, 2000:169-188.

Coucill W, Bryan S, Bentham P, Buckley A, Laight A. EQ-5D in dementia: an investigation of inter-rater agreement. Medical Care 2001;39(8):760-771.

Curran D, Fayers P M, Molenberghs G, Machin D. Analysis of incomplete quality of life data in clinical trials. In: Staquet M J, Hays R D, Fayers P M, editors. Quality of Life Assessment in Clinical Trials. Oxford: Oxford University Press, 1998.

Delate T, Coons S J. The use of 2 health-related quality-of-life measures in a sample of persons infected with human immunodeficiency virus. Clinical Infectious Diseases 2001;32(3):E47-E52.

Devlin N J, Ashton T, Cumming J. Rationing and health care: how should the HFA proceed? New Zealand Medical Journal 1999;112(1097):369-370.

Devlin N J, Hansen P, Kind P, Williams A. The health state preferences and logical inconsistencies of New Zealanders: A tale of two tariffs. Discussion Paper No 180. York Centre for Health Economics UK and University of Otago New Zealand, 2000a.

Devlin N J, Hansen P, Herbison P. Variations in self-reported health status: results from a New Zealand survey. The New Zealand Medical Journal 2002b;113(1123): 517-520.

Devlin N J, Maynard A, Mays A. New Zealand's new health sector reforms: Back to the future? [unpublished paper]. Dunedin: Department of Economics, University of Otago, 2000c.

Deyo R A, Diehr P, and Patrick D L. Reproducibility and responsiveness of health status measures. Controlled Clinical Trials 1991;12:142S-158S.

Diaz-Prieto A, Gorriz M T, Badia X, et al. Proxy-perceived prior health status and hospital outcome among the critically ill: is there any relationship? Intensive Care Medicine 1998;24:691-698.

Dolan P, Gudex C, Kind P, Williams A. The measurement and valuation of health. Report to the Department of health. York Centre for Health Economics, University of York, 1994.

Dolan P, Gudex C, Kind P, Williams A. The time trade-off method: results from a general population study. Health Economics 1996a;5:141-154.

Dolan P, Kind P. Inconsistency and health state valuations. Social Science & Medicine 1996b;42(4):609-615.

Dolan P. Modeling valuations for EuroQol health states. Medical Care 1997;35(11): 1095-1108.

Donovan J L, Frankel S J, Eyles J D. Assessing the need for health status measures. Journal of Epidemiology & Community Health 1993;47:158-162.

Dorman P, Slattery J, Farrell B, Dennis M, Sandercock P. Are proxy assessments of health status after stroke with the EuroQol questionnaire feasible, accurate, and unbiased? Stroke 1997;28(10):1883-1887

Durie M. Whaiora. Maori Health Development, Oxford: Oxford University Press, 1998.

Essink-Bot M L, Stouthard M, Bonsel G J. Generalizability of valuations on health states collected with the EuroQol questionnaire. Health Economics 1993;2:237-246.

Essink-Bot M L, van Royen L, Krabbe P, Bonsel G J, Rutten F F. The impact of migraine on health status. Headache 1995;35(4):200-206.

EuroQol Group. EuroQol - a new facility for the measurement of health-related quality of life. Health Policy 1990;16:199-208.

Fox-Rushby J, Badia X. Reviewing the development of international language versions of the EuroQol instrument: Challenges for the future. In: Badia X, Herdman M, Segura A, editors. EuroQol Plenary Meeting, Barcelona 1995, 3-6 October 3-6. Institut de Salut Pública de Catalunya, Spain, 1996:123-134.

Fox-Rushby J. First steps to assessing semantic equivalence of the EQ-5D: Results of a questionnaire survey to members of the EuroQol Group. In: Nord E, editor. EuroQol Plenary Meeting, Oslo 17-18 October 1996. Conference Proceedings. Working paper No 2/97. National Institute of Public Health, Oslo, Norway, 1997.

Fox-Rushby J, Nzioka C, Nganda B, Mugo M. Are health state valuation techniques likely to be understood in the same way in Kenya? Moving towards an assessment of conceptual equivalence. Background paper presented at workshop 'Assessing HRQOL - what can the cognitive science contribute?' Hull University, 2000.

Gaminde I, Cabasés J. Measuring valuations for health states among the general population in Navarra (Spain). In: Badia X, Herdman M, Segura A, editors. EuroQol Plenary Meeting, Barcelona 1995, 3-6 October 3-6. Institut de Salut Pública de Catalunya, Spain, 1996:113-122.

Gandek B, Ware J E, for the IQOLA Project Group. Methods for validating and norming translations of health status questionnaires: the IQOLA project approach. Journal of Clinical Epidemiology 1998;51(11):953-959.

Gelber S, Gelber R D, Cole B F, Goldhirsch A. Using the Q-TWIST method for treatment comparisons in clinical trials. In: Staquet M J, Hays R D, Fayers P M, editors. Quality of Life Assessment in Clinical Trials. Oxford University Press, 1998.

Gifi A. Nonlinear Multivariate Analysis. Wiley, New York, 1990.

Gold M R, et al. Identifying and valuing outcomes: Appendix 4.1: Generic preference-based measures for use in CEA. Cost effectiveness in health and medicine 1996;124-125.

Goldhirsch A, Gelber R D, Simes R J, Glasziou P, Coates A S. Costs and benefits of adjuvant therapy in breast cancer: a quality-adjusted survival analysis. Journal of Clinical Oncology 1989;7:36-44.

Goldstein H. Multilevel statistical models. London: Edward Arnold, 1995.

Gudex C. Are we lacking a dimension of energy in the EuroQol instrument? In: Björk S, editor. Discussion paper no 1. EuroQol Conference Proceedings, Lund, October 1991. IHE working paper 1992:2. Institute of Health Economics, Lund, Sweden, 1992:61-82.

Gudex C. Time trade-off user manual: Props and self-completion methods. Report of the Centre for Health Economics, University of York, 1994.

Gudex C. The development of the EuroQol descriptive system: A review. In: Badia X, Herdman M, Segura A, editors. EuroQol Plenary Meeting, Barcelona 1995, 3-6 October 3-6. Institut de Salut Pública de Catalunya, Spain, 1996:23-32.

Gudex C, Dolan P H, Kind P, Thomas R, Williams A H. Valuing health states. Interviews with the general public. European Journal of Public Health 1997;7:441-448.

Guillemin F, Bombardier C, Beaton D. Cross-cultural adaptation of health-related quality of life measures: literature review and proposed guidelines. Journal of Clinical Epidemiology 1993;46:1417-1432.

Guyatt G H, Deyo R A, Charlson M, Levine M N, Mitchell A. Responsiveness and validity in health status measurement. Journal of Clinical Epidemiology 1989;42:403-406.

Guyatt G H. The philosophy of health-related quality of life translation. Quality of Life Research 1993;2:461-465.

Guyatt G H, Juniper E F, Walter S D, Griffith L E, Goldstein R S. Interpreting treatment effects in randomised trials. British Medical Journal 1998;316:690-693.

Haley E C Jr, Kassell N F, Apperson-Hansen C, Maile M H, et al. A randomized, double blind, vehicle-controlled trial of tirilazad mesylate in patients with aneurismal subarachnoid hemorrhage: a cooperative study in North America. Journal of Neurosurgery 1997;86:467-474.

Hadorn D, Uebersax J. Large-scale health outcomes evaluation: how should quality of life be measured? Part 1: Calibration of a brief questionnaire and a search for preference subgroups. Journal of Clinical Epidemiology 1995;48:607-618.

Hays R D, Hadorn D. Responsiveness to change: an aspect of validity, not a separate dimension. Quality of Life Research 1992;1:73-75.

Health Funding Authority. How shall we prioritise health and disability services? Discussion paper. Wellington: Health Funding Authority, 1998.

Herdman M, Fox-Rushby J, Badia X. A model of equivalence in the cultural adaptation of HRQoL instruments: The universalist approach. Quality of Life Research 1998;7:323-335.

Hurst N P, Kind P, Ruta D, Hunter M, Stubbings A . Measuring health-related quality of life in rheumatoid arthritis: validity, responsiveness and reliability of EuroQol (EQ-5D). British Journal of Rheumatology 1997;36:551-559.

Ikeda S, Tamura M, Mori K, Tsuchiya A, Takefumi K. EuroQol and quality-adjusted life expectancy. Kosei no Shihyo 1999;46(4):46-49.

Ikegami N, Hisashige A. Introduction (to the special issue on Japan). International Journal of Technology Assessment in Health Care 1994;10(3):341-345.

Ikegami N, Campbell J C. Health care reform in Japan: The virtues of muddling through. Health Affairs 1999;18(3):56-75.

Jelsma J, Chivaura V, De Cock P, De Weerdt W. A bridge between cultures: A report on the process of translating the EQ-5D instrument into Shona. South African Journal of Physiotherapy 2000a;53:3-9.

Jelsma J, Mhundwa K, Chivaura V, De Weerdt W, De Cock P. The global burden of disease disability weights. Lancet 2000b;355:2079.

Jelsma J, Hansen K, De Weerdt W, De Cock P. How do Zimbabweans value health states? In: Jelsma J. The burden of disease due to disability in a high density area in Harare, Zimbabwe, PhD Thesis. Leuven: Catholic University of Leuven, 2002a:64-79.

Jelsma J, De Weerdt W, De Cock P, Mielke J, Mhundwa K. The validity of the Shona version of the EQ-5D quality of life measure. South African Journal of Physiotherapy 2002b;58:8-12.

Jobe J B, Mingay D J. Cognitive research improves questionnaires. American Journal of Public Health 1989;1053-1055.

Johnson J A, Coons S J, Ergo A, Szava-Kovats G. Valuation of EuroQol (EQ-5D) health states in a U.S. sample. Pharmacoeconomics 1998a;13:421-433.

Johnson J A, Coons S J. Comparison of the EQ-5D and SF-12 in an adult US sample. Quality of Life Research 1998b;7:155-166.

Johnson J A, Ohinmaa A, Murti B, Sintonen H, Coons S J. Comparison of Finnish and U.S.-based visual analog scale valuations of the EQ-5D measure. Medical Decision Making 2000a;20:281-289.

Johnson J A, Pickard S. Comparison of the EQ-5D and the SF-12 health surveys in a general population survey in Alberta, Canada. Medical Care 2000b;38:115-121.

Johnson J A, Connolly M, Zuberbuhler P, Brown N E. Health-related quality of life for adults with cystic fibrosis: A regression approach to assessing the impact of recombinant human DNase. Pharmacotherapy 2000c;20:1167-1174.

Juniper E F, Guyatt G H, Jaesche R. How to develop and validate a new health-related quality of life instrument. In: Spilker B, editor. Quality of Life and Pharmacoeconomics in Clinical Trials. Philadelphia: Lippincott-Raven publishers, 1996.

Keller S D, Ware J E, Gandek B, Aaronson N K, Alonso J, Apolone G, et al. Testing the equivalence of translations widely used response choice labels: results from the IQOLA project. Journal of Clinical Epidemiology 1998;51(11):933-944.

Kind P, Dolan P, Gudex C, Williams A. Variations in population health status: results from a United Kingdom national questionnaire survey. British Medical Journal 1998;316:736-741.

Krabbe P F M, Essink-Bot M L, Bonsel G J. On the equivalence of collectively and individually collected responses: Standard gamble and time-trade-off judgments of health states. Medical Decision Making 1996;16:120-132.

Krabbe P F M. The valuation of health outcomes: a contribution to the QALY approach, Phd thesis. Erasmus University Rotterdam, the Netherlands, 1998.

Laheij R J F, Krabbe P F M, Jong C A J de. Rapid heroin detoxification under general anesthesia. JAMA 2000;283(3):1143.

Langenhoff B S, Peerenboom L, Krabbe P F M, Wobbes Th, Ruers T J M. Quality of life as an outcome measure in surgical oncology. British Journal of Surgery 2001;88:643-652.

Larson M L. Meaning Based Translation: A guide to cross-language equivalence. University Press of America, 1984.

Leew E de, Nicholls W. Technological innovations in data collection: Acceptance, data quality and costs. Vol. No. 1. Sociological Research Online, 1996.

Macran S, Kind P. Valuing EQ-5D health states using a modified MVH protocol: Preliminary results. In: Badia X, Herdman M, Roset M, editors. 16th Plenary Meeting of the EuroQol Group. Sitges, 6-9, November 1999. Discussion Papers. Institut de Salut Pública de Catalunya, Spain, 2000:205-240.

Macran S. Kind P. EQ-5D Valuations from a British national postal survey. In: Cabasés J M, Gaminde I, editors. 17th Plenary Meeting of the EuroQol Group, Pamplona, 28-29 September 2000. Discussion Papers. Universidad Pública de Navarra, Spain, 2001: 87-102.

Magaziner J, Simonsick E M, Kashner T M, et al. Patient-proxy response comparability on measures of patient health and functional status. Journal of Clinical Epidemiology 1998;41:1065-1074.

Mararike C G. Survival strategies in rural Zimbabwe. Harare: Mond Books, 1999.

Mayo N, Goldberg M, Kind P. Performance of the EuroQol EQ-5D in a Canadian Population. Paper presented at the EuroQol Plenary Meeting, Rotterdam, the Netherlands, 1997.

Murti B, Johnson J, Ohinmaa A, Sintonen H, Coons SJ. Comparison of Finnish- and US-based VAS valuations of the EQ-5D. In: Rabin R E, Busschbach J J V, Charro F Th de, Essink-Bot M L, Bonsel G J, editors. EuroQol Plenary Meeting, Rotterdam 1997, 2-3 October. Discussion papers. Centre for Health Policy & Law, Erasmus University, Rotterdam, the Netherlands, 1998: 115-138.

MVH Group. The Measurement and Valuation of Health. Final report on the modelling of valuation tariffs. York: MVH Group, Centre for Health Economics, 1995.

National Health Committee. The social, cultural and economic determinants of health in New Zealand: action to improve health. Wellington: NHC, 1998.

Nawata S, Yamada Y, Ikeda S, Ikegami N. EuroQol study of the elderly general population: Relationship with IADL and other attributes (in Japanese). Journal of Health Care and Society 2000;10(2):76-86 (in Japanese).

Neal J M, Liebert R M. Science and behaviour: an introduction to methods of research. New Jersey: Prentice/Hall International, 1986.

Norman G R, Stratford P, Regehr G. Methodological problems in the retrospective computation of responsiveness to change; the lesson of Cronbach. Journal of Clinical Epidemiology 1997;50:869-879.

O'Hanlon M, Buxton M. Brunel. Pfizer utility assessment study: quality of life of people with rheumatoid arthritis. Report of pilot phase, 1993.

Ohinmaa A, Eija H, Sintonen H. Modelling EuroQol values of the Finnish adult population. In: Badia X, Herdman M, Segura A, editors. EuroQol Plenary Meeting, Barcelona 1995, 3-6 October 3-6. Institut de Salut Pública de Catalunya, Spain, 1996:67-76.

Ohinmaa A. Sintonen H. (1999). Inconsistencies and modelling of the Finnish EuroQol (EQ-5D) preference values. In: Greiner W, Schulenburg J-M Graf v.d, Piercy J, editors. EuroQol Plenary Meeting, 1-2 October 1998. Discussion papers. Centre for Health Economics and Health Systems Research, University of Hannover, Germany. Uni-Verlag Witte, 1999:57-74.

Patrick D L, Starks H E, Cain K C. Measuring preferences for health states worse than death. Medical Decision Making 1994;14:9-18.

Pedersen K M, Gudex C, Brooks R. Qualitative exploration of meaning attached to key words in the EQ-5D. Paper presented at the 17th EuroQol Plenary Meeting, Pamplona, Spain, 2000.

Perkins M, Devlin N, Hansen P. Maori health state preferences: a pilot study. Discussion Paper No. 0101, Economics Department, University of Otago, 2001.

Pharmac. Prescription for pharmacoeconomic analysis, 1999. Available from: URL: http://www.pharmac.govt.nz/download/pfpa.pdf

Pickard A S, Weijnen T J G, Nieuwenhuizen M G M, Johnson J A, Charro F Th de. A comparison of Canadian and European VAS-based valuations of EQ-5D health states. Canadian Association of Population Therapeutics Annual Meeting, 2001, April 1-3, Banff, AB, Canada. Canadian Journal of Clinical Pharmacology 2001;8:23.

Poissant L, Mayo NE, Wood-Dauphinee S, Clarke A. A stroke-specific utility-based module to the EQ-5D: Developmental steps. Paper presented at the 17th EuroQol Plenary Meeting, Pamplona, Spain, 2000.

Robinson A, Dolan P, Williams A. Valuing Health Status Using VAS and TTO: What lies behind the numbers? Social Science and Medicine 1997;45(8):1289-1297.

Sakamaki H, Uchigata Y, Origasa H, Otani T, Ikeda S, Ikegami N, Otani Y, Iwamoto Y. Measurement of HRQL using EuroQol (EQ-5D) in patients with type 2 diabetes mellitus in Japan. 7th Annual Conference of the International Society of Quality of Life Research, 2000, Vancouver, Canada.

Sartorius N, Kuyken W. Translation of health status instruments. In: Orley J, Kuyken W, editors. Quality of Life Assessment: International Perspectives. Heidleberg: Springer-Verlag, 1994.

Schulenburg J-M Graf v.d, Claes C, Greiner W, Uber A. The German version of the EuroQol quality of life questionnaire. In: Badia X, Herdman M, Segura A, editors. EuroQol Plenary Meeting, Barcelona 1995, 3-6 October 3-6. Institut de Salut Pública de Catalunya, Spain, 1996:135-160.

Selai C E, Rosser R M. Eliciting EuroQol descriptive data and utility scales from inpatients: A feasibility study. PharmacoEconomics 1995a;8(2):147-158.

Selai C E. The use of the EuroQol (pages 2 & 3) with patients at the Institute of Neurology, London. In: O'Hanlon M, Buxton M, editors. EuroQol Plenary Meeting London, October 1994. Conference Proceedings. Health Economics Research Group Report No. 20, Brunel University, Uxbridge, UK, 1995b:1-14.

Selai C E, O'Hanlon M. Using the EuroQol instrument. In: Badia X, Herdman M, Segura A, editors. EuroQol Plenary Meeting, Barcelona 1995, 3-6 October 3-6. Institut de Salut Pública de Catalunya, Spain, 1996:13-22.

Selai C E. Further testing of the EuroQol 3-level and 4-level classification systems: (i) cognitive debriefing and (ii) test-retest reliability. In: Nord E, editor. EuroQol Plenary Meeting, Oslo 17-18 October 1996. Conference Proceedings. Working paper No 2/97. National Institute of Public Health, Oslo, Norway, 1997.

Selai C E. Using the EuroQol EQ-5D in dementia. In: Rabin R E, Busschbach J J V, Charro F Th de, Essink-Bot M L, Bonsel G J, editors. EuroQol Plenary Meeting, Rotterdam 1997, 2-3 October. Discussion papers. Centre for Health Policy & Law, Erasmus University, Rotterdam, the Netherlands, 1998a:157-174.

Selai C E. Scaling the EQ-5D middle-level quantifiers. In: Rabin R E, Busschbach J J V, Charro F Th de, Essink-Bot M L, Bonsel G J, editors. EuroQol Plenary Meeting, Rotterdam 1997, 2-3 October. Discussion papers. Centre for Health Policy & Law, Erasmus University, Rotterdam, the Netherlands, 1998b:79-92.

Selai C E, Elstner K, Trimble M R. Is the EuroQol EQ-5D sensitive to clinically defined treatment outcome in epilepsy? In: Greiner W, Schulenburg J-M Graf v.d, Piercy J, editors. EuroQol Plenary Meeting, 1-2 October 1998. Discussion papers. Centre for Health Economics and Health Systems Research, University of Hannover, Germany. Uni-Verlag Witte, 1999:262-278.

Selai C E, Trimble M R, Rossor M, Harvey R. The Quality of Life Assessment Schedule (QOLAS) - a new method for assessing Quality of Life (QOL) in dementia. In: Albert S M, Logsdon R G, editors. Assessing Quality of Life in Alzheimer's Disease. Springer Publishing Company, Inc. New York, 2000a:31-48.

Selai C E, Elstner K Trimble M R. Quality of life pre- and post epilepsy surgery. Epilepsy Research 2000b;38:67-74.

Selai C E. The problem of inconsistencies in elicited EuroQol values: discussion paper. In: Badia X, Herdman M, Roset M, editors. 16th Plenary Meeting of the EuroQol Group. Sitges, 6-9, November 1999. Discussion Papers. Institut de Salut Pública de Catalunya, Spain, 2000c:93-98.

Selai C E, Trimble M R, Rossor M, Harvey R. Assessing quality of life in dementia. Preliminary psychometric testing of the Quality of Life Assessment Schedule. Neuropsychological Rehabilitation 2001;11(3/4): 219-243.

Siegel S, Castellan N J. Nonparametric Statistics for the Behavioral Sciences. New York: McGraw-Hill Book Company, 1988.

Smith R, Dobson M. Measuring utility values for QALY's: Two methodological issues. Health Economics 1993;2:349-355.

Stolk E A, Busschbach J J V, Vogels T. Performance of the EuroQol in children with imperforate anus. Quality of Life Research 2000;9:29-38.

Stone A A, Turkkan J S, Bachrach, et al., editors. The science of self-report: Implications for research and practice. Mahway (NJ): Erlbaum, 2000.

Streiner D L, Norman G R. Health measurement scales: a practical guide to their development and use. Oxford: Oxford University Press, 1995.

Tabachnick B G, Fidell L S. Using multivariate statistics. Northridge: Harper Collins Publishers, 1989.

Tandon Y. Human Development Report 1999 Zimbabwe. Harare: United Nations Development Programme, Poverty Reduction Forum, Institute of Development Studies, University of Zimbabwe, 2000:1-119.

Tanur J M. Questions about questions: Inquiries into the cognitive bases of surveys. Russell Sage Foundation, 1994.

Torrance G W. Measurement of health state utilities for economic appraisal. Journal of Health Economics 1986;5:1-30.

Tsuchiya A, Ikeda S, Ikegami N, Nishimura S, Sakai I, Fukuda T, Hamashima C, Hisashige A, Tamura M. Estimating an EQ-5D population value set: The case of Japan, Health Economics 2002; 11:341-353.

Ustun T B, Rehm J, Chatteri S, Saxena S, Trotter R, Room R, Bickenbach J. Multiple-informant ranking of the disability effects of different health conditions in 14 countries Lancet 1999; 354(9173):111-115.

Ware J E, Keller S D, Gandek, Brazier J E, Sullivan M. The IQOLA Project Group. Evaluating translations of health status questionnaires. International Journal of Technology Assessment in Health Care 1995;11(3):525-551.

WHOQOL Group. The development of the WHO Quality of Life Assessment Instrument (the WHOQOL). In: Orley J, Kuyken W, editors. Quality of Life Assessment: International Perspectives. Heidelberg: Springer-Verlag; 1994:41-60.

Williams A. The measurement and valuation of health - a chronicle. York: Centre for Health Economics, University of York, 1995.

Wittrup-Jensen K U, Lauridsen J T, Gudex C, Brooks R, Pedersen K M. Estimating Danish EQ-5D Tariffs using the Time Trade-off (TTO) and Visual Analogue Scale (VAS) method. In: Norinder A L, Pedersen K M, Roos P, editors. Proceedings of the 18th Plenary Meeting of the EuroQol Group, 6-7 September 2001, Copenhagen, Denmark. IHE, The Swedish Institute for Health Economics, 2002:257-292.

Wolfe F, Hawley D J. Measurement of the quality of life in rheumatic disorders using the EuroQol. British Journal of Rheumatology 1997;36:786-793.

World Health Organisation. WHOQOL Protocol for New Centres. Geneva: WHO, 1994.

World Health Organisation. The International classification of functioning and disability - Beta draft. Geneva: WHO, 1999.

World Health Organisation. The World Health Report 2000 Health Systems: Improving Performance. Geneva: WHO, 2000.

World Health Organization Quality of Life Assessment (WHOQOL). Development and general psychometric properties. Social Science & Medicine 1998;46:1569-1585.

Wright J G, Young N L. A comparison of different indices of responsiveness. Journal of Clinical Epidemiology 1997;50:239-246.

Wu A W, Jacobson D L, Berzon R A, Revicki D A, van der Horst C, Fichtenbaum C J, Saag M S, Lynn L, Hardy D, Feinberg J. The effect of mode of administration on Medical Outcomes Study health ratings and EuroQol scores in AIDS. Quality of Life Research 1997a;6:3-10.

Wu W, Jacobson D, Clark R, et al. Responsiveness of the EuroQol in a clinical trial in advanced HIV disease. Quality of Life Research 1997b;6:438.

Appendices

APPENDIX 1

THE EQ-5D VALUATION QUESTIONNAIRE (INCLUDES EQ-5D)

Health Questionnaire

We are trying to find out what people think about health. We are going to describe a few health states that people can be in. We want you to indicate how good or bad each of these states would be for a person like you. There are no right or wrong answers. Here we are interested only in your personal view.

But first of all we would like you to indicate (on the next page) the state of your own health today.

By placing a tick in one box in each group below, please indicate which statements best describe your own health state today.

Mobility

I have no problems in walking about	☐
I have some problems in walking about	☐
I am confined to bed	☐

Self-Care

I have no problems with self-care	☐
I have some problems washing or dressing myself	☐
I am unable to wash or dress myself	☐

Usual Activities *(e.g. work, study, housework, family or leisure activities)*

I have no problems with performing my usual activities	☐
I have some problems with performing my usual activities	☐
I am unable to perform my usual activities	☐

Pain/Discomfort

I have no pain or discomfort	☐
I have moderate pain or discomfort	☐
I have extreme pain or discomfort	☐

Anxiety/Depression

I am not anxious or depressed	☐
I am moderately anxious or depressed	☐
I am extremely anxious or depressed	☐

To help people say how good or bad a health state is, we have drawn a scale (rather like a thermometer) on which the best state you can imagine is marked 100 and the worst state you can imagine is marked 0.

We would like you to indicate on this scale how good or bad your own health is today, in your opinion. Please do this by drawing a line from the box below to whichever point on the scale indicates how good or bad your health state is today.

Your own health state today

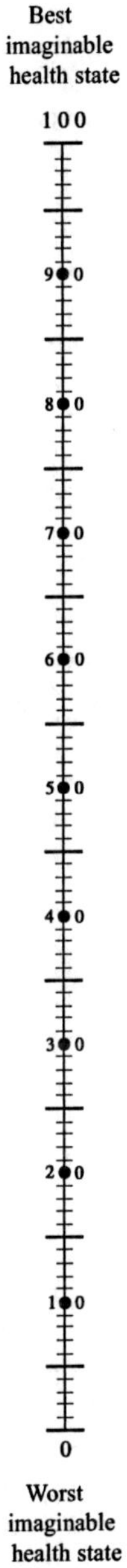

- We now want you to consider some other health states.
- Remember, we want you to indicate how good or bad each of these states would be for a person like you.
- They are described, on either side of the scale, on the page opposite.
- When thinking about each health state imagine that it will last for one year. What happens after that is not known and should not be taken into account.

- Please draw **one line from each box** to whichever point on the scale indicates how good or bad the state described in that box is.
- It does not matter if your lines cross each other.

Best imaginable health state

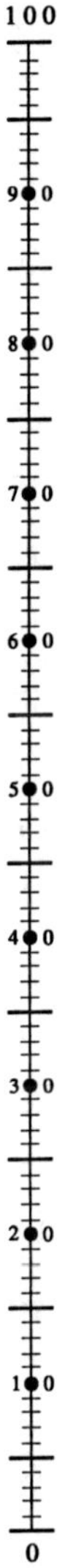

Worst imaginable health state

No problems in walking about
No problems with self-care
Some problems with performing usual activities *(e.g. work, study, housework, family or leisure activities)*
No pain or discomfort
Not anxious or depressed

No problems in walking about
No problems with self-care
No problems with performing usual activities *(e.g. work, study, housework, family or leisure activities)*
Moderate pain or discomfort
Not anxious or depressed

No problems in walking about
No problems with self-care
No problems with performing usual activities *(e.g. work, study, housework, family or leisure activities)*
No pain or discomfort
Not anxious or depressed

Some problems in walking about
Some problems with washing or dressing self
Some problems with performing usual activities *(e.g. work, study, housework, family or leisure activities)*
Extreme pain or discomfort
Extremely anxious or depressed

Some problems in walking about
No problems with self-care
Some problems with performing usual activities *(e.g. work, study, housework, family or leisure activities)*
Extreme pain or discomfort
Moderately anxious or depressed

Confined to bed
Unable to wash or dress self
Unable to perform usual activities *(e.g. work, study, housework, family or leisure activities)*
Extreme pain or discomfort
Extremely anxious or depressed

No problems in walking about
No problems with self-care
No problems with performing usual activities *(e.g. work, study, housework, family or leisure activities)*
Moderate pain or discomfort
Moderately anxious or depressed

Confined to bed
Unable to wash or dress self
Unable to perform usual activities *(e.g. work, study, housework, family or leisure activities)*
Moderate pain or discomfort
Not anxious or depressed

PLEASE CHECK THAT YOU HAVE DRAWN ONE LINE FROM EACH BOX (THAT IS, 8 LINES IN ALL)

IN THE SAME WAY AS ON THE PREVIOUS PAGE, PLEASE INDICATE HOW GOOD OR BAD THESE ADDITIONAL STATES ARE, BY DRAWING A LINE FROM EACH BOX TO A POINT ON THE SCALE.

YOU WILL FIND THAT 2 OF THESE STATES (MARKED *) ARE REPEATED FROM THE PREVIOUS PAGE.

Best imaginable health state

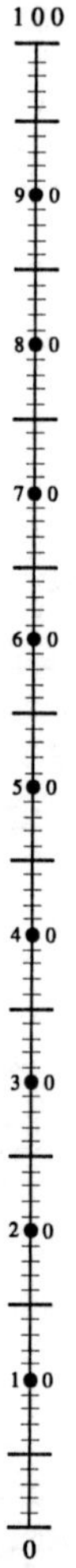

Some problems in walking about
No problems with self-care
No problems with performing usual activities *(e.g. work, study, housework, family or leisure activities)*
No pain or discomfort
Not anxious or depressed

No problems in walking about
No problems with self-care
No problems with performing usual activities *(e.g. work, study, housework, family or leisure activities)*
No pain or discomfort
Moderately anxious or depressed

*
No problems in walking about
No problems with self-care
No problems with performing usual activities *(e.g. work, study, housework, family or leisure activities)*
No pain or discomfort
Not anxious or depressed

Confined to bed
Some problems with washing or dressing self
Some problems with performing usual activities *(e.g. work, study, housework, family or leisure activities)*
No pain or discomfort
Not anxious or depressed

Unconscious

*
Confined to bed
Unable to wash or dress self
Unable to perform usual activities *(e.g. work, study, housework, family or leisure activities)*
Extreme pain or discomfort
Extremely anxious or depressed

No problems in walking about
Some problems with washing or dressing self
No problems with performing usual activities *(e.g. work, study, housework, family or leisure activities)*
No pain or discomfort
Not anxious or depressed

Some problems in walking about
Some problems with washing or dressing self
Unable to perform usual activities *(e.g. work, study, housework, family or leisure activities)*
Moderate pain or discomfort
Extremely anxious or depressed

Worst imaginable health state

PLEASE CHECK THAT YOU HAVE DRAWN ONE LINE FROM EACH BOX (THAT IS, 8 LINES IN ALL)

- In the previous pages we asked you to say how good or bad various health states are in your view.
- We would now like you to tell us how good or bad you feel the state 'dead' is, compared with being in the other states for one year.
- Please turn back to pages 5 **and** 6 and draw one line across the thermometer at the point you would locate the state 'dead'.
- Remember we would like you to do this on **both** pages 5 and 6.

Because all replies are anonymous, it will help us to understand your answers better if we have a little background data from everyone, as covered in the following questions. (At the end there is space to add anything else you think may be helpful to us).

1. Have you experienced serious illness?

	Yes	No	
in you yourself	☐	☐	PLEASE TICK APPROPRIATE BOXES
in your family	☐	☐	
in caring for others	☐	☐	

2. What is your age in years? ☐

3. Are you:

Male	Female	
☐	☐	PLEASE TICK APPROPRIATE BOX

4. Are you:

a current smoker	☐	PLEASE TICK APPROPRIATE BOX
an ex-smoker	☐	
a never smoker	☐	

5. Do you now, or did you ever, work in health or social services?

Yes	No	
☐	☐	PLEASE TICK APPROPRIATE BOX

If so, in what capacity? ☐

6. Which of the following best describes your main activity?

in employment or self employment	☐	PLEASE TICK APPROPRIATE BOX
retired	☐	
housework	☐	
student	☐	
seeking work	☐	
other (please specify)	☐	☐

7. Did your education continue after the minimum school leaving age?

Yes	No	
☐	☐	PLEASE TICK APPROPRIATE BOX

8. Do you have a Degree or equivalent professional qualification?

Yes	No	
☐	☐	PLEASE TICK APPROPRIATE BOX

9. Please add here any comments you may wish to make which might help us to understand your answers better:

10. Did you find filling in this questionnaire:

very difficult ☐
fairly difficult ☐
fairly easy ☐
very easy ☐

PLEASE TICK APPROPRIATE BOX

11. Could you please let us know roughly how long it took you to complete (in minutes): ☐

12. If you know your postcode, would you please write it here: ☐

Thank you for being so helpful

APPENDIX 2

SUGGESTIONS FOR EQ-5D TELEPHONE ADMINISTRATION

GENERAL INSTRUCTION

It is suggested that the telephone administrator follows the script of the EQ-5D. Although allowance should be made for the interviewer's particular style of speaking, the wording of the questionnaire instructions should be followed as closely as possible. In the case of the EQ-5D descriptive system on page 2, the precise wording must be followed.

It is recommended that the administrator has a copy of the EQ-5D in front of him or her as it is administered over the telephone. This enables the respondent's answers to be entered directly on the EQ-5D by the administrator on behalf of the respondent (i.e. the appropriate boxes on page 2 are marked and the scale on page 3 is marked at the point indicating the respondents 'own health state today'). If the respondent asks for clarification, the administrator can help by re-reading the question verbatim. The administrator should not try to offer his or her own explanation but suggest that the respondent uses his or her own interpretation.

If the respondent has difficulty with regard to which box to mark, the administrator should repeat the question verbatim and ask the respondent to answer in a way that most closely resembles his or her thoughts about his or her health state today.

INTRODUCTION TO EQ-5D

We are trying to find out what you think about your health. I will first ask you a few brief and simple questions about your own health state today. I will then ask you to do a rather different task that involves rating your health on a measuring scale. I will explain the tasks fully as I go along but please interrupt me if you do not understand something or if things are not clear to you. Please also remember that there are no right or wrong answers. We are interested here only in your personal view.

EQ-5D DESCRIPTIVE SYSTEM - PAGE 2: INTRODUCTION

First I am going to read out some questions. Each question has a choice of three answers. Please tell me which answer best describes your own health state today.

Do not choose more than one answer in each group of questions.

(Note for administrator: it may be necessary to remind the respondent regularly that the timeframe is today.)

EQ-5D DESCRIPTIVE SYSTEM - PAGE 2: TASK

Mobility

First I'd like to ask you about mobility.

Question 1: Would you say you have…

1. No problems in walking about?
2. Some problems in walking about?
3. Are you confined to bed?

So, would you say you have no problems in walking about, some problems in walking about or are you confined to bed?

(Note for administrator: mark the appropriate box on EQ-5D)

Self-Care

Next I'd like to ask you about self-care.

Question 2: Would you say you have…

1. No problems with self-care?
2. Some problems washing or dressing yourself?
3. Are you unable to wash or dress yourself?

So, would you say you have no problems with self-care, some problems washing or dressing yourself or are you unable to wash or dress yourself?

(Note for administrator: mark the appropriate box on EQ-5D)

Usual Activities

Next I'd like to ask you about usual activities, for example work, study, housework, family or leisure activities.

Question 3: Would you say you have…

1. No problems with performing your usual activities?
2. Some problems with performing your usual activities?
3. Are you unable to perform your usual activities?

So, would you say you have no problems performing your usual activities, some problems performing your usual activities or are you unable to perform your usual activities?

(Note for administrator: mark the appropriate box on EQ-5D)

Pain/Discomfort

Next I'd like to ask you about pain or discomfort.

Question 4: Would you say you have…

1. No pain or discomfort?
2. Moderate pain or discomfort?
3. Extreme pain or discomfort?

So, would you say you have no pain or discomfort, moderate pain or discomfort or extreme pain or discomfort?

(Note for administrator: mark the appropriate box on the EQ-5D questionnaire)

Anxiety/Depression

Finally I'd like to ask you about anxiety or depression.

Question 5: Would you say you are…

1. Not anxious or depressed?
2. Moderately anxious or depressed?
3. Extremely anxious or depressed?

So, would you are not anxious or depressed, moderately anxious or depressed or extremely anxious or depressed?

(Note for administrator: mark the appropriate box on the EQ-5D questionnaire)

EQ VAS - PAGE 3: INTRODUCTION

(Note for administrator: If possible, it might be useful to send a visual aid (i.e. the EQ VAS) before the telephone call so that they can have this in front of them when completing the task).

I would now like to ask you to do a rather different task.

To help you say how good or bad your health state is, I'd like you to try to picture in your mind a scale that looks a bit like a thermometer. Can you do that? The best health state you can imagine is marked 100 (one hundred) at the top of the scale and the worst state you can imagine is marked 0 (zero) at the bottom.

EQ VAS - PAGE 3: TASK

I would now like you to tell me the point on this scale where you would put your own health state today.

Thank you for taking the time to answer these questions.

APPENDIX 3

SUGGESTIONS FOR SELF-COMPLETION OF THE EQ-5D IN THE PRESENCE OF AN INTERVIEWER

The EQ-5D may be completed alone or it may be completed in the presence of an interviewer. When an interviewer is present, he or she can either give the EQ-5D to the respondent for self-completion or read out the questions. If the respondent asks for clarification, the administrator can re-read the question verbatim. The administrator should not try to offer his or her own explanation but should suggest that the respondent uses his or her own interpretation.

If the respondent has difficulty choosing which box to mark, the interviewer should repeat the question verbatim. He or she should not offer any suggestions or advice but should ask the respondent to answer in a way that most closely resembles his or her thoughts about his or her health state today.

APPENDIX 4

SUGGESTIONS FOR ADMINISTRATION OF THE EQ-5D IN FACE-TO-FACE INTERVIEWS

It is suggested that the interviewer follows the script of the telephone administration of the EQ-5D. Although allowance should be made for the interviewer's particular style of speaking, the wording of the questionnaire instructions should be followed as closely as possible. In the case of the EQ-5D dimensions on page 2, the precise wording must be followed.

It is recommended that the interviewer gives a copy of the EQ-5D to the respondent. This enables the respondent's answers to be entered directly on the EQ-5D by the administrator on behalf of the respondent (i.e. the appropriate boxes on page 2 are marked and the scale on page 3 is marked at the point indicating the respondent's 'own health state today').

If the respondent asks for clarification, the interviewer can help by re-reading the question verbatim. The interviewer should not try to offer his or her own explanation but suggest that the respondent uses his or her own interpretation.

If the respondent has difficulty with regard to which box to mark, the administrator should repeat the question verbatim and ask the respondent to answer in a way that most closely resembles his or her thoughts about his or her health state today.

APPENDIX 5

SCRIPT FOR PROXY VERSION OF THE EQ-5D: VERSION 1

(asking the proxy to rate how he or she (i.e. the proxy) would rate the subject's health)

Proxy version of the EQ-5D: 1

By placing a tick in one box in each group below, please indicate which statement best describes (*insert name of person whose health is being assessed e.g. Mr. Smith's or John's*) health state today.

Do not tick more than one box in each group

Mobility
No problems in walking about ☐
Some problems in walking about ☐
Confined to bed ☐

Self-Care
No problems with self-care ☐
Some problems washing or dressing myself ☐
Unable to wash or dress myself ☐

Usual Activities (*e.g. work, study, housework, family or leisure activities)*
No problems with performing usual activities ☐
Some problems with performing usual activities ☐
Unable to perform usual activities ☐

Pain/Discomfort
No pain or discomfort ☐
Moderate pain or discomfort ☐
Extreme pain or discomfort ☐

Anxiety/Depression
Not anxious or depressed ☐
Moderately anxious or depressed ☐
Extremely anxious or depressed ☐

To help people say how good or bad a health state is, we have drawn a scale (rather like a thermometer) on which the best state you can imagine is marked 100 and the worst state you can imagine is marked 0.

We would like you to indicate on this scale how good or bad the subject's health is today, in your opinion. Please do this by drawing a line from the box below to whichever point on the scale indicates how good or bad you think the subject's health is today.

(N.B: "The subject's health" may be replaced by e.g. "Mrs. Smith's health)

The subject's own health state today

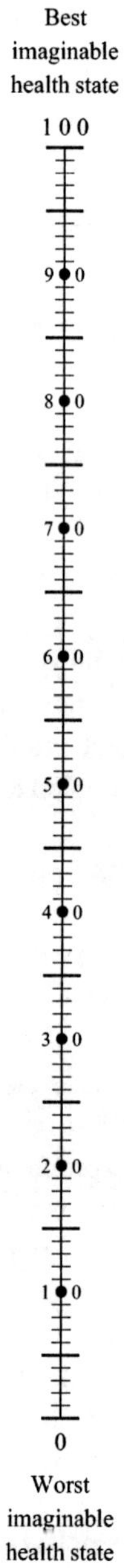

APPENDIX 6

SCRIPT FOR PROXY VERSION OF THE EQ-5D: VERSION 2

(asking the proxy to rate how he or she, (i.e. the proxy), thinks the subject would rate his or her own health if he or she could communicate it).

Proxy version of the EQ-5D: 2

By placing a tick in one box in each group below, please indicate which statement (*insert name of person whose health is being assessed e.g. Mr. Smith or John*) would choose to describe his or her health state today if he or she were able to tell us.

Do not tick more than one box in each group

Mobility
No problems in walking about ☐
Some problems in walking about ☐
Confined to bed ☐

Self-Care
No problems with self-care ☐
Some problems washing or dressing myself ☐
Unable to wash or dress myself ☐

Usual Activities (*e.g. work, study, housework, family or leisure activities)*
No problems with performing usual activities ☐
Some problems with performing usual activities ☐
Unable to perform usual activities ☐

Pain/Discomfort
No pain or discomfort ☐
Moderate pain or discomfort ☐
Extreme pain or discomfort ☐

Anxiety/Depression
Not anxious or depressed ☐
Moderately anxious or depressed ☐
Extremely anxious or depressed ☐

To help people say how good or bad a health state is, we have drawn a scale (rather like a thermometer) on which the best state you can imagine is marked 100 and the worst state you can imagine is marked 0.

We would like you to indicate on this scale how good or bad <u>the subject</u> would say his or her health is today, if he or she was able to tell us. Please do this by drawing a line from the box below to whichever point on the scale indicates how good or bad <u>you think the subject</u> would say his or her health is today.

(N.B: "The subject's health" may be replaced by e.g. "Mrs. Smith's health)

The subject's own health state today

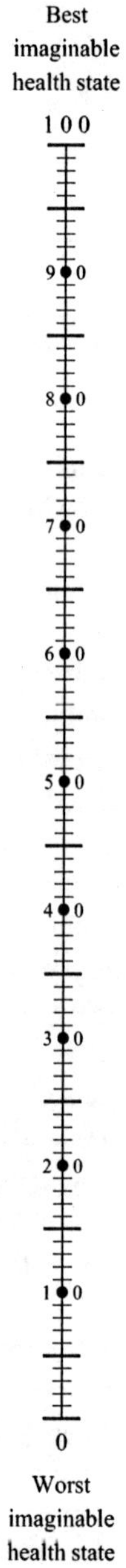

APPENDIX 7

DEFINITION OF EQ-5D CONCEPTS
EQ-5D DESCRIPTIVE SYSTEM, EQ-VAS AND EQ-5D VAS

Health

A general term relating to physical, emotional and social functioning; is wider than a strict medical interpretation (e.g. absence of illness), as it also includes emotional and social well-being. Includes both negative aspects of health (illness) as well as positive aspects (well-being).

Your own health state

Emphasis on the respondent's own judgement of his/her health state; relates to the individual and depends on the respondent's own situation.

Today

The day of completing the questionnaire (this particular calendar day).

Mobility

This refers to the physical ability to walk or move about, both inside and outside. It does not refer to the use of bicycle, car or public transport.

1. *Walking about:* The ability to walk or move about independently from one place to another, both inside and outside. It does not refer to walking about an object such as a building. In some languages, where the concept of walking 'about' does not exist, the translation of simply 'walking' has been accepted. 'Walking about' does not refer to running, strenuous activities, country walks or sport.

2. *Confined to bed:* Restricted to staying in bed (except to use the toilet). It includes being confined to a chair (but not wheelchair) all day (e.g. where someone is moved from bed to a chair and returned to bed at the end of the day). This can be a long-term condition or short term (e.g. in bed because of influenza). What is important is that the subject is confined to bed on the day the EQ-5D questionnaire is administered.

Thus, the 3 levels of mobility could be interpreted as:

Level 1: Can walk (about) without help or aids.
Level 2: Needs to use stick, crutches, walking frame, when walking. Would include people in a wheelchair (although they may not classify themselves in level 2).
Level 3: Confined to bed or chair all of the day (except to use the toilet). Excludes people in a wheelchair.

Self-Care

The term self-care refers to independence in daily personal care. It specifically covers washing and dressing, but also includes feeding oneself, personal hygiene, brushing teeth, grooming and going to the toilet. It does not include social or role activities, or the ability to manage personal finances or household affairs.

Washing self

Ability to take a bath or shower without help from someone else; washing whole body and not just face and hands.

Usual activities

This refers to activities such as work (paid and unpaid), study, housework, leisure and social activities. 'Usual' means activities carried out on a regular basis, but not necessarily on a daily basis. The activities should be 'usual for you', i.e. the respondent personally. The ability to perform usual activities refers to the ability to be able to participate in these activities today, rather than to accomplish or complete them.

Pain/Discomfort

1. *Pain:* Physical or bodily hurt. Does not refer to psychological or mental suffering.

2. *Discomfort:* Uncomfortable physical sensation, of a lower grade of intensity than pain. Includes ache(s), breathlessness, itching, palpitations, nausea, tiredness, dizziness, bloatedness, pins and needles, ringing in the ears. Does not include psychological or mental disturbance.

Anxiety/Depression

1. *Anxiety:* Psychological sensation relating to 'worry'; covers general feelings of feeling tense, troubled, nervous, apprehensive, fearful. An example of extreme anxiety may be panic or dread.

2. *Depression:* Psychological sensation relating to lowness of spirit. Does not refer only to clinical depression; covers feeling cheerless, gloomy, dejected, down, sad, miserable, unhappy. No inherent time element i.e. not defined by length of time for which it has been experienced.

Some/moderate problems

Ranges from a small number or a small degree of difficulty to many problems or difficulties. Should indicate a middle level between no problems and extreme problems. More severe than mild.

Extreme

Indicating a very severe or very bad level - the highest (outermost) level.

Best imaginable health state

The most optimal, desirable, ideal health state a person can imagine.

Worst imaginable health state

The most bad, undesirable health state a person can imagine. Unable to function independently in all areas of life.

A person like you

The respondent personally in terms of his/her characteristics (may include socio-demographic factors).

Personal view

The respondent's own subjective opinion or perception.

When thinking about each health state imagine that it will last for one year. What happens after that is not known and should not be taken into account

The respondent should think about the particular health state for a period of a year. He/she should not think about what happens after the year (i.e. getting better, worse, same, die) because this is uncertain. It is important that when judging the health state, the respondent should not take prognosis into account.

Unconscious

Being alive but not awake or aware of surroundings.

The state dead

Deprived of life. All functions have ceased and are incapable of being restored or revived. Does not include the process of dying.

APPENDIX 8

TRANSLATION GUIDELINES FOR THE EQ-5D DEVELOPED BY THE EUROQOL GROUP

Before beginning the process of translating the EQ-5D, the Project Manager in the country where the EQ-5D is being translated should contact the Business Manager of the EuroQol Group, Dr. Frank de Charro, who will ensure that he/she receives all of the relevant materials and information. These include a copy of the official English version of the EQ-5D, definitions of key words and phrases contained in the EQ-5D, as well as these guidelines which should be read carefully. The EuroQol Business Manager is also responsible for organising the communication procedure between the Project Manager and EuroQol Group members during the process. This involves an on-going communication with members of a translation review team within the EuroQol Group who will be continually involved in the process. Time should be allowed at each stage for the EuroQol review team to provide feedback and comments on the reports they receive.

If these guidelines are not followed, the EuroQol Group will not be able to approve translations.

The process of translation should consist of the following steps:

Forward Translation

*Two forward translations into the target language by qualified and/or experienced translators who should be native speakers of the target language, and fluent in English.

*The production of a first consensus version from the two forward translations in a meeting with the Project Manager.

*The production of a report on the forward translation process.

*Submission of full report on the process to the EuroQol Business Management before proceeding to the next stage.

Back translation

*Two back translations of the consensus version into English.

*Comparison of the back translations with the original version.

*Production of a report on the back translation process.

*Production of a second consensus version, incorporating changes decided upon after comparison between the back translations and the original version.

*Submission of a full report on the process to the EuroQol Business Management before proceeding to the next stage.

Respondent testing

*Testing of the second consensus version on a sample of lay respondents, native speakers of the target language. The lay respondents should include healthy individuals as well as patients.

*Production of third consensus version based on comments from lay subjects.

*Production of final version incorporating comments from the EuroQol translation review team.

It is important to realise that these instructions are designed to ensure that the version of the EQ-5D for use in your country will be as *semantically equivalent* as possible to other language versions used around the world (in other words that the meaning of individual words and phrases is similar to that used in other language versions). These guidelines cannot ensure that the questionnaire *per se* will be appropriate in terms of its content and purpose. That is matter for your judgement, and should be determined before undertaking the translation exercise.

In order to help you achieve an operationally equivalent version of the questionnaire, you will be provided with an electronic format of the EQ-5D which you should use to ensure an identical layout and style.

References are available on request from the EuroQol Business Management which should be helpful in understanding the aims and problems of the translation process.

Forward translations into the target language

The first stage in the translation process is to produce 2 *forward* translations, i.e. translations from English into the 'target' language. These 2 forward translations (from the official EQ-5D English version), should be carried out independently by 2 qualified and/or experienced translators who are native speakers of the target language, and fluent in English. At least one of the translators should be someone *un*connected with the health field. Details of translators' qualifications and/or experience should be provided in the report.

The forward translators should be briefed on the nature of the task by the Project Manager. The aim is to produce clear and natural-sounding translations which are acceptable to respondents in the target language, but which transmit the meaning of the original. Care should be taken to ensure the use of simple, non-technical language. Translators should note alternative wordings and difficulties encountered.

Production of first consensus version

Once the 2 forward translations are completed, the 2 forward translators should meet with the Project Manager to produce the *first consensus version* of the EQ-5D in the target language.

The questionnaire should be reviewed sentence by sentence *to produce a single version in the target language* on which all participants agree. The criteria of simplicity, clarity, and natural language should guide decision-making, particularly as the EQ-5D is used by a wide variety of respondents, some of who may have only a low level of education. Alternatives and difficulties noted by the translators should be taken into account.

Report on the forward translation process

Details of the forward translation meeting should be included in a report produced for the EuroQol translation review team. The report should include:

i) Copies of the 2 forward translations (clearly indicated).
ii) Copies of the final consensus version (clearly indicated).
iii) Qualifications and/or experience of translators.
iv) Problematic words, phrases or items encountered.
v) Points of disagreement.
vi) Alternatives considered.
vii) Solutions/consensus items.

It should be remembered that those reviewing the process will normally not understand the target language, and that the quality of translated versions will be judged largely on the reports produced.

The report should be sent to the EuroQol Business Management who will distribute copies to members of the EuroQol translation review team, who will then comment on the process and ask for clarification where necessary. Their comments and queries should be answered by the Project Manager before moving onto the next stage.

Back translations of the consensus version into English

Once the first consensus version has been agreed upon, 2 back translations of that version should be produced by 2 qualified and/or experienced translators whose native language is English, but who are bilingual in the target language. The 2 back translators should work independently.

One back translator should be asked to produce a relatively literal translation, the other a more polished version. Translators should note any difficulties encountered, as well as formulations which sound unnatural in the target language.

Back translation meeting

Once the back translations are completed, the Project Manager should meet with the back translators to discuss the process. The aim of this meeting is to produce a *report on the back translation process.*

At the meeting the Project Manager and the back translator should:

i) Discuss problems the translators had in translating the questionnaire.
ii) Compare the back translations with the original English version of the questionnaire, noting any discrepancies. The translators should also be asked to comment on their perceptions of the first consensus version of the questionnaire in the target language.

Report on the back translation process

The report should therefore mention:

i) Differences between the original version and the back translations, or between the 2 back translations.
ii) The quality and adequacy of the first consensus version.

The Project Manager should produce a report of the meeting which will include:

i) Copies of the 2 back translations (clearly indicated).
ii) Copies of the final consensus version (clearly indicated).
iii) Qualifications and/or experience of translators.
iv) Differences with original English version.
v) Differences between back translations.
vi) Comments on first consensus version.

The report should be sent to the EuroQol Business Management who will distribute copies to members of the EuroQol translation review team. They will comment on the process and ask for clarification where necessary. Their comments and queries should be answered by the Project Manager before moving onto the next stage. Suggestions made by the Project Manager and the EuroQol translation review team may lead to changes to the first consensus version. The version produced after back translation is *the second consensus version*.

Respondent testing

There are separate guidelines for respondent testing (Appendix 9).

The report on respondent testing should be sent to the EuroQol Business Management. They will distribute the report to members of the EuroQol translation review team, who will comment on the process and ask for clarification where necessary. They will liaise with the Project Manager, and final changes will be agreed upon, taking into account comments and queries made at earlier stages in the process. The version produced at this stage will be the final version, and should be proof-read by at least 2 native speakers of the target language.

Translated versions of the EQ-5D are given the official seal of approval by the EuroQol Translation Committee based on the recommendations of members of the EuroQol translation review team who carried out the work. Recommendation for official approval is based on the quality of the process followed, particularly the quality and detail of the reports provided to the EuroQol Translation Committee (Examples of previous reports are available on request from the EuroQol Business Management). Please follow guidelines and recommendations as closely as possible, and make reports as detailed as possible.

If you wish to carry out a translation of the EQ-5D, please contact the EuroQol Business Manager. His details are:

Dr. Frank de Charro
EuroQol Business Manager
PO Box 4443
3006 AK Rotterdam
The Netherlands
Tel: +31 10 4081545
Fax: +31 10 4525303
E-mail: fdecharro@compuserve.com

APPENDIX 9

RESPONDENT TESTING OF EQ-5D

The second consensus version of the EQ-5D should be tested on 8 respondents, who are native speakers of the target language. The questionnaire should be self-administered in the presence of the Project Manager or other members of the research team. The aim of respondent testing is to evaluate the clarity, understandability, naturalness and adequacy of wording. Respondents should represent a range of socio-demographic and health characteristics, and should include healthy individuals as well as patients, with a bias towards those in lower educational categories. Respondents should not have seen the questionnaire before, and should not be connected with the health professions.

The aim of this testing is to identify any items which respondents: have difficulty understanding; think are inappropriate for any reason. Where respondents have difficulties understanding, it is important to determine what the problems are and how *he/she* would word the question.

The interview should be conducted as follows:

(i) First ask the respondent to complete the EQ-5D. Explain that it is a brief questionnaire on health that has been translated from English, and that you want to check that it is clear and well-written in his/her language.

Ask the respondent to answer the questions as carefully as possible, but remind him/her that there are no right or wrong answers, and that you are primarily interested in the respondent's opinions regarding the quality of the questionnaire. Explain that when the respondent has completed the questionnaire you will ask some further questions regarding the respondent's impression of the questionnaire.

(ii) Once the respondent has completed the questionnaire, record his/her age and the time it took to complete the questionnaire.

Record the respondent's general impression about the EQ-5D as follows:

- Is it clear, easy to understand, easy to answer?
- Is it too long?
- Are the instructions clear?

(iii) Once you have recorded the respondent's general impression you should go through the whole questionnaire item by item (including response options and instructions) and check whether:

- The question/instruction was difficult to understand or answer. If so, why?
- Wording was ambiguous.
- The language used was easy to understand and colloquial.
- The respondent would ask the question or formulate the instruction in another way.

It is helpful to standardise questioning as follows: For each instruction in the EQ-5D, you should ask respondents:

- Are there words that you find difficult to understand?
- Would you change anything in the instructions?
- Would you add anything to the instructions?

To get a better understanding of respondents' interpretation of key words and concepts in the instructions, the following questions can be used.

- What does [*INSERT WORD*] mean for you?
- What were you thinking about when you read the instructions?

In the instructions, key words tested should include 'health status' and 'today'

For each question, you should ask the respondents:

- Do you understand the question?
- What does it mean for you?
- What were you thinking about when you answered the question? Were you thinking about any particular aspect of your health or your current situation?
- Would you make any changes to the question? If so, what?

To get a better understanding of respondents' interpretation of key words and concepts in the questions, the following questions can be used:

- What does [*INSERT WORD*] mean for you?
- What were you thinking about when you answered this question? Were you thinking about any particular aspect of your health or your current situation when you answered this question
- What does the word [*INSERT WORD*] make you think of?

Key words tested should include ‘mobility’, ‘walking about’, ‘confined to bed’, ’self-care’ ‘wash’, ‘discomfort’ ‘moderate’ ‘extreme’ ‘anxious’ ‘depressed’.

(iv) The aim of respondent testing is to make any final adjustments to the translated version of the EQ-5D so that it is clear and acceptable to respondents.

Once the 8 respondents have been interviewed, their comments should be summarised in a report in English and returned to the Business Management of the EuroQol Group. The report should be approximately 2-3 pages long and should give a brief summary of the comments of the respondents in relation to each question and instruction text in the EQ-5D. The report should be accompanied by a summary of the demographic characteristics of the respondents (see summary form).

Wherever possible, it would be helpful for future analysis of respondents’ impressions of the EQ-5D, to record the respondent testing interviews on cassette or video recorder. Copies of the tapes should be provided to the EuroQol Business Management, and respondents’ permission to record the interview should be sought.

Below is an example of a patient testing report. This form is available from the EuroQol Business Management on request.

Cognitive Debriefing

Data summary

Questionnaire: EQ-5D developed by the EuroQol Group

Country:

Language:

Specify age, sex, profession and time taken to complete the EQ-5D of each respondent

	Age	Sex	Profession	Time needed
R 1		☐ male ☐ female		
R 2		☐ male ☐ female		
R 3		☐ male ☐ female		
R 4		☐ male ☐ female		
R 5		☐ male ☐ female		
R 6		☐ male ☐ female		
R 7		☐ male ☐ female		
R 8		☐ male ☐ female		

Mean age .... Mean time ....

Median age .... Median time ....

APPENDIX 10

GUIDELINES FOR EQ-5D LANGUAGE ADAPTATIONS

These guidelines apply to situations where it may be unnecessary to perform a complete translation process, due to the similarities between the language spoken in a given country and an existing EQ-5D language version. This applies for example to South America where the Spanish spoken in Spain is similar to that spoken in countries like Venezuela and Peru or where the French spoken in Quebec, Canada is similar to the French spoken in France.

Before beginning the process of adapting EQ-5D, the Project Manager in the country where the EQ-5D is being adapted should contact the Business Manager of the EuroQol Group, who will ensure that he/she receives all of the relevant materials and information. Together with these guidelines, these include:

i) A copy of the official English version of the EQ-5D.
ii) A copy of the 'mother' language version to be adapted. This should also be used as a 'template' for changes (if any) so that the standard format of the questionnaire can be maintained.
iii) Definitions of key words and phrases contained in the EQ-5D.
iv) An example of a report on a previous EQ-5D language adaptation.

The EuroQol Business Manager is also responsible for organising the communication procedure between the Project Manager and EuroQol Group members during the process. This involves an on-going communication with a translation review team member within the EuroQol Group who will be continually involved in the process. Time should be allowed at each stage for the EuroQol Group reviewer to provide feedback and comments on the reports he/she receives.

If these guidelines are not followed, the EuroQol Group will not be able to approve language adaptation.

References are available on request from the EuroQol Business Management which should be helpful in understanding the aims and problems of the translation process.

The process of adapting EQ-5D language versions should consist of the following steps:

Review by a translation consultant

The translation consultant should be a qualified and/or experienced translator who is a native speaker of the target language, and fluent in English.

He/she should be briefed on the nature of the task by the Project Manager. The aim is to produce a clear and natural-sounding version that is acceptable to respondents in the target language. This is especially important as EQ-5D is used by a wide variety of respondents some of whom may have only a low level of education. Alternatives and difficulties noted by the translators should be taken into account.

First consensus version

When the consultant has reviewed the existing "mother" version he/she should meet with the Project Manager to produce a *first consensus version* of EQ-5D in the target language.

Report on the review of the mother version by the consultant.

A full report on the review process of the mother version outlining the suggested changes should be submitted to the EuroQol Business Management.

The report should include.

(i) Copy of the first consensus version (using the standard layout of EQ-5D).
(ii) Names, qualifications and/or experience of consultant.
(iii) Problematic words, phrases or items encountered.
(iv) Alternatives considered.
(v) Solutions offered.

It should be remembered that those reviewing the process from the EuroQol Group will normally not understand the target language, and that the quality of translated versions will be judged largely on the reports produced.

The report should be sent to the EuroQol Business Management who will distribute copies to a member of the EuroQol translation review team. He/she will comment on the process and ask for clarification where necessary. Comments and queries from the EuroQol reviewer should be answered by the Project Manager before moving onto the next stage. Suggestions made by the Project Manager and the EuroQol translation reviewer may lead to changes to the first consensus version.

Respondent testing

Guidelines for respondent testing for language adaptations are the same as for full translations except that the number of participants is less (5).

The report on respondent testing should be sent to the EuroQol Group Business Management. They will distribute the report to a member of the EuroQol translation review team, who will comment on the process and ask for clarification where necessary. He/she will liase with the Project Manager, and final changes will be agreed upon, taking into account comments and queries made at earlier stages in the process. The version produced at this stage will be the final version, and should be proof-read by at least two native speakers of the target language.

All translations and adaptations of EQ-5D are given the official seal of approval by the EuroQol Translation Committee based on the recommendations of members of the EuroQol translation review team who carried out the work. Recommendation for official approval is based on the quality of the process followed, particularly the quality and detail of the reports provided to the EuroQol Translation Committee. Please follow guidelines and recommendations as closely as possible, and make reports as detailed as possible.

If you wish to carry out a translation or adaptation of EQ-5D, please contact the EuroQol Business Manager. His details are:

Dr. Frank de Charro
EuroQol Business Manager
PO Box 4443
3006 AK Rotterdam
The Netherlands
Tel: +31 10 4081545
Fax:+31 10 4525303
E-mail:fdecharro@compuserve.com

Index

Africa 167, 186
Age 4, 32, 44, 48, 58, 59, 61, 62, 66, 68, 70, 75, 77, 78, 83, 85, 86, 87, 89, 90, 92, 94, 100, 130, 144, 149, 210, 231
Aggregation 33, 34
Application 1, 4, 7, 8, 11, 29, 33, 34, 39, 95, 106, 172, 229
Asia 167
Australasia 167

Back translation 183, 184, 185, 191, 192, 193, 195, 201, 203
Background variables 24, 55, 56, 57, 63, 66, 75, 77, 78, 79, 81, 82, 84, 85, 91, 99, 103, 113, 117, 129, 130, 144, 148, 231, 232, 233, 235
Best imaginable health state 3, 10, 30, 176, 177, 188
Biomed II 4, 229

Canada 40, 167, 186, 208
CANALS 117, 118, 119, 120, 121, 122, 123, 233
Cardinal index 1
Catalonia 58, 62, 71, 78, 82, 83, 85, 112
Clinical decision-making 38
Clinical studies 7, 8, 9, 12, 13, 14, 32, 38, 39, 195
Cognitive debriefing 172
Communication 4, 5, 229
Computer-assisted methods 4, 23
Cornellà de Llobregat 58, 62, 83, 112, 146
Cost-benefit analysis 8
Cost-effectiveness analysis 8
Cost-utility analysis 8, 35, 41, 211
Cross-cultural measurement 183

Dementia 9, 24, 25, 173, 174, 176
Denmark 40, 177, 179, 197
Descriptive system 3, 7, 10, 11, 12, 14, 15, 21, 22, 24, 29, 30, 43, 44, 55, 59, 63, 67, 81, 93, 103, 107, 108, 112, 114, 125, 131, 145, 148, 167, 173, 176, 192, 193, 195, 210, 230, 231, 235
Disease-specific 1, 2, 8, 143

Economic evaluation 2, 8, 10, 34, 130, 131, 231, 234
Education 4, 13, 14, 56, 66, 67, 69, 70, 75, 76, 77, 78, 83, 85, 87, 91, 93, 100, 113, 129, 149, 179, 197, 199, 210, 212, 231, 232, 235
England 59, 146
Epilepsy 173, 174, 175, 176
EQ SDQ 4, 197
EQ-5D index 10, 11, 14, 31, 230
EQ-net 4, 5, 37, 39, 55, 63, 64, 66, 78, 191, 192, 198, 202, 204, 205, 207, 229, 230, 231
EQ-net TTO 57, 62, 63, 71, 74, 77, 79
EQ-net VAS 38, 39, 41, 55, 57, 58, 59, 63, 68, 71, 72, 75, 78, 79, 103, 199
Equivalence 5, 172, 180, 183, 188, 191, 205
Europe 167, 177, 192, 207
European Union 4
European VAS-based health state valuations 99
EuroQol Business Management 23, 299
Exclusion criteria 57, 83, 99, 100, 104, 147, 231, 235
Exclusions 55, 57, 71, 72, 73, 74, 75, 77, 78
Experience of illness 66, 212, 231
Experimental 7, 9, 11, 13, 14, 22, 25

Face-to-face 2, 22, 61, 145, 229, 277
Finland 40, 56, 59, 64, 65, 68, 69, 71, 72, 73, 82, 85, 87, 94, 95, 96, 112, 113, 115, 129, 132, 133, 184, 197, 199, 218
Forward translation 183, 184, 185, 191
Framing effects 23
Frome IV 59

Generic 1, 2, 7, 10, 29, 31, 54, 167, 180, 191, 230
Generic instrument 8, 167, 188, 208, 229
Germany 40, 56, 60
Guidelines 4, 5, 7, 143, 183, 185, 186, 187, 189, 191, 192, 205, 229

Health profile 3
Health states 1, 2, 3, 5, 8, 10, 11, 13, 27, 29, 30, 31, 33, 34, 35, 37, 39, 41, 55, 56, 57, 58, 59, 60, 61, 62, 63, 64, 65, 78, 81, 82, 83, 85,

88, 89, 90, 93, 97, 99, 100, 101, 103, 105, 106, 107, 109, 110, 112, 114, 124, 125, 126, 127, 128, 129, 130, 131, 134, 135, 136, 137, 138, 139, 140, 141, 142, 143, 144, 145, 146, 147, 148, 149, 167, 171, 176, 177, 189, 192, 198, 199, 200, 201, 202, 203, 204, 209, 210, 212, 231, 232, 233, 234, 235
Health status index 10, 11
Health status measurement 2, 38
Health-related quality of life (HRQoL) 1, 2, 5, 7, 8, 9, 10, 12, 13, 25, 26, 29, 30, 31, 32, 34, 81, 101, 103, 143, 167, 168, 176, 180, 183, 184, 188, 189, 191, 192, 203, 208, 209, 229, 230, 233

Inconsistencies 55, 57, 58, 62, 71, 72, 73, 74, 78, 83, 85, 100, 104, 109, 110, 111, 112, 113, 130, 147, 170, 172, 181, 211, 212, 231, 233
Interpretation 13, 25, 26, 27, 31, 53, 148, 149, 167, 168, 172, 177, 178, 179, 180, 181, 186, 205, 271, 275, 277
Interview 2, 21, 22, 23, 24, 32, 44, 55, 58, 59, 61, 62, 63, 64, 65, 71, 78, 82, 83, 85, 108, 112, 130, 145, 146, 147, 172, 173, 174, 175, 178, 198, 199, 200, 201, 202, 209, 229, 231, 234, 235, 271, 275, 277
Intra-class correlation coefficient (ICC) 43

Japan 40, 186, 207, 208, 209, 210

l'Hospitalet del Llobregat 58, 64, 65, 71, 82, 83, 112
Language versions 5, 167, 180, 183, 184, 185, 186, 187, 189, 191, 192, 193, 201, 203, 205
Latin America 167

Maori 207, 212, 213
Meaning 1, 47, 168, 170, 171, 172, 175, 179, 180, 188, 189, 194, 195, 196, 203, 204
Medical effectiveness 4
Missing data 11, 12, 13
Mode of administration 2, 21, 22, 23, 27, 31
Modelling 1, 14, 33, 34, 57, 106, 147, 175, 233, 234
Multi-level model 107, 148

N2 variable 125
N3 variable 107, 109, 122, 125
Navarra 40, 61, 64, 65, 68, 69, 71, 72, 73, 82, 83, 85, 87, 93, 94, 95, 96, 97, 98, 99, 100, 113, 115, 132, 133, 198, 200
Netherlands 40, 56, 61, 62, 65, 71, 81, 82, 85, 112, 113, 129, 177, 179, 184, 186, 197, 199, 204
New Zealand 40, 186, 207, 211, 212, 213
Non-linear regression analysis 117, 129, 233
Norway 184, 204
Nottingham Health Profile (NHP) 2

Observational 8, 9, 11, 14
Observer 2, 4, 29
OLS regression 12, 107, 113, 114, 116, 117, 118, 119, 129, 233
Outcomes 3, 7, 8, 12, 13, 14, 32, 34, 39, 95, 99, 113, 114, 118, 122, 130, 183, 191, 229, 233, 234

Pacific Islands 207, 212
Paired comparisons 33
Pakeha 212
Parkinson's disease 22, 26, 173, 175, 210
Patient 4, 5, 7, 9, 11, 13, 14, 22, 24, 25, 26, 27, 29, 32, 35, 37, 38, 40, 44, 54, 58, 167, 173, 174, 175, 176, 183, 210, 212, 214, 230
Person Trade-Off (PTO) 33, 180
Perspective 11, 35, 37, 164
Population health 2, 4, 7, 8, 9, 10, 14
Population studies 3
Preference weights 11
Proxies 2, 22, 24, 25, 27
Proxy report 23, 24, 229

Quality-adjusted life-year (QALY) 1, 10, 11, 35, 214, 231
Quasi-experimental 9, 10, 11

Ranking 33, 59, 61, 64, 83, 85, 130, 131, 145, 204, 209, 214, 234, 235
RCTs 7, 8, 9, 11
Reliability 1, 4, 43, 44, 45, 46, 48, 50, 51, 53, 54, 189, 230
Reproducibility 43, 53, 230
Rescaling 106, 114, 127, 130, 131, 233, 234

Resource allocation 4, 32
Respondent characteristics 55, 56, 57, 63, 66, 67, 68, 70, 75, 77, 78, 82, 83, 84, 85, 86, 87, 99, 100, 113, 205, 231, 232
Rheumatoid arthritis 9, 44, 48, 49, 50, 51, 52, 54, 176, 230

Sample features 55, 63, 64, 65, 78, 231
Scotland 44, 59, 146, 230
Self-completion 2, 22, 23, 29, 31, 172, 229, 275
Self-report 2, 3, 4, 21, 22, 23, 24, 26, 52, 53, 54, 209, 212
Self-reported problems 3, 41
Semantic 5, 168, 172, 179, 180, 185, 188, 189, 191, 204, 205
Sex 4, 32, 58, 61, 62, 68, 75, 84, 86, 87, 146, 148, 149, 210, 231
SF-36 2, 210
Sickness Impact Profile (SIP) 2
Singular value decomposition (SVD) 84
Spain 40, 56, 100, 101, 143, 144, 148, 184, 186, 195, 200, 202, 204, 232, 235
Standard Gamble (SG) 33
Statistical models 12, 14
Stroke 24, 209
Study designs 8, 14, 58
Sweden 40, 56, 62, 64, 65, 68, 69, 71, 72, 73, 81, 82, 84, 85, 87, 95, 96, 99, 112, 113, 115, 132, 133, 184, 204

Telephone 2, 4, 21, 22, 23, 32, 60, 61, 62, 147, 229, 271, 274, 277
Test-retest 4, 43, 44, 45, 49, 53, 54, 229, 230
Time trade-off (TTO) 33, 143, 204
Transformation 30, 33, 34, 104, 105, 114, 117, 118, 120, 122, 123, 129, 233
Translation 4, 5, 100, 112, 167, 168, 170, 172, 173, 177, 179, 180, 183, 184, 185, 186, 187, 188, 189, 191, 192, 193, 194, 195, 196, 197, 198, 201, 202, 203, 204, 205
Treatments 2
TTO database 55, 57, 62, 63, 65, 66, 67, 70, 71, 74, 77, 78, 79, 231, 235

UK MVH 37, 44, 45, 46, 47, 48, 49, 50, 51, 53, 58, 59, 62, 63, 65, 68, 69, 70, 71, 72, 73, 74, 82, 85, 87, 95, 96, 97, 99, 100, 108, 112, 115, 132, 133, 144, 145, 146, 147, 199, 201, 202, 208, 210, 213, 230, 236
UK TTO A1 37, 38, 41
UK VAS A3 39, 41
Unconscious 3, 29, 55, 56, 58, 59, 60, 61, 62, 63, 105, 112, 129, 146, 147, 169, 170, 199, 202, 231
United Kingdom 56, 59, 143, 172
United States 40, 101, 167, 186, 204, 208, 232
Utility weights 35, 37, 41, 81

Valuation 1, 2, 3, 39, 40, 78, 112, 176, 230
Value sets 3, 29, 31, 35, 39, 40, 41, 143, 144, 212, 213, 214, 229, 230
VAS database 55, 57, 58, 59, 63, 64, 65, 66, 67, 68, 71, 72, 75, 78, 79, 103, 199

Wales 59, 146
Weighted health state index 3
working 231
Working status 56, 66, 75, 76, 78, 231
World Health Organisation 183
Worst imaginable health state 3, 10, 169, 171, 172, 176

Zimbabwe 40, 186, 188, 207, 208

Printed in the United Kingdom
by Lightning Source UK Ltd.
9821500001B/49